Zimbabwe in the Post-COVID-19 Era

This comprehensive book brings together reflections, lessons, and insights relating to the post-COVID-19 era in Zimbabwe.

The outbreak of the COVID-19 pandemic has immensely affected all facets of humanity globally. Its impact on Zimbabwe is evident through its effect on socio-economic and education systems, politics, religion, infrastructural development, and health delivery systems. This book provides scholarly introspections into the lessons drawn from the pandemic in an effort to re-imagine future possibilities of public health in Zimbabwe and beyond. Providing a platform for research that seeks to re-think global public health matters from a decolonial school of thought, the book asks questions such as: What is the role of religion, linguistics, communication, education, economics, politics, and science in preparing Zimbabwe for possible future pandemics? How can the lessons drawn from the pandemic inform scholars to re-imagine future trajectories of the country in the various domains? How can researchers evaluate the power and economic dialectics of COVID-19, navigate the tumultuous challenges generated, and come up with appropriate systems for future pandemics?

Offering a realistic picture of the post-COVID-19 era in Zimbabwe, the book will be a key resource to students and researchers across the fields of political communication, science communication, decolonial discourse, language, and culture, as well as African Studies more broadly.

Esther Mavengano is a lecturer who teaches Linguistics and Literature in the Department of English and Media Studies, Faculty of Arts, at the Great Zimbabwe University in Masvingo, Zimbabwe. She holds a PhD in Linguistics and Literary Studies obtained from the University of North West in South Africa. Her research areas maintain the interface of linguistics and poetics. She has interests in language policy and planning, sociolinguistics, language practices and linguistic ideologies, media and political discourses, cultural and religious discourses, English as foreign/second language, rhetoric and language use, translingual practices in fictional writings, identity issues in contemporary transnational Anglophone/African literature, religion and gender, discourse analysis, stylistics, Zimbabwean literature, and language education in "multi" contexts. She has published in reputed international journals including *Cogent Arts and Humanities*, *African Identities*, *Literator*, and *Journal of Multicultural Discourses*. She is a member of the Circle of Southern African Women and Zimbabwean Circle Chapters. She is a Research Fellow at the Research Institute for Theology and Religion, College of Human Sciences, UNISA, South Africa, and a Georg Forster Postdoctoral Research Fellow at Alexander von Humboldt, Germany TU (Techische Universistat Dresden) Institut of English and American Studies, Department of English.

Tobias Marevesa is a New Testament senior lecturer in the Department of Philosophy and Religious Studies, under the Joshua Nkomo School of Arts and Humanities at the Great Zimbabwe University where he teaches New Testament Studies and New Testament Greek. He holds a PhD from the University of Pretoria in South Africa. He is also Research Fellow at the Research Institute for Theology and Religion (RITR) in the College of Human Sciences University of South Africa (UNISA). His areas of interest are New Testament studies and politics, Pentecostal expressions in Zimbabwean Christianity, culture, human rights, and gender-based violence. He has also published in the area of New Testament studies and conflict-resolution in the Zimbabwean political landscape.

Ernest Jakaza is a senior lecturer in the Department of Media, Communication, Film, and Theatre Arts at Midlands State University, Zimbabwe, and Research Fellow at the University of South Africa. He is the External Examiner for the Center for Languages and Communication Studies at Chinhoyi University of Technology in Zimbabwe. He has published edited books, a number of book chapters, and journal articles with accredited publishers. His research interests are in the areas of discourse analysis, political discourse, argumentation, appraisal discourse, and language and communication aspects.

Routledge Studies in Health in Africa

Series Editor: Pieter Fourie

1. **The Normalization of the HIV and AIDS Epidemic in South Africa**
   Katinka de Wet

2. **Preventing HIV Among Young People in Southern and Eastern Africa**
   Emerging Evidence and Intervention Strategies
   Edited by Kaymarlin Govender and Nana K. Poku

3. **The Political Economy of Mental Illness in South Africa**
   The Life Esidimeni Tragedy
   André J van Rensburg

4. **The South African Response to COVID-19**
   The Early Years
   Edited by Pieter Fourie and Guy Lamb

5. **Zimbabwe in the Post-COVID-19 Era**
   Reflections, Lessons, and the Future of Public Health
   Edited by Esther Mavengano, Tobias Marevesa, and Ernest Jakaza

Zimbabwe in the Post-COVID-19 Era

Reflections, Lessons, and the Future of Public Health

Edited by Esther Mavengano, Tobias Marevesa, and Ernest Jakaza

Routledge
Taylor & Francis Group

LONDON AND NEW YORK

First published 2024
by Routledge
4 Park Square, Milton Park, Abingdon, Oxon OX14 4RN

and by Routledge
605 Third Avenue, New York, NY 10158

Routledge is an imprint of the Taylor & Francis Group, an informa business

© 2024 selection and editorial matter, Esther Mavengano,
Tobias Marevesa, and Ernest Jakaza; individual chapters, the contributors

The right of Esther Mavengano, Tobias Marevesa, and Ernest Jakaza to
be identified as the authors of the editorial material, and of the authors for
their individual chapters, has been asserted in accordance with sections 77
and 78 of the Copyright, Designs and Patents Act 1988.

British Library Cataloguing-in-Publication Data
A catalogue record for this book is available from the British Library

Library of Congress Cataloging-in-Publication Data
Names: Mavengano, Esther, editor. | Marevesa, Tobias, editor. | Jakaza,
Ernest, 1977-editor.
Title: Zimbabwe in the post-Covid-19 era: reflections, lessons and the
future of public health/edited by Esther Mavengano, Tobias Marevesa and
Ernest Jakaza.
Other titles: Routledge studies in health in Africa.
Description: Abingdon, Oxon; New York, NY: Routledge, 2023. |
Series: Routledge studies in health in Africa | Includes index. |
Identifiers: LCCN 2022061214 | ISBN 9781032487748 (hardback) |
ISBN 9781032487755 (paperback) | ISBN 9781003390732 (ebook)
Subjects: LCSH: Public health–Zimbabwe. | Public health–Economic
aspects–Zimbabwe. | COVID-19 Pandemic, 2020–Zimbabwe–Influence. |
Medical policy–Zimbabwe. | Language policy–Zimbabwe.
Classification: LCC RA552.Z55 Z563 2023 | DDC 362.1096891–dc23/
eng/20230419
LC record available at https://lccn.loc.gov/2022061214

ISBN: 978-1-032-48774-8 (hbk)
ISBN: 978-1-032-48775-5 (pbk)
ISBN: 978-1-003-39073-2 (ebk)

DOI: 10.4324/9781003390732

Typeset in Bembo
by Deanta Global Publishing Services, Chennai, India

Contents

List of Contributors   vii

Preface   xi

Acknowledgements   xiii

1 **Introduction: Reflections, Lessons, and Future Possibilities**   1
ESTHER MAVENGANO

2 **The Socratic Sieve, Post COVID-19 Public Health and Zimbabwean Social Media**   14
EPHRAIM TAURAI GWARAVANDA

3 **Negotiating the Shifting Sands of Time: The Future Possibilities of Journalism Education and Research in Zimbabwe, Post-Covid-19 Era**   24
ELIZABETH F. HOVE AND LAST ALFANDIKA

4 **Communication and New Cultural Order in Zimbabwean Public Health: Reflections from COVID-19**   37
GIFT GWINDINGWE AND TICHAONA ZINHUMWE

5 **The Dialectics of Language in Zimbabwe's Public Health Communication: Reflections on English as a Lingua Franca in (Post) COVID-19 Era**   49
ESTHER MAVENGANO

6 **A Language-Policy-Inspired Lesson for the Zimbabwean Post-COVID-19 Era**   65
ISAAC MHUTE

7 Language Change beyond the COVID-19 Pandemic:
   The Case of Shona Language   75
   MIKA NYONI AND TSITSI NYONI

8 COVID-19 Related Communications on Zimbabwean
   Online Health Communities: A Netnographic Study   91
   SHUPIKAI KEMBO

9 Ndebele Funeral Rites and COVID-19: Deciphering
   Public Health in Spirituality   106
   SAMBULO NDLOVU

10 Securitization of COVID-19 and the Imagination of
    Post-COVID-19 Burial Ceremonies in Kenya and
    Zimbabwe   121
    LOREEN MASENO AND SIBANDA FORTUNE

11 Karanga-Shona Funeral and Post-Funeral Rites in
    the COVID-19 Era: A Case Study of the VaDuma in
    Bikita, Zimbabwe   135
    BEATRICE TARINGA AND SOPHIA CHIRONGOMA

12 The COVID-19 Restrictions and Clashes with Shona
    Cultural Practices and Values: Post-COVID Era
    Lessons for Zimbabwe   153
    LIVESON TATIRA, SHAMISO TATIRA, AND GAYNOR PARADZA

13 Beyond COVID-19: Reimagining Religious and
    Political Futures in Zimbabwe: A Decolonial Paradigm   163
    TOBIAS MAREVESA

14 The Socioeconomic Ramification of COVID-19 to
    the Economically Disadvantaged Members of the
    Community in Harare during 2020 Lockdowns: A
    Practical-theological Approach to the Post-COVID-19 Era   174
    GUSHA ISHEANESU SEXTUS

15 Conclusion: The Post-COVID-19 – The Future of
    Public Health in Zimbabwe   194
    ERNEST JAKAZA

    Index   197

Contributors

Last Alfandika is Media and Cultural Studies Lecturer at Great Zimbabwe University. He obtained his PhD at the University of the Witwatersrand, South Africa, in 2019. Alfandika writes about media policy; audience, text, and reception processes; political economy of the news media; and political communication. He is currently working on his first book titled *Democratising Communication: Media Reform and Media Activism in Zimbabwe*.

Sophia Chirongoma is Senior Lecturer in the Religious Studies Department at Midlands State University, Zimbabwe. She is also an Academic Associate/ Research Fellow at the Research Institute for Theology and Religion (RITR) in the College of Human Sciences, University of South Africa (UNISA). Her research interests and publications focus on the interface between culture, ecology, religion, health, and gender justice.

Ephraim Taurai Gwaravanda holds a PhD in philosophy from the University of South Africa (UNISA). He is Associate Professor of philosophy in the Department of Philosophy and Religious Studies (Great Zimbabwe University) and Research Associate at the Ali Mazrui Centre for Higher Education Studies (University of Johannesburg). He has published several scholarly articles and book chapters in African epistemology, higher education, critical thinking, and indigenous knowledge systems. He has co-edited two books namely, *African Higher Education in the 21st Century: Epistemological, Ontological and Ethical Perspectives* (Brill/Sense, 2021) and *Mediating Learning in Higher Education in Africa: From Critical Thinking to Social Justice Pedagogies* (Brill/Sense, 2021).

Gift Gwindingwe is Media and Cultural Studies Lecturer at Great Zimbabwe University, Mashava Campus. He holds a PhD in Communication from the University of Fort Hare, South Africa. He is a former member of the Research Committee and currently a member of the Great Zimbabwe University International Relations Committee. He has published articles in local (South African) accredited journals. His research interests are in the following areas: cultural studies, post-colonialism, politics, and the pervasive nature of digital media in shaping today's communication terrain.

Elizabeth F. Hove is Media and Cultural Studies Lecturer (Media Studies), in the English and Media Studies Department, Simon Muzenda School of Arts, Culture and Heritage, Great Zimbabwe University, Masvingo, Zimbabwe. Research interests include media, gender, and development, new media, social media and journalism, and audience research.

Shupikai Kembo is doing her PhD with the University of South Africa (UNISA)'s Department of Marketing and Retail Management. She is an upcoming researcher with interests in health marketing; social marketing; crisis, emergency, and risk communication; marketing communications; and social media.

Loreen Maseno is Senior Lecturer at the Department of Religion, Theology and Philosophy, Maseno University, Kenya, and Research Fellow at the Department of Biblical and Ancient Studies, University of South Africa. She was a Humboldt Fellow at the University of Bayreuth, Germany. Her research interests include feminist christology, eco-feminism, gender, and theology.

Isaac Mhute is Associate Professor at Midlands State University's Department of Language, Literature, and Culture Studies. He is a chief examiner for language and literature with an international examining board, professional editor, and translator/back translator (English and Shona). He graduated with a Doctor of Literature and Philosophy in African Languages from the University of South Africa whose focus was on the morphological, syntactic, and semantic representation of grammatical relations. His research interests are in both theoretical and applied linguistic areas such as language policy and development, syntax and semantics, onomastics, as well as language and strategic communication issues in education, among others.

Sambulo Ndlovu is Humboldt Research Fellow in the Department of Anthropology and African Studies at The Johannes Gutenberg University Mainz, Germany, and Professor in the Department of African Languages and Culture at the Great Zimbabwe University. He holds a PhD in linguistics from the University of Cape Town. His research interests are theoretical and applied linguistics, onomastics, and cultural studies.

Mika Nyoni holds a Doctor of Literature and Philosophy (English) from the University of South Africa. He is currently Associate Professor in the Department of Curriculum Studies of the Great Zimbabwe University where he teaches English modules. His research interests are in semiotics, social media, popular culture, and sociolinguistics. He is also a published poet and fiction writer.

Tsitsi Nyoni holds a Doctor of Philosophy in Languages, Linguistics, and Literature from the University of South Africa. She is also an Associate Professor in the department of Teacher Development at Great Zimbabwe University. Currently she is Senior Lecturer at Great Zimbabwe University,

Zimbabwe. Her research interests lie in language, literature, indigenous knowledge systems, pedagogics, and contemporary issues such as gender, child abuse, and domestic violence. She has published several journal articles, book chapters, and books in these areas. She has also done consultancy work on translation for government and nongovernmental organizations.

Gaynor Paradza holds a Master's in Rural and Urban Planning from the University of Zimbabwe and a Doctoral Degree in Law and Governance from Wageningen University. Currently she is at the University of Witwatersrand's Public Affairs Research Institute where she leads the Land Sector Program. Her interests are in land tenure, gender mainstreaming, biodiversity management, land policy development, large-scale land-based investment, agricultural value and chain governance, land reform, and sustainable livelihoods. She has published in the above areas of interest.

Gusha Isheanesu Sextus holds a PhD in Theology, specializing in New Testament, from the University of Pretoria, South Africa (2018); Master's in Theological Studies, specializing in Old and New Testament, from Nashotah House Theological Seminary, Wisconsin, USA (2017); MA in Religious Studies, specializing in New Testament (2012); BA in Religious Studies (2007); Diploma in Religious Studies (2004) from the University of Zimbabwe; and Diploma in Pastoral Studies from Bishop Gaul Theological Seminary, Harare, Zimbabwe (2002). He is formerly Senior Lecturer of the New Testament and Biblical Greek at the University of Zimbabwe and Former Lecturer of the following seminaries: Bishop Gaul Theological Seminary, Arrupe Jesuit University, United Theological College, and Wadzanai Training Centre. He is currently serving as parish priest in Palma de Mallorca, Spain, in the Anglican Diocese in Europe. His research interests are in Biblical exegesis, Biblical theology, Interfaith/Interreligious Dialogue, and Peace Building. He is a fellow of the following international schools: New Era Educational and Charitable Support-Jos, Nigeria, 2011; Communities Engaged in Development and Religion-Yogyakarta and Bali, Indonesia, 2012; Septuagint Studies-Gottingen, Germany, 2013; International School for Jain Studies—Delhi, Jaipur, Pune, and Mumbai, India, 2014 and 2015; SAFCEI-Cape Town, South Africa, 2015; KAICIID-Abuja, Nigeria, and Vienna, Austria, 2018 and 2019.

Fortune Sibanda (PhD) is a Professor of Religious Studies in the Department of Theology and Religious Studies, University of Eswatini, Eswatini & Department of Philosophy and Religious Studies, Great Zimbabwe University, Masvingo. He is also a Research/Academic Associate, Research Institute for Theology and Religion Studies, UNISA, South Africa.

Beatrice Taringa holds a Doctor of Philosophy in Education Degree, Master of Education Degree, Bachelor of Education Degree in Curriculum and Arts Education specialising in Indigenous Language Education, ChiShona, all from the University of Zimbabwe. She also attained a Diploma in

Education specialising in ChiShona and History from Gweru Teachers College. She is a Lecturer and the Coordinator of Research Methods and Statistics at Belvedere Technical Teachers College in the Department of Professional Studies and Contemporary Subjects.

Liveson Tatira holds a Bachelor of Arts Honours in Shona, a Master of Arts in African Languages and Literature, a Graduate Certificate in Education, a Doctoral Degree in Novel (Shona), all from the University of Zimbabwe, and a Doctoral Degree in Humanities (Onomastics) from Atlantic International University, USA. He is Professor in the Department of Languages and Arts Education at the University of Zimbabwe where he has taught for over two decades. His research interests are in folklore, language education, indigenous knowledge systems, literature, and onomastics. He has published in several academic books and journals. He is also a published Shona poet.

Shamiso Tatira holds a Bachelor of Arts general degree, Graduate Certificate in Education, Post-Graduate Diploma in Education, and Masters of Education Degree in Curriculum (Shona) all from the University of Zimbabwe and a Doctoral Degree in Language and Media Studies from KwaZulu-Natal, South Africa. She is a principal lecturer at Morgan Teachers College. She has been in Teacher Education for over two decades. Her research interests are language education, curriculum, indigenous knowledge systems, literature, and folklore. She has published in academic books and journals.

Tichaona Zinhumwe is PhD student in Film and Television at the University of Johannesburg. He is Lecturer at Great Zimbabwe University teaching television and radio journalism under the English and Media Studies Department. His research interests cover television and radio news and current affairs programming. His desire is to discover how television and radio current affairs programming can be harnessed for deliberations to create a genuine democratic dispensation in Zimbabwe. He is also interested not only in linguistic research of broadcast discourse in genres such as news and current affairs but would also want to unravel the pictorial and visual discourses and semiotics of television images and how they contribute to telling the television story.

Preface

The outbreak of the COVID-19 pandemic has affected human lives in several ways, that is, public life, working schedules, health delivery systems, and environmental challenges. The effects of the coronavirus disease did not spare Zimbabwe's religious and political life, social media, cultural order, and language in public health communication, language policy, funeral rites, practical theology, and constitutionalism among others. Zimbabwe and beyond have been affected by a number of natural disasters and pandemics such as cyclones and coronavirus among other calamities. The human race was perplexed by the viciousness of the novel coronavirus disease when globally the death toll continued to skyrocket. This resulted in the World Health Organization (WHO) proclaiming that the COVID-19 pandemic was a global public health threat and announcing a variety of mitigatory measures worldwide. The COVID-19 pandemic affected different institutions and organizations through lockdowns that crippled the public health delivery system, education, economy, food supply, transportation, and other valuable sectors in Zimbabwe. All these facets mentioned were affected by COVID-19 in a number of ways. This necessitated the basis for and urgent need to re-imagine the alternative future that would be better prepared to handle pandemics in terms of public health and preparedness for future pandemics in Zimbabwe. This volume's focus is to examine the confronted challenges and lessons and suggest possible solutions in an attempt to create an alternative post-COVID-19 era.

This volume examines the existing incapacitation of the public health system in Zimbabwe, which was hindered by the non-availability of essential medicines and equipment during the outbreak of the COVID-19 pandemic, a situation that caused public panic. The public consciousness of the pandemic was much needed to save the populace from the deadly rage of COVID-19. However, the availability of this necessary information was unfortunately hampered by language choices that reverenced the use of the English language and ignored indigenous languages in Zimbabwe. The volume debated the alternative use of post-COVID-19 journalism, religious beliefs and practices, political experiences, disaster communication, and indigenous languages in Zimbabwe.

Bearing in mind the various catastrophes, disasters, and pandemics that have affected Zimbabwe and the world over, this edited book is a valued academic resource for scholars globally. This volume is going to be an important resource book for academics from various disciplines.

Acknowledgements

First and foremost, we want to thank God, Almighty, *'Musikavanhu'* in *ChiShona* for giving us guidance and wisdom throughout the editorial journey of this volume. We wish to express our heartfelt gratitude to colleagues and friends, particularly external reviewers whose constructive criticism and comments provoked further reflections on the initial proposal. We are indebted to them in terms of sharing ideas and reassurance during the editorial progression. For this volume to be a success, it is due to the team spirit which was prevalent throughout the editorial process. As the editorial team of this volume, we give credit to the meticulous work done by reviewers of the chapters whose professional conduct improved the ultimate quality attained. Their contributions to this volume will conscientize the people of Zimbabwe to have a future pandemic preparedness that will help save lives. We are indebted and thankful to Routledge for giving us the opportunity to edit and publish this volume. We are also thankful to the editorial and publishing team for their responsiveness and positive guidance.

1 Introduction

Reflections, Lessons, and Future Possibilities

Esther Mavengano

The book titled *Zimbabwe in the Post-COVID-19 Era: Reflections, Lessons, and the Future of Public Health* is born at a time when humanity is threatened by unprecedented COVID-19-induced challenges. The outbreak of COVID-19 towards the end of 2019, in China's Wuhan Province and its swift spread across the world to become a full-scale pandemic in 2020, has profoundly affected all spheres of human life. The world was brought to a halt as humanity in both the Global South and Global North was astounded by uncertainties (Wright & Campbell, 2020; Mutanda, 2022). Paradoxically, the advent of the coronavirus pandemic irrefutably exposed lack of human alertness and capacity to deal with global public health catastrophes thereby deconstructing a long-standing Cartesian perspectivism which is deeply embedded in geopolitical subjectivities and North–South divide in a global context. Countries with more vigorous public healthcare systems such as the United States, Italy, Spain, United Kingdom, and France among others were astonishingly not spared from the severity of the Acute Respiratory Syndrome Coronavirus (SARS-CoV-2) infection, which causes COVID-19 disease. For instance, the cited nations account for 70% of recorded deaths internationally by mid-2020, although they comprise merely 7.5% of the world's population (Schellekens & Sourrouille, 2020). These figures speak about the ambiguities in Western discourses and perhaps such a new paradigm that shifts from binary thinking as high COVID-19 mortality rates were recorded in developed countries (Campbell & Doshi, 2020; Schellekens & Sourrouille, 2020). This puzzling reality in the context of the COVID-19 pandemic should evoke an enormous debate among academics as rightly argued by Ndlovu-Gatsheni (2020). Nevertheless, this does not connote that developing nations are spared from the adverse socioeconomic and public-health threats posed by the pandemic. Similarly, it was observed that the impact of COVID-19 was amplified in countries with least-performing health systems and fragile governance and economies. Zimbabwe, which unquestionably falls under this descriptive classification, was caught by the novel COVID-19 pandemic amidst a tremendously debilitated and insubstantial public healthcare system, insufficient equipment, and medical supplies together with a host of other problems. The alarming realities of frustrated public health practitioners compounded by collapsed public health infrastructure, poor sanitary services,

DOI: 10.4324/9781003390732-1

and cynic state–citizen liaison in contemporary Zimbabwe further troubled the instantly desired response to the pandemic and the far-reaching ravages of the coronavirus disease (Mutanda, 2022). For instance, Zimbabwe's public health sector struggled to provide intensive care to patients severely affected by COVID-19 owing to the scarcity of intensive care units, ventilators, and Personal Protective Equipment, a situation that is evidence of poor standards of Occupation Health and Safety (Mutanda, 2022). The cracks that exist between government health workers and the state should be fixed to pave the way for a harmonious rapport.

Against this background, it is thus an opportune time to provide rigorous scholarly introspections into the Zimbabwean experience of COVID-19. Cognizant of the tragic loss of human lives caused by the current pandemic, the essential focus is to draw lessons from the experience with the quest to prioritize and enhance post-COVID-19 public health security. Surely, the pandemic has not merely upended regular procedures and practices but also altered academic agendas. It is the aim of this book to provide thought-provoking and perceptive academic conversations about the unique Zimbabwean experience of the pandemic. Contributors to this volume interrogate the context of COVID-19 from different epistemic orientations and methods with the intention to produce prisms that invite a more robust debate on the subjects of the pandemic and the future of public health service in Zimbabwe. The inter-disciplinary nature of the chapters in this volume is envisioned to offer diversified critical empirical insights that would be an impetus in finding a sustainable vision for the future trajectories that would bring about the desired transformations in Zimbabwe's post-COVID-19 public health system. The volume is a well-timed resource for public health policymakers and practitioners, the Zimbabwean government, World Health Organization, academics, human rights activists, researchers, students, and the general populace in Zimbabwe, Africa, and beyond.

Reflections on Zimbabwe's Experience of COVID-19 Pandemic

While COVID-19 caused excruciating pain and humanitarian crisis, as the world continues to battle the rage of the coronavirus, it cannot be refuted that the pandemic shook humanity out of its nap and stimulated action towards addressing vexing issues that hamper public health service delivery. This hasty activity could positively transform the planet into a better space. The COVID-19 pandemic challenges the academic world as it demands urgency in finding public health solutions. Scholars across the globe are obliged to participate in polemic philosophical dialogues about public health matters and human safety in (post)-COVID-19 context. Such an intellectual endeavor would offer empirical substantiation that informs possible transformative actions. The scholarly reflections in this volume are framed around the following questions: What are the challenges encountered by Zimbabwe during the pandemic which should be addressed to improve public health delivery in post-COVID-19? How does the prevailing socioeconomic environment obstruct efforts to combat the pandemic in Zimbabwe? How can the lessons drawn from the pandemic contribute towards addressing the current problems vis-à-vis dealing with public health emergencies? What will be the role of the Zimbabwean government in promoting the recovery process and reshaping a post-COVID-19 future? Which steps are vital for setting Zimbabwe on a pedestal and path towards safeguarding public health security in post-COVID-19 era? In addition, the outbreak of the COVID-19 pandemic exacerbated binary conceptualization of humanity, dogmatic power dynamics, and de/colonial logics (Quijano 2000), which should be interrogated in order to suggest appropriate transformations in the post-COVID-19 era. What elements of biopolitics and pejorative logics are at play in times of crises? What is the role of language/languaging and communication in public health education during emergencies in preparing Zimbabwe and Africa for possible future pandemics? These reflections come at a time when humanity is yet to find a permanent solution to the depredations of coronavirus disease.

Zimbabwe had its first COVID-19 infection case on 20 March 2020, a Zimbabwean national and a returnee from Britain tested positive, which marked the arrival of the pandemic in a Southern African country (Mutanda, 2022). The first mortal case followed on 22 March 2020, with the death of Zororo Makamba who had visited the United States (Mavengano, 2021). The World Health Organization (WHO) had two months earlier declared the COVID-19 pandemic as a public health crisis of global concern (WHO, 2020a, 2020b; Chitsamatanga & Malinga, 2021). On 27 March 2020, the Government of Zimbabwe pronounced the pandemic a national public health disaster, which impelled an instantaneous response such as a national lockdown, increased public health awareness among others, to counter the rapid spread of coronavirus. By mid-April 2020, Zimbabwe had recorded 14 cases of COVID-19 including 3 deaths (Mavengano, 2021).

Zimbabwe's population is highly mobile due to the reality of deepening poverty and socioeconomic disparities. The initial recorded cases were linked to this mobility of Zimbabwean nationals in and out of the country. Cognizant of the fact that a substantial number of Zimbabweans cross national borders every day into neighboring countries like South Africa, Botswana, Mozambique, and Zambia among others. The national lockdowns, border closures, and other measures, which were put in place, did not deter hungry citizens whose economic precarity and urgency for survival were more pressing issues than the government's COVID-19 preventive regulations (Mavhinga, 2020). This sad scenario compromised public health security and posed a grave health threat to the poor marginal sections of the society, who had no substantial provision whatsoever to anchor them from the COVID-19 impact. Melber (2020) postulates that COVID-19 vulnerability in Africa is likely more linked to primary health problems than in other parts of the globe, where the aged population is most affected. These challenges, as Melber further observes, that emanate from the pathetic economic reality of the populace, commonly poor health conditions, poor state of public health systems, and widespread mistrust of state institutions mean that COVID-19 poses a huge challenge for African societies and governance (Melber, 2020). Guided by the WHO's COVID-19 protocols and considering the highly infectious nature of the coronavirus disease and the fragility of the public health sector, Zimbabwe's restrictions on movement and prohibitions on public associations were most important. Yet, the lockdown measures were weakened by informal trading, which comprises 60% of the country's economy and illegal border-crossing business among other factors. It is hence anticipated that despite the government's efforts to combat the COVID-19 pandemic, Zimbabwe's coronavirus infection cases increased to an estimated 40,314 with 1,637 fatalities within a year from the initial detection (Chitsamatanga & Malinga, 2021). It is by factoring in economic impact on all domains of life within a national space that studies (Masunungure, 2020; Chitsamatanga & Malinga, 2021, Mavengano, 2021) affirm that Zimbabwe's public health system has been in a fragile state for more than two decades.

Lessons Drawn from COVID-19 Pandemic

Although the Zimbabwean government promptly enforced a national lockdown in March 2020 when the country recorded its first case of coronavirus infection, the country's economic, social, and political conditions hamper the effectiveness of its responses to COVID-19. The enforced lockdown measures generated socio-economic precarity of the powerless masses whose bare lives (Agamben, 1998) became more vulnerable (Chagonda, 2020). Similarly, the WHO Director General Tedros Adhanom Ghebreyesus has also pointed out that "The human cost of COVID-19 has been devastating, and the so-called lockdown measures have turned lives upside down" (WHO, 2020a). The economic problems in Zimbabwe had the effect of obstructing the country's attentiveness to the coronavirus calamity. Certainly, the government should think about investing towards the public emergency fund and social welfare programs, which will go a long way to alleviate the economic impact on poor sections of the society. In other words, the ecological crisis triggered by the coronavirus disease turns out to be multi-faceted and context specific. Whereas some developed nations could cope as enclosed states, most poverty-stricken populations felt the heavy burden of being suddenly cut off from the world. Although necessary, the lockdown measures did not go along with important community programs meant to support the less-privileged (Shumba et al., 2020). The government should awaken to the task of alleviating poverty among its citizens in Zimbabwe.

Biopolitics of COVID-19 Pandemic

The discourse of public health outcry and management of the COVID-19 pandemic in Zimbabwe generated a nuanced environment that brought to the fore entrenched political pragmatism and biopolitics to borrow Giorgio Agamben's (1998, 2005) and Foucault's (1979) theorization of state power. It is on record that totalitarianism characterizes governance issues in Zimbabwe (Mavhunga, 2020; Masunungure, 2020). The upsurge of coronavirus disease facilitated the use of both national and global health discourses as spaces for the expression of power tussle. The government justified that lockdown measures were allegedly meant to save lives from the daggers of the coronavirus and contain growing cases of COVID-19. Nevertheless, civil organizations, human rights activists, and government critics contended that the curfew and other restrictions were aimed at suppressing anti-government protests planned for 31 July 2020 (Mavhunga, 2020). The spectacle of authoritarian power further amplifies the state–citizens conflict. The citizens disregarded most of the restrictions and preventive measures as they went about their business in several parts of the country (Mavhunga, 2020). What also exuberated citizenry defiance in the context of Zimbabwe is the challenge of public distrust of state institutions as rightly noted by Melber (2020) and Mavhunga (2020). Ordinary people's cynical view of the government should be addressed to create trust and cooperation. The prevailing strained state–citizen relationship has glaring complications and is a cause for concern particularly with regard to human security during public health emergencies. It is generally alleged that the COVID-19 pandemic environment is used as a facet of regimes of power in Foucauldian vocabulary. For instance, Zimbabwe's poorly remunerated public health workers who became frontline soldiers in the battle against COVID-19 were an army without armory (Mavengano, 2021) due to a lack of essential medical equipment, poor sanitation, crippled medical facilities, insufficient supplies of medicines, PPEs among others. Biopolitical power was instrumental in issuing orders to these workers to desist from strikes or any form of protest. Since the pandemic has created what Agamben (1998) calls a state of exception, the government justifies its dictatorial powers. For instance, the powerless workers were forced to work under what Fanon (1963/2001) could describe as hellish conditions with full awareness of the lingering danger and possible premature deaths.

The political conflict between the Zimbabwean government and the West also came to light. Such politicized schisms and ill-conceived responses to the global health crisis have some catastrophic implications on both citizens' health behavior and diplomatic relations, as the regrettable statement escalates existing tensions. Political reasons such as the view that the COVID-19 pandemic came as God's wrath against the West were quite unfortunate as this hampered efforts meant to control the spread of coronavirus in Zimbabwe. Although the government distanced itself from such a misleading pronouncement and othering logic, it can be argued that some citizens took the public official seriously at the detriment of their health security. The pandemic should not be politicized since mutual partnerships are obligatory. Page (2020) cogently contends that politicizing the pandemic is not only harmful to national [and global] health but also problematic and divisive.

Public Service Delivery

One of the fundamental lessons that the coronavirus reinforced is the requirement to invest in service delivery in order to ameliorate human security (Mutanda, 2022). Whilst affirming that lockdowns and other restrictive measures were necessary for the well-being of the entire nation, it should also be highlighted that poor service delivery and an ailing economy are on the list of key drivers of deviant behavior among citizens in Zimbabwe during the pandemic. The nation should desist from extreme reliance on global supplies of medical equipment, medicines, food, and other essentials that sustain life. The outbreak of COVID-19 led to the closure of borders, and global markets and supply chains came to a halt (Campbell & Doshi, 2020). What does this entail? The pandemic presents a telling moment about the danger of over-reliance on foreign-based services and supplies. Hence it cannot be overemphasized that each government across the world was put to test. Certainly, there is a need to develop self-sufficient local mechanisms as a prerequisite for the possible recurrence of pandemics in the future. It is also impetus to strengthen home-grown production of pharmaceutical industries in order to safeguard human health in times of emergencies. In addition, it is apparently impossible for citizens to practice safety protocols in a country facing water, starvation, and transport crises among other inherently constraining aspects (Mutanda, 2022). With the closure of both public and private sectors during national lockdowns, service delivery was seriously affected in Zimbabwe. In view of the post-COVID-19 future, there is an urgent mandate to think critically about possible new working modalities that would ensure services are continuously offered in times of unexpected disruptions. The pandemic to some extent re-enacts the discourses about geographies of scarcity and geographies of wealth in the public health domain at a global level. The Government of Zimbabwe needs to increase investment towards public healthcare amenities, emergency budget allocation, and medical equipment since this sector has been adversely affected for a very long time. Mandaza and Reeler (2020, p.1) submit illuminating remarks on the state of affairs in Zimbabwe:

> COVID-19 may be a unique problem being faced by the country, but it is superimposed on all the problems that existed prior to the epidemic. It is a moot point whether Zimbabwe was fragile or failed prior to COVID-19: what is unarguable is that the state was broken already, reeling from, an absence of visionary leadership, incoherent policies (even admitted by the Finance minister), a broken economy, broken services, and the spectre of mass hunger and starvation. Zimbabwe was in the deepest trouble it could be, even before COVID-19.

Clearly, Zimbabwe was already a troubled land when the current pandemic broke out worsening its encumbrance. Whereas the nation is exceptionally rich in terms of natural resources, its inhabitants have been enduring poverty and hunger for more since the year 2000 to date. This disquieting state in

Zimbabwe explains why it was predicted by critics that the country was going to be a vortex of contagion.

Vigorous Public Health Education

The media perform an indispensable role in providing accurate information to citizens during health emergencies (UNESCO, 2020). From the public health promotion perspective, it is imperative to have reliable and effective information dissemination outlets during life-threatening epidemic and pandemic emergencies (WHO, 2020a). This includes verification of facts before they are published and truthful reporting of COVID-19 cases, preventive measures, information on mortality cases, vaccination, and so on. This will arguably make a milestone in transforming Zimbabwe's media landscape that has currently been accused of being captured by the state (Mavengano & Marevesa, 2021). An effective information dissemination system is fundamental in reducing anxiety and uncertainties triggered by COVID-19. According to Shumba et al. (2020) there was profound apprehension over the Government of Zimbabwe's ability to manage the coronavirus pandemic, as some people dreaded that there was no transparency and distortion of figures in the way in which confirmed COVID-19 cases were reported in the country. The Zimbabwean government has an arduous task to regain public confidence and support in the post-COVID era. It is also necessary for the government to engage its citizens in decision making that affects the public's daily lives as well as finding lasting solutions to internal tensions that impede national cooperation.

Language and Communication in Management of Public Health Crises

Language plays a fundamental communicative role in all discourse domains (Mavengano, 2021). Hence, it cannot be exaggerated that language is an essential aspect in the present context of the pandemic specifically with regard to constructing and influencing public understanding of the coronavirus disease, how it is transmitted, its treatment, and mitigatory measures (Bates, 2020). This rekindles the language debate and its relevance in public health matters. The pandemic exposed severe limitations of monolingual practices and marginalization of other linguistic communities through English-centric ideologies in mass media, public health literature, and political debates (Piller et al., 2020). This is part of the contestations in discourses on (inter)national (in)justices, linguistic human rights, systematic silencing, and marginalization of othered sections of humanity. The most challenging questions to be addressed are: Which language/s should be used to disseminate vital information on health emergencies? What will happen to linguistic minorities during public health disasters? Is the use of a few languages in a multilingual context like Zimbabwe effective in delivering health information for the wellbeing of all citizens? Scholars in this volume who have attended to the subjects of language and communication are also convinced that there is a need for intercultural dialogue or multilingual communicative repertoires to ensure that the entire populace is well informed about the menace of the pandemic. Xiang et al. (2020) indicated that during a disaster obtainability of well-timed, high-quality information becomes even more vital, not only for the common public but also health experts and decision makers at all stages. This implies that removal of communication barriers will position the nation on a sure footing for a combative journey and finding a lasting solution to the pandemic.

A Preview of the Chapters in this Volume

Chapters in this volume are arranged thematically. Following this introductory chapter, Chapter 2, authored by Gwaravanda Ephraim Taurai, explores the intersection between post-COVID-19 public health and the future of Zimbabwean social media using the Socratic sieve as a tool of ethical reading. Gwaravanda underscores the point that social media is frequently characterized by falsity, unfounded claims, and distorted ideas. The Socratic sieve is an imperative framework for attaining goodness, truthfulness, and usefulness which are requisite ethical aspects for post-COVID-19 social media use in case of future pandemics. Elizabeth Hove and Last Alfandika's chapter entitled "Negotiating the shifting sands of time: The future possibilities of journalism education and research in Zimbabwe, Post-Covid-19 Era," interrogates how the emergence of COVID-19 has transformed the journalism profession. They argued that due to the explosion of information and shift from traditional media to digital modes there is a need for critical and reflective journalism and media practitioners require to catch up with the demand for technological skills in a fast-changing world. This is one salient way of survival in times of pandemics like COVID-19. Their chapter underlines the assertion that effective journalism is one of the key areas when fighting against public health threats.

Similarly, Gift Gwindingwe and Tichaona Zinhumwe in Chapter 4 examine emerging communication culture in the context of COVID-19 and how it has redefined a cultural communication order for the post-pandemic era in Zimbabwe. In Chapter 5, Esther Mavengano examines the dialectics of language questions in Zimbabwe's public health communication with particular attention to the use of English as a lingua franca during the COVID-19 pandemic. Drawing analytical insights from linguistic human rights and decolonial theorizations, Mavengano contends that the COVID-19 pandemic generated sites of language inquiry to quiz abyssal thinking and provide discursive contours around (in) equalities and linguistic subjectivities of the Zimbabwean people. Whereas Mavengano's study acknowledges the fact that English has become an important linguistic link between Zimbabwe and the world, it remains necessary to guard against subtle othering practices which are often hidden in discourses on globalization. The study concludes that there is a need to adopt language use which considers situated demands for multilingual communicative practices for increased collaboration. Chapter 6 authored by

Isaac Mhute is framed within Cultural Dependency Theory to account for the Zimbabwe/African COVID-19 fight's weakness from a language policy perspective in a bid to prepare for better responses to such pandemics in the post-COVID-19 era. The author draws insights from the lived realities of marginalization of indigenous languages and the sad consequences of such language policy in Africa vis-à-vis finding medical solutions to public health challenges. The chapter illuminates the fact that Africa remains pushed into oblivion with regard to finding COVID-19 vaccinations and other medical interventions. Local communities, if empowered through the use of indigenous languages can provide long-term solutions to pandemics like COVID-19. In other words, the relegation of these languages is done at the detriment of public well-being. The local languages could be used to tap into Africa's Indigenous Knowledge Systems (IKS). The IKSs could go a long way towards empowering local communities, ecological sustenance, and Planet Earth health maintenance.

Mika Nyoni and Tsitsi Nyoni's chapter, Chapter 7, draws attention to how the COVID-19 pandemic has changed Zimbabwe's linguistic landscape with a particular reference to ChiShona, which is one of Zimbabwe's Indigenous languages. It also elucidates the imperative of adaptive linguistic practices that embrace contextualized communicative and linguistic changes in (post) COVID-19 Zimbabwe. In Chapter 8, Shupikai Kembo employs netnography to examine COVID-19-related communications in virtual health communities specifically, Facebook groups for Zimbabweans. The results show the importance of information dissemination and in influencing members to adopt recommended behaviors and the need for public health officials to consider utilizing online health communities as vehicles for health communications and marketing interventions.

Sambulo Ndlovu, in Chapter 9, taking the IKS topic further from a different conceptual standpoint, argues for serious consideration of IKS and the need for decolonial thinking to contain the spread of communicable pandemics such as COVID-19. The study draws its framing praxes from the cultural realities of the Ndebele people in Zimbabwe and their funeral practices. The chapter establishes that COVID-19 has vindicated the value of African systems in global development. Maseno Loraine and Sibanda's Chapter 10 deliberates on burial rites in Kenya and Zimbabwe in the context of COVID-19. One of the fundamental aspects of African religion is the reverence it has for its dead and the profound link between the ancestral and living. The study proffers suggestions on how the challenges encountered could be solved for the new post-pandemic African world. In Chapter 11, Beatrice Taringa and Sophia Chirongoma foreground the sociocultural funeral rites of the Karanga Indigenous people who are also known as VaDuma in Bikita, a district in Masvingo, Zimbabwe. Their study interrogates how the pandemic generated monopolizing habits, which disregarded sacred cultural ethos. The pandemic reconfigured religio-sociocultural terrain in Zimbabwe with regard to the funeral rituals of the Karanga people based in Bikita. The religious landscape of the country also informed issues of adherence to preventive measures pronounced by the government and WHO.

To buttress the subject of religio-cultural conflict that was generated by the pandemic, a subsequent Chapter 12, authored by Liveson Tatira, Shamiso Tatira, and Gaynor Paradza also probes the COVID-19 restrictions and their effects on Shona cultural practices and values. The chapter concludes by reflecting on the possible ways of taking aboard some cultural practices and values whilst taking precautions against the spreading of the virus. In doing so, the country would be better placed to deal with similar situations in future. Tobias Marevesa's Chapter 13 focuses on Zimbabwe's religious and political post-COVID-19 future from a decolonial perspective. The chapter illuminates the problematic terrain of decolonial conversations in the context of public healthcare. It explicates how the use of traditional medicines in Africa has been ignored in the global arena during the pandemic. Isheunesu Sexus Gusha's study, Chapter 14, brings to the fore theological and socioeconomic reflections on COVID-19 and its impact on the economically disadvantaged members of the community in Harare Zimbabwe during the 2020 lockdowns. The research proposed that in the future, the government should set aside funds to subsidize economically disadvantaged people in terms of food; engage other key stakeholders like the church, NGOs, and civic organizations in helping the needy during disasters; and ensure accountability to disaster grants and donations. Investment in research and home-grown policy development on disaster preparedness should be a priority.

Conclusion

It is profoundly clear that the COVID-19 pandemic has endangered several areas of public wellbeing by exacerbating economic and social vulnerabilities in Zimbabwe and other poor African nations. It is also ostensible from the contributions in this volume that indeed the outbreak of the COVID-19 pandemic has exposed the prevailing inequities and teething troubles that really hamper the public health system and all other domains of human life in Zimbabwe. This illumination certainly compels us in many ways, to radically shift from historical practices, binary thinking, and stigmas which created dichotomies and negatively affected the public health service delivery and the general wellbeing of the entire humanity. It is evident that Zimbabwe, just like any other countries, cannot return to the ecosphere that existed before the COVID-19 pandemic strike. The authors in this volume engaged in diverse polemical discourses with regard to theCOVID-19 pandemic experience in Zimbabwe and proffered suggestions on steps needed to recreate new national space and modalities of the public health sector in the post-COVID era. One of the foregrounded messages in this volume is that our shared humanity dictates regional and global *esprit de corps*. The polysemic readings of the pandemic proffered in this volume underscore the urgent plea to think about the future in the post-COVID world. The magnitude of the damage to human relations in the context of the COVID-19 pandemic caused by Cartesian thinking and other forms of discrimination cannot be overstated. Ironically, there is no single zone across the globe that has proven to be beyond vulnerability to ecological disasters. Like Santos (2007, 2018), some of the scholars in this volume argue that another medical knowledge (IKS) from Africa is possible and can save the world from the pandemic. It is mostly significant that the state–citizen relationship is built on accountability, trust, unanimity, public engagement, and democratic state institutions to avoid rebellious behavior and practices that would jeopardize response to future public health emergencies. The present pandemic crisis reminds us how essential it is to prioritize a sustainable and efficient public health system in Zimbabwe, as well as nurture healthy human relations. This book reflects on some of the cutting-edge issues concerning understanding public health security in Zimbabwe and taking novel directions towards improving the existing conditions.

References

Agamben, G. (1998). *Homo sacer: Sovereign power and bare life* (translated by Heller-Roazen, D.). Redwood: Stanford University Press.

Agamben, G. (2005). *State of exception*. Chicago: University of Chicago Press.

Bates, R. B. (2020). The (In) appropriateness of the WAR metaphor in response to SARS-COV-2: A rapid analysis of Donald, J. Trump's Rhetoric. https://doi.org/10.3389/fcomm.2020.

Campbell, K. M., & Doshi, R. (2020, March 18). The coronavirus could reshape global order. *Foreign Affairs*, 99(2). Retrieved March 27, 2020, from https://www.foreignaffairs.com/articles/china/2020-03-18/coronavirus-could-reshape-global-order.

Chagonda, T. (2020). *Zimbabwe's shattered economy poses a serious challenge to fighting COVID-19*. Retrieved May 21, 2020, from https://theconversation.com/zimbabwes-shattered-economy-poses-a-serious-challenge-to-fighting-covid-19-135066.

Chitsamatanga, B. B., & Malinga, W. (2021). 'A tale of two paradoxes in response to COVID-19': Public health system and socio-economic implications of the pandemic in South Africa and Zimbabwe. *Cogent Social Sciences*, 7(1), 1–19.

Fanon, F. (1963 [2001]). *The wretched of the earth*. London: Penguin Books.

Foucault, M. (1979). *Discipline and punish: The birth of the prison* (translated by Sheridan, A.).New York: Vintage Books.

Mandaza I., & Reeler T. (2020, May 3). There is no other way than a National Transitional Authority. *The Standard*. https://www.thestandard.co.zw/2020/05/03/no-way-national-transitional-authority/.

Masunungure, Eldred V. ed. (2020). *Zimbabwe's trajectory: Stepping forward or sliding back?* Harare: Weaver Press.

Mavengano, E., & Marevesa, T. (2021). Media landscape and political conflict in Zimbabwe: A critical discourse analysis. In *Emerging trends in strategic communication in the Sub Saharan Africa* (edited by Mhute, I., Mangeya, H., & Jakaza, E.). London: Routledge Publishers, pp. 224–240. https://www-lehmanns-de.translate.goog/shop/sozialwissenschaften /57252303-9781032123387-strategic-com.

Mavengano, E. (2021). Metaphor and representation of COVID-19 pandemic: A cognitive linguistic perspective. In *Covid-19 and the dialectics of global pandemics in Africa: Challenges, opportunities and the future of the global economy in the face of Covid-19* (edited by Mawere, M., Chazovechii, B., & Machingura, F.). Cameroon: Langaa RPCIG. ISBN: 9789956552023. https://www.africanbookscollective.com/books/covid-19-and-the -dialectics-of-globalpandemics-in-africa.

Mavhinga, D. (2020). Lockdown laws draconian, excessive. *The Independent.* Retrieved November 20, 2022, from https://www.theindependent.co.zw/2020/04/03/lockdown -laws-draconian-excessive/.

Melber, H. (2020). *Africa needs tailored responses to coronavirus.* Retrieved November 25, 2022, from https://nai.uu.se/news-and-events/news/2020-04-03-africa-needs-tailored -responses-to-coronavirus.html.

Mutanda, D. (2022). Challenges and opportunities for Zimbabwe's responses to COVID-19. *Cogent Social Sciences*, 8(1), 1–15.

Page, C. (2020). Politicising coronavirus is hazardous to our national health [Blog post]. https://ww.telegraphherald.com/ap/commentary/article-58ffbb41-ob5d-5ac2-bfc1 -bc590ad5a699.html.

Ndlovu-Gatsheni, S. J. (2020). Geopolitics of power and knowledge in the COVID-19 pandemic: Decolonial reflections on a global crisis. *Sage Publications*, 36(4), 366–389.

Piller, I., Zhang, J., & Li, J. (2020). Linguistic diversity in a time of crisis: Language challenges of the COVID-19 pandemic. *Multilingua*, 39(5), 503–515.

Quijano, A. (2000). The coloniality of power and social classification. *Journal of World Systems*, 6(2), 342–386.

Santos, B. de S. (Ed.). (2007). *Another knowledge is possible: Beyond northern epistemologies.* New York: Verso.

Santos, B. de S. (2018). *The end of the cognitive empire: The coming of age of epistemologies of the south.* Durham: Duke University Press.

Schellekens, P., & Sourrouille, D. (2020). Tracking COVID-19 as cause of death: Global estimates of relative severity. *JEL*, I10(J11), 1–16.

Shumba, K., Nyamaruze, P., Nyambuya, V. P., & Meyer-Weitz, T. (2020). Politicising the COVID-19 pandemic in Zimbabwe: Implications for public health and governance. *African Journal of Governance and Development*, 9(1), 270–285.

United Nations Department of Economic and Social Affairs, UNDESA. (2020, May 15). Data tells the story on how Covid-19 is changing the world. New York. https://www .un.org/development/desa/en/news/statistics/data-tells-the-story-on-how-covid-19-is -changing-theworld.html.

World Health Organisation (WHO). (2020a). *Statement on the second meeting of the International Health Regulations (2005) emergency committee regarding the outbreak of novel coronavirus (2019-nCoV).* Retrieved November 20, 2022, from https://www. who.int/ newsroom/detail/30-01-2020

World Health Organisation (WHO). (2020b). *WHO announces COVID-19 outbreak a pandemic.* Retrieved November 27, 2022, from http://www.euro.who.int/en/health -topics/health-emergencies/coronaviruscovid-19/news/news/2020/3/who-announces -covid-19-outbreak-apandemic

Wright, T., & Campbell, K. (2020). The Coronavirus is exposing the limits of populism. *Brookings*, March 5, Retrieved March 18, 2020, from https://www.brookings.edu/blog /order-from-chaos/2020/03/05/the-coronavirus-is-exposing-the-limits-of-populism/.

Xiang, Y.-T., Li, W., Zhang, Q., Jin, Y., Rao, W.-W., Zeng, L.-N., Lok, G. K. I., Chow, I. H. I., Cheung, T., & Hall, B. J. (2020). Timely research papers about COVID-19 in China. *The Lancet*, 395(10225), 684–685.

Yafei, H. (2020). 'It takes a globe' China US Focus, March 3, Retrieved March 23, 2020, from https://www.chinausfocus.com/foreign-policy/it-takes-a-globe.

2 The Socratic Sieve, Post COVID-19 Public Health and Zimbabwean Social Media

Ephraim Taurai Gwaravanda

Introduction

The sudden outbreak of a deadly disease called COVID-19 caused by a coronavirus (SARS-CoV-2), which started in December 2019 in China and spread across the globe by March 2020, shook the entire world. Information about the causes, transmission, effects, and cure for COVID-19 was mixed and confusing. As a result, many countries, including Zimbabwe, found themselves ill-prepared to deal with the pandemic. The lack of credible information about COVID-19 resulted in social media filling in the gap with both misinformation and disinformation. Information about the pandemic is high around the globe and social media occupied the information gap given that government and health institutions were on the slow side in providing information. Social media have occupied a central role during the ongoing pandemic and the resulting wave of content related to COVID-19 has been referred to as an infodemic (Fallis, 2014; Marin, 2020; WHO, 2020). Misinformation about COVID-19 can be dangerous to public health for the reason that it may divert people away from taking appropriate health decisions and actions that would help protect their health and the health of others. Furthermore, misinformation could lead them to take actions that may spread the virus or engage in other problematic behaviors such as violating rules of social distancing, sanitizing, wearing masks, and vaccination. The World Health Organization (WHO) has already recognized the importance of COVID-19-related misinformation and is participating in an awareness campaign aimed at encouraging people to check information with trusted sources. In the context of COVID-19, the trusted sources are the health professionals and it appears where social media users are concentrated numerically, there is also a good supply of medical professionals. It is important to distinguish between misinformation, defined as incorrect or false information that is shared without the intent to harm, and disinformation, defined as incorrect or false information that is shared with the aim of causing harm. However, making this distinction involves assessing the intent of the person spreading the information, which may be problematic at this point and time given that this may be difficult to judge in the Zimbabwean context under study. Consequently, in this chapter, I use misinformation as an embracing term

DOI: 10.4324/9781003390732-2

for incorrect or false information, regardless of intent. This chapter focuses on misinformation that appeared from the onset of the pandemic, transmissions, infections, treatments, and vaccinations in the Zimbabwean context.

Research about the role of social media in spreading misinformation is not entirely new, with a plurality of studies raising alarms about the prevalence of misinformation across social media platforms for emerging diseases and enduring health issues (Marin, 2020; Nguyen & Nguyen, 2020; Weinberg, 2020; Cinelli et al., 2020; Costa-Font, 2020). The contribution of this chapter is the application of the Socratic sieve as an ethical framework to guide against misinformation in the context of the COVID-19 pandemic while at the same time, drawing important information for the responsible use of social media in the future.

This chapter is divided into three sections. The first section examines the extent of misinformation in the various stages of the COVID-19 pandemic that include causes, transmission, treatment, side effects, and vaccination as experienced in Zimbabwean social media. The second section provides an analysis of the Socratic sieve as an ethical framework that can be used to achieve truth, goodness, and usefulness in passing information. The last section provides social media lessons that can be drawn from COVID-19 social media experiences for the future.

COVID-19 and Social Media in Zimbabwe

Social media is defined as "online services that allow users to create profiles which are public, semi-public or both" (Barret-Maitland & Lynch, 2020: 1). Forms of social media include WhatsApp, Twitter, Instagram, YouTube among others. The World Health Organization (WHO) has called attention to the "infodemic" that exists alongside the COVID-19 pandemic, arguing that social media plays a dangerous role in amplifying the spread of misinformation (WHO, 2020). For COVID-19, misinformation has been documented on a number of topics, including official governmental and medical organization actions – how the virus originated, how it spreads, ways to prevent or treat infection, and vaccination (Brennen et al., 2020; Howard, 2021). In Zimbabwe, social media played a role in passing information that failed to meet the credibility test. The misinformation may be categorized as myth, humor, and deliberate falsity. While certain sections of the society could easily identify myths, jokes, and false information about COVID-19, other sections may have missed the jokes thereby ending up being misinformed.

In analyzing the extent of misinformation about COVID-19 in Zimbabwe, I will focus on the origins, transmission, treatment, and vaccination. In Zimbabwe, a lot of misinformation circulated concerning the origins of the virus with both internal and external information filling social media. One key theory which spread in social media is that the coronavirus started as an experiment for biological weapons in China. So it was understood as an artificial rather than a natural virus. In Zimbabwe, the Minister of Defence pronounced coronavirus as a punishment from God to rich nations such as the US, UK, and the EU for imposing sanctions on Zimbabwe (Ndebele, 2020). The pronouncement spread through social media and online news items but it took a day or two before other government officials corrected the minister. However, despite the efforts to correct, the damage had already been done and it is highly probable that the corrective efforts were missed by a significant population in Zimbabwe.

Regarding the transmission of the virus, there is misinformation that relates to the Defence Minister's punishment from God theory that sees COVID-19 as a disease for the rich or the affluent. This means that COVID-19 is seen as affecting developed countries only. Linked to that, COVID-19 was also viewed as a disease for the aeroplane and there was misinformation that pedestrians were spared from the virus. This misinformation was further deepened in the early stages of the virus in Zimbabwe (March 2020) by the absence of local transmissions.

Concerning the treatment of the virus, there was a lot of misinformation about the use of hot tea or hot water as it was believed that the virus does not spread under hot conditions. In addition to these, herbs that were traditionally used to treat common cold were also suggested and among them were *zumbani*, lemon, guava, mango, and gumtree leaves. This information led to delays in informing health officials and certain individuals who may have otherwise been saved lost their lives. Based on the fact that sanitizers are alcohol based, there was a wide circulation of misinformation that alcohol consumption can cure coronavirus infection.

Vaccination misinformation was around vaccine efficacy, side effects, and even the real purpose of the vaccine. In the context of COVID-19 vaccination, misinformation was around efficacy, side effects, and even deformation. Social media circulated material indicating left-wing scientists who argued that the vaccines were rushed and they are ineffective. Side effects were even more and there was a lot of circulation of misinformation about deaths due to vaccination, dizziness, and fainting. A more serious news that was widely circulated on social media was the death of a Gutu health official who died one week after receiving the Sinopharm COVID-19 first vaccine (Chagonda, 2021). Such incidents created a strawman argument that sideswept the good sides of the vaccines in the light of COVID-19 deaths. There was also misinformation that COVID-19 virus causes infertility among men and women. This kind of misinformation resulted in the production, selling, and buying of fake vaccination cards as a way of trying to avoid vaccination (The Herald, 2021). Vaccination cards were also bought by employees whose employers demanded proof of vaccination.

Considered jointly, the impact of misinformation on social media has far-reaching effects on the Zimbabwean population and gives a lot of work to the health officials who try to combat the virus. Health education begins by demystifying the myths before the actual health education can be offered. The examined misconceptions make it necessary to adopt a framework of ethical analysis in social media as discussed in the next section.

The Socratic Sieve

The Socratic sieve is an ethical test that was developed by Socrates that subjects information to a three-step test of truth, goodness, and usefulness before it can pass as credible and worth spreading to other people (Beversluis, 2000; Ahbel-Rappe & Rachana, 2005; Rudebusch, 2009; Morrison, 2010). The test is presented as a story where Socrates is in dialogue with his interlocutor.

The first sieve, Socrates explained, is the sieve of truth. According to Socrates, a story is worth hearing and sharing if it is true. That means it must be possible to confirm the truth of any piece of information. Otherwise, it is better to remain silent. Socrates proceeds to consider the second sieve, which is goodness. For Socrates, if the story does good, if it contributes something positive to the person who hears it, then no doubt it is worth telling (Teloh, 1986). In a more modern context, it would be interesting to ask about the information's intention: does the story aim to shock, create fear, convince, or manipulate. Finally, the third sieve is the sieve of usefulness. The philosopher asked the person if his story contained any useful information. Given a third negative answer, he concluded: "If what you want to tell me is neither true nor good nor useful, why bother telling me at all?" (Reshotko, 2006: 38). This theory looks simplistic. But if everyone filtered their comments and assertions through these three sieves before making them public, there would certainly be less disinformation. And probably there would be a lot less "noise" on social media.

By way of application, the three sieves test can be used to test information about the origins, transmission, treatment, and prevention of the COVID-19 pandemic by subjecting each of the misinformation to the test. To begin with, testing the "news" that the COVID-19 virus was a laboratory experiment would require one to provide proof of scientific evidence so as to demonstrate the truth of the claim. There is a need to check facts before one passes that to the next person. An ethically responsible use of social media would indicate that unverified "news" items are not worth passing. This means that when one has not proved the veracity of something, one should not pass it to the next person.

The second sieve is goodness. In ethics, goodness is defined as rightness or correctness. In other words, it refers to the right action. It is seen as an intrinsic quality of moral actions. In the context of the sieve, goodness is measured by the extent to which it benefits people who hear the "news." If for example, one spreads the misinformation that COVID-19 vaccination will result in deformation and eventual death after two years, such news becomes harmful to the extent to which it threatens public health given that such information results in people shunning the vaccine. Manipulations and scapegoats are therefore inconsistent with goodness and this can be seen in the way Donald Trump accused China of manufacturing the coronavirus, even if he did not have the evidence and again this accusation was made prior to the WHO fact-finding mission to China.

The third sieve is usefulness. According to Socrates, information has to be useful to the recipients before it can be passed from one person to the other. In other words, this sieve requires that information must have practical benefits to the recipients. It has to be beneficial to their everyday lives. In the context of COVID-19 social media postings, damaging information is still being passed without due consideration of the associated harms.

There is a close connection among the three requirements of the triple-test filter. For anything to pass as worth spreading, it has to pass all three stages. If a piece of information just passes one stage and fails the other two then it is not worth spreading. Again, if information passes only two filters and fails in one, that information is not worth spreading. The triple-test filter requires that if information passes all three filters then it can be worth spreading. This means that the filters are individually necessary and jointly sufficient in their application. So in the context of COVID-19 origins, transmission, treatment, vaccination, and mutation of the virus, it is important that ethical responsibility is exercised to avoid spreading false information that may go against efforts to fight COVID-19.

Despite the potential significance of the Socratic sieve in addressing misinformation, critics of the sieve have identified conceptual and practical limitations associated with it. Firstly, it can be argued that the triple test is too abstract and remote from daily moral reasoning procedures. While this objection may be noted, it can still be maintained that the level of abstraction can be reduced significantly, if the triple test is expressed in simple language and even indigenous language for the ordinary person to grasp and appreciate. The second possible limitation is that it may be difficult to identify the real experts as sources of truth and this may result in social media playing the expert role. In response to this objection, it can be argued that while social media may play the role of experts, it is still possible to distinguish truth and falsity in the context of social media by verifying social media claims with health authorities. The third limitation that critics point out is that goodness appears to be more subjective than an objective concept and what may be good for one person may be bad for the next person. To answer this objection, it can be argued that while the appreciation of goodness may involve subjective sentiments, it does not necessarily follow that the evaluation of moral goodness is also subjective given that each moral theory has objective evaluative criteria in terms of motives (Kantian ethics), consequences (utilitarianism), virtues (virtue ethics), rights (rights-based ethics), or communal values (Ubuntu ethics). Lastly, critics have pointed out that usefulness varies with cultures and places and it is difficult to obtain a universal or pluriversal understanding of usefulness. In response to such an objection, it may be true that the concept of usefulness may be difficult to universalize but the context in the Socratic sieve is not about universal application but it measures the extent to which an individual benefits and it goes beyond individual levels by assessing the overall benefits to the community. The next section focuses on important lessons that can be drawn from the triple-test filter for use against misinformation for the COVID-19 pandemic and even future pandemics and or natural disasters.

Lessons for the Future

In this section, I will discuss three important lessons corresponding to each of the filters in the Socratic sieve for future responsible use of social media in the context of the COVID-19 pandemic, in particular, and future pandemics in general. The lessons are drawn from misinformation about COVID-19 origins, transmission, treatment, and vaccination.

As indicated earlier, social media is promoting and disseminating untrustworthy information. To counter this, it can be that suggested addressing; rebutting or refuting misinformation can be done by health authorities by posting accurate information on social media platforms. This implies that misinformation could be replaced by facts and accurate information, or health authorities could debunk myths and help answer people's queries (Dreyfus, 2001). Public broadcasters and the print media can also be used to correct misinformation on COVID-19. Increasing the health literacy of social media users can help individuals to decide on information before passing it to the next person: there is a need to educate social media users on how to determine what information is reliable and to encourage them to assume personal responsibility for not circulating false information. In addition, the circulation of information should be done by authorities on experts in the area and in this particular context, health experts. Responsible analysis can be drawn from the principle of verification which states that a statement is meaningful if and only if it can be proved true or false, at least in principle, by means of the experience. In other words, the meaning of a statement is its method of verification; that is, we know the meaning of a statement if we know the conditions under which the statement is true or false. This appears to be a strict and difficult requirement because if and only if we are able to exactly describe the conditions in which it is possible to answer "yes," or, respectively, the conditions in which it is necessary to answer with a "no." The meaning of a statement is thus defined only through the specification of conditions of truth and falsity.

A scientific theory, and in this context, a medical theory is an axiomatic system that obtains an empirical interpretation through appropriate statements called rules of correspondence, which establish a correlation between real objects (or real processes) and the abstract concepts of the theory. These statements are often expressed by experts or professionals who actually identify themselves with such statements (Elder, 2014). Contrary to social media postings that are often anonymous, the lesson that can be drawn is that anonymous postings are often false and therefore unreliable to be passed on to the next person or groups. However, sometimes a false name is given to a statement or a medical expert's name is misquoted and this means it does not necessarily follow that postings with names are indications of truth. There is a need for scrutiny of the postings and social media users should first verify claims with medical professionals before passing them to the next person. Where one is unsure of the contents of social media, it is better to completely refrain from posting to the next person. The language of a theory is expressed in two terms, observational and theoretical, and these correspond to analytic and synthetic statements. Analytic statements refer to relations of ideas and the truth of such statements is tested through the logical relationship of the subject and the predicate terms. Synthetic statements are obtained by joining two unrelated concepts and the truth of such statements is obtained via empirical observation. Analytic statements are *a priori* and their truth is based on the rules of the language; on the contrary, synthetic statements depend on experience, and their truth can be acknowledged only by means of the experience. This conception about the structure of scientific theories is perhaps the most durable philosophical principle of logical positivism.

The lesson that can be drawn is that, in relation to COVID-19, the truth of circulating social media postings can be established through both a logical and factual criterion. In terms of logical analysis, a statement can be judged as untrue by virtue of contradicting known facts. Furthermore, two contradictory theories cannot be simultaneously true (Ess, 2006). Rather, contradictory statements may be both false. For example, it can be established by logical analysis that claim A which states that the COVID-19 virus was manufactured in a laboratory and claim B that the virus came as a result of fifth-generation technology. Such statements may not both be true; rather they may both be false. In the context of factual claims, the truth of such statements should be verified using established medical facts about COVID-19. While some thinkers propose that social media should be supervised by an authority or government to avoid misinformation, this line of thought is inconsistent with the principles of democracy. Instead, this could be addressed by the government providing more comprehensive reports on the current epidemiological situation.

The second lesson relates to goodness or moral uprightness. Irresponsible posting of unverified claims about COVID-19 may do more harm than good to individuals because they violate the principle of respect for persons, which holds that individual persons have the right to make their own choices and develop their own life plans. In the context of COVID-19 social media misinformation, the principle implies that individuals have the right to true and correct information. The principle requires individuals to be competent, that is, capable of understanding the consequences of the information and capable of making a free choice. Since this cannot be easily determined prior to posting messages, it is important for one to refrain from making any potentially harmful postings because it may be far more dangerous to pass false information that threatens public health.

The ethical principle of goodness requires people to judge what is best not only for themselves or other individuals but also what is best for groups, such as friends, families, religious groups, one's country, etc. Social media is characterized by mixed populations in terms of literacy levels, age groups, religions, and cultural backgrounds, hence the important lesson is that one must be sensitive to demographic factors before irresponsible postings. To promote goodness and well-being, social media users must think whether postings would maximize the well-being of the relevant group. Their method for determining the well-being of a group involved adding up the benefits and losses that members of the group would experience as a result of adopting one action or policy. The well-being of the group is simply the sum total of the interests of all of its members.

While there are circumstances in which moral goodness focuses on the interests of specific individuals or groups, goodness also requires that moral judgments be based on equal consideration of interests. Goodness is approximated by the extent to which social media information is impartial and not from a partiality perspective that favors ourselves, our friends, or others we especially care about.

If this impartial perspective is seen as necessary for measuring goodness, then both self-interest and partiality to specific groups will be rejected as deviations from goodness. For example, the so-called "ethical egoism," which says that goodness requires people to promote their own interest, would be rejected either as a false morality or as not a morality at all (Feenberg, 1999). While morality implies that it is rational for people to maximize their own well-being or the well-being of groups that they favor, goodness would reject this as a criterion for determining what is morally right or wrong.

In the context of social media, it may be difficult to decide whether judgments of right and wrong should be based on the actual consequences of actions or their foreseeable consequences. This problem arises when the actual effects of actions differ from what we expected. Foreseeable consequence moral philosophers such as Jeremy Bentham and John Stuart Mill accept the distinction between evaluating actions and evaluating the people who carry them out, but they see no reason to make the moral rightness or wrongness of actions depend on facts that might be unknowable. For them, what is right or wrong for a person depends on what is knowable by a person at a given time.

Another way to describe the actual versus foreseeable consequence dispute is to contrast two thoughts. The first one, the actual consequence view, states that to act rightly is to do whatever produces best consequences. The second view claims that a person acts rightly by doing the action that has the highest level of "expected utility." The expected utility is a combination of the good (or bad) effects that one predicts will result from an action and the probability of those effects occurring. What this shows is that actual consequence and foreseeable consequence provide difficulties in measuring what is morally justifiable. Foreseeable consequence is understood as a decision-making procedure while actual consequence gives a criterion of right and wrong. Foreseeable consequence moral philosophers claim that the action with the highest expected utility is both the best thing to do based on current evidence and the right action. Actual consequence moral philosophers might agree that the option with the highest expected utility is the best thing to do but they claim that it could still turn out to be the wrong action (Frick and Oberprantacher, 2011).

This would occur if unforeseen bad consequences reveal that the option chosen did not have the best results and thus was the wrong thing to do.

As far as usefulness is concerned, the third lesson to be drawn from the COVID-19 and future pandemics in this chapter, is that social media postings are to be judged primarily by their fruits and consequences, not by their origins or their relations to antecedent data or facts. Social media should be used as an instrument or tool for coping with reality. This means that useful information must be measured in terms of its problem-solving power rather than emotional consolation or subjective comfort. What is important is that social media postings can be relied upon time and again to solve pressing problems and to clear up significant difficulties confronting inquirers in terms of the COVID-19 pandemic. To the extent to which social media information "works" practically in this way (Manders-Huits, 2010), it makes sense to keep using it – though we must always allow for the possibility that it will eventually have to be replaced by some information that works even better as health science improves. This can be evidenced by WHO in its shift of positions regarding social distancing, face masks, treatment, and vaccination (WHO, 2020). Again, important lessons can be drawn in the case of the mutations of the coronavirus (such as delta and omicron variants) thereby placing a greater need for credible information.

Conclusion

The chapter has examined the proliferation of social media messages about COVID-19 and it has shown that the pandemic is characterized by misinformation. I have argued that the use of the Socratic sieve as a framework of ethical analysis allows individuals to test the truth, goodness, and usefulness of social media postings before they can be passed to the next person or group of persons. I have also drawn lessons from the Socratic triple-sieve test, for the responsible use of social media both for the COVID-19 pandemic and future pandemics. Verification, awareness of well-being, and practical outcomes are to be given serious consideration to avoid situations where social media postings threaten public health due to misinformation. Having explored the ethical dimension of the use of social media in the context of COVID-19, future research may focus on epistemic and logical dimensions of social media postings in the context of COVID-19.

References

Ahbel-Rappe, S., & Rachana, K. (2005). *A companion to Socrates*. Oxford: Blackwell Publishers.

Barret-Maitland, N., & Lynch, J. (2020). Social media, ethics and the privacy paradox. In C Kalloniatis & C Travieso-Gonzalez (Eds.) Security and privacy from a legal, *ethics, and technical perspective* (pp. 1–15). London: IntechOpen.

Beversluis, J. (2000). *Cross-examining Socrates: A defense of the interlocutors in Plato's early dialogues*. Cambridge: Cambridge University Press.

Brennen, J. S., Simon, F., Howard, P. N., & Nielsen, R. K. (2020). *Types, sources, and claims of COVID-19 misinformation*. Retrieved October 25, 2021, from https://reute rsinstitute .politics.ox.ac.uk/types-sources-and-claims-covid-19-misinformation.

Changonda, C. (2021, March 5). Gutu man dies after taking Covid19 vaccination. *The Mirror*. Available at: Gutu man dies after taking Covid19 vaccination | The Mirror (masvingomirror.com)

Cinelli, M., Quattrociocchi, W., Galeazzi, A., Valensise, C. M., Brugnoli, E., Schmidt, A. L. et al. (2020). *The Covid-19 social media infodemic*. Retrieved October 30, 2021, from https://arxiv.org/pdf/2003.05004v1.

Costa-Font, J. (2020). *Dealing with Covid-19 requires pre-emptive action to realistically communicate risks to the public*. Retrieved October 24, 2021, from https://blogs.lse.ac.uk/impactofsoc ialsciences/2020/03/25/dealing-with-covid-19-requires-preemptive-risksto-.

Dreyfus, H. (2001). *On the internet*. New York: Routledge.

Elder, A. (2014). Excellent online friendships: An Aristotelian defense of social media. *Ethics and Information Technology, 16*(4), 287–297.

Ess, C. (2006). Ethical pluralism and global information ethics. *Ethics and Information Technology, 8*(4), 215–226.

Fallis, D. (2014). The varieties of disinformation. In L. Floridi & P. Illiari (Eds.), *Philosophy of information quality* (pp. 135–162). Cham: Springer.

Feenberg, A. (1999). *Questioning technology*. New York: Routledge.

Frick, M., & Oberprantacher, A. (2011). Shared is not yet sharing, or: What makes social networking services public? *International Review of Information Ethics, 15*, 18–23.

Herald. (2021, September 13). Zimbabwe: Nurse in trouble over vaccination cards. *The Herald*. Available at: Zimbabwe: Nurse in Trouble Over Vaccination Cards - allAfrica .com

Howard, P. (2021). *Misinformation and the coronavirus resistance*. Retrieved October 15, 2021, from https://www.oii.ox.ac.uk/blog/misinforma tion-and-the-coron aviru s-resis tance/.

Manders-Huits, N. (2010). Practical versus moral identities in identity management. *Ethics and Information Technology, 12*(1), 43–55.

Marin, L. (2020). Three contextual dimensions of information on social media: Lessons learned from the COVID19 infodemic. *Ethics and Information Technology*. https://doi.org /10.1007/s10676-020-09550-2.

Morrison, D. R. (2010). *The Cambridge companion to Socrates*. Cambridge: Cambridge University Press.

Ndebele, L. (2020, March 16). Zim minister's bizarre coronavirus claim: 'It's to punish the West for sanctions'. *Sunday Times*, 3–4. Available at: Zim minister's bizarre coronavirus claim: 'It's to punish the West for sanctions' (timeslive.co.za)

Nguyen, H., & Nguyen, A. (2020). Covid-19 misinformation and the social (media) amplification of risk: A Vietnamese perspective. *Media and Communication, 8*(2), 444–447.

Reshotko, N. (2006). *Socratic virtue: Making the best of the neither-good-nor-bad*. Cambridge: Cambridge University Press.

Rudebusch, G. (2009). *Socrates*. Oxford: Wiley-Blackwell.

Teloh, H. (1986). *Socratic education in Plato's early dialogues*. Notre Dame, IN: University of Notre Dame Press.

Weinberg, J. (2020). *The role of philosophy and philosophers inthe coronavirus pandemic*. Retrieved October 14, 2021, from https://dailynous.com/2020/03/27/role-philosophy-philosophe rs-coronavirunous.com/2020/03/27/role-philosophy-philosophers-coronaviru.

World Health Organisation. (2020). *Novel coronavirus, situation report 13*. Retrieved October 15, 2021, from https://www.who.int/docs/defau lt-sourc e/coron aviru se/situa tion-repor ts/20200 202-sitrep-13-ncov-v3.pdf.

3 Negotiating the Shifting Sands of Time

The Future Possibilities of Journalism Education and Research in Zimbabwe, Post-Covid-19 Era

Elizabeth F. Hove and Last Alfandika

Introduction

While still contending with *the constantly changing circumstances or aspects of the media due to the ever-changing digital technology,* the coming in of the COVID-19 pandemic has further compounded journalism education in Zimbabwe, Africa, and the world at large. The advancement of digital media technology and the emergence of COVID-19 have transformed the profession *making it difficult to understand or contend with* thereby calling for new ways to train media practitioners around the globe. The shift from breaking the news to citizen journalism, calls for a new set of technical skills to provide the ever-changing and difficult-to-please audience with befitting content. Mere reporting of the facts is no longer adequate in a world awash with fake news; misinformation and disinformation. The growing demands of digital media technology require journalists who are critical, reflective, and multi-skilled.

Besides, the COVID-19 pandemic has brought to the fore challenges to traditional practices in journalism. Thus, the challenges of online learning and research in journalism have necessitated the need for alternative learning methods to impart requisite practical skills. Although Zimbabwe and the rest of Africa are behind in technological innovation, the rapid changes in digital technology have had a profound impact on our journalism hence, the need to begin the conversation on future possibilities for journalism education and research in Zimbabwe, Africa, and the world.

In Southern Africa, journalism education and training has come a long way; however, there is still more to be done to catch up with the demands of the modern world of digital technology. In this region and beyond, journalism education and training are struggling due to several challenges such as failure to disentangle itself from western-oriented models of education and training, which are still rooted in colonial systems, yet in the Global South, they have moved ahead. The training currently offered in most of the schools does not hone critical skills that can be imparted to a community to open up democratic space for debates. In some authoritarian regimes such as Zimbabwe, repressive

DOI: 10.4324/9781003390732-3

legal environments ushered around 2000–2005 are still limiting media freedom and freedom of expression hindering the growth of the journalism industry. In addition, some journalists are yet to come to terms with digital communication technologies and the "ethical implications of using them" (Banda et. al., 2010: 168). The digital revolution has not just transformed the media industry but is calling upon new ways to define the profession and train media practitioners.

It is however necessary to provide a brief background to understand the scenario of the training institutions in Zimbabwe as it is from these that the data will be derived. Zimbabwe's journalism education and training can be traced back to 1987 when Zimbabwe had only two institutions offering diplomas in journalism and media namely, Harare Polytechnic and the Christian College of Southern Africa (CCOSA). From 1993, the University of Zimbabwe started offering a one-year postgraduate diploma in Media and Communication Studies, and then in 1998 an MA degree in Media and Communication was introduced sponsored by the Norwegian Agency for Rural Development (NORAD). This marked the beginning of the teaching of media and journalism in higher education. By 2005, three universities, Midlands State University (MSU), National University of Science and Technology (NUST), and Zimbabwe Open University (ZOU), were offering programs in media and journalism (Banda et al., 2010). Today, the country has various universities and other institutions offering journalism programs. In terms of digital equipment, these institutions are poorly equipped.

Thus, still contending with the ever-shifting sands of the digital technology, the COVID-19 pandemic has accelerated these changes putting more pressure on journalism training institutions to wholly embrace digital communication technologies' skills in their training curriculum. For instance, measures enforced by the Zimbabwean government to combat the scrounge of COVID-19, such as restrictions, have further resulted in a "new normal" that is reliant on digital technologies hence, the need for journalism training in Zimbabwe to start preparing media students to meet the demands of future journalism with confidence. Using original data collected from news editors, media, and journalism trainers in Zimbabwean training institutes, this chapter interrogates future possibilities for journalism education and training in Zimbabwe. It examines the skills and knowledge that media and journalism schools in Zimbabwe should hone to produce a complete journalist who can effectively work in this ever-shifting digital technology-induced environment.

Journalism Education in Africa – Pedagogical Theory to Meaning-based Practice

The literature on media and journalism education pre-COVID-19 can be looked at as debates on how media and journalism ought to be taught: decolonizing or de-westernizing journalism education versus internationalizing journalism education. It can be further seen as a means to understand how repressive governments have affected journalism and the extent to which digital media comes in as solace. While these debates have shaped journalism in Africa and the world at large, they have continued to be issues of concern in journalism education and training in Zimbabwe. Based on the complications added by COVID-19, there is a need to reflect on these concerns.

Journalism education is a complex concept. The field itself cannot be clearly defined because it "brings together two areas that are in constant flux. Each is based on a series of theoretical suppositions, some of which are based in the historical, cultural, and industrial experiences of a rather narrow slice of people coming from, and/or educated by colonial powers" Hochheimer (2001: 98). Education is a word derived from the Latin word "educare," meaning, to draw out (ibid). Thus, to educate is to provide the context and the support within which students can learn to reach within themselves, to discover the power and abilities that lie within them, and to take control of their own lives (Hochheimer, 2001: 101). Defining "journalism education" Hochheimer (2001) contends that it is the "means to teach students the norms and processes of news work to provide them with the skills they need to succeed within the journalism industries" (Hochheimer, 2001: 101). However, he further argues that it "poses the students as blank slates to be drawn upon; they are seen as people with no previous knowledge into which the teacher will pour relevant facts and skills, which the student is obliged to learn to succeed" (Hochheimer, 2001: 101). It is based on this argument that we seek to review journalism training in Zimbabwe.

Another dimension this debate takes is the theory versus skills debate. Wasserman (2005) argues that "theory vs skills debate" is redundant and not helpful to cope with the new challenges to journalism such as the increasing multicultural nature of international societies, the rise of infotainment genres, the meaning of the modernistic view of journalism as "intrinsically objective, free and fair," the convergence of media, and "the globalisation of the media" (2005: 65). In light of these challenges, Wasserman advocates for the praxis approach to journalism education, which "would mean that theory, research and practice would be seen as mutually constitutive instead of separate ingredients that need to be present in the right quantities as in a recipe" (2005: 165). However, Banda et al. (2010) note that achieving this may be a long way as the greatest challenge for training institutions is the lack of funding and equipment: "In an environment where training institutions are ill equipped and where there are too few media companies to facilitate 'industry attachments," practical courses rarely achieve their objectives" (2010: 167). Thus, theoretical modules largely dominate most programs in Zimbabwe and Southern Africa.

The debate to teach students the norms and processes of news work and provide them with the skills they need to succeed in the modern journalism industry engulfed by digital technology is very complex. The current ways of delivering have been slated as it does not acknowledge the existence of some skills naturally embedded in the students, thus, they are taken as a tabula rasa. As the debate unfolds, some researchers believe that there is a need for a praxis approach to journalism education. This entails that theory should come in to explain praxis. In other words, theory comes in to theorize practice as theory, research, and practice are supposed to be seen as mutually constitutive instead of separate ingredients that need to be present in the right quantities as in a recipe.

Liberalizing Journalism and Media Education: Can It Serve the Profession?

The dominance of Western-based knowledge in the production, organization, and dissemination of information in non-western countries is a direct result of the journalism training systems (Ake, 1979; Wa Thiong'o, 1986; Chabal, 2012). In contextualizing journalism education and training in Southern Africa, Banda et al. argue that "Journalism education in Southern Africa must further contend with defining a new academic identity for itself, extricating itself from dependency on western-oriented models of journalism education and training" (2010: 157). This process of finding a new identity has been widely explored by journalism and media scholars in Africa. Pieter J. Fourie (2013: 223) summarizes these debates in journalism education as the "crisis of journalism" and also raises concerns among others on the commercialization of journalism and its influence on the quality of journalism, and the rise of tabloid journalism. Willems (2014) traces the emergence of media and communication studies in West Africa and Southern Africa. She points to the emerging literature that has critiqued the Eurocentric nature of existing research and has called for a need to ensure that research is rooted more clearly in the African context. "These alternative genealogies of the field have frequently and actively challenged the presumed universality of media and communication training, thereby pointing to much longer histories of 'de westernising' or 'internationalising' not driven by the 'centre' but propagated from the 'periphery'" (2014: 3).

As Hochheimer (2001: 100) puts it, "if these current news values don't serve Americans well, there seems to be no way they can serve African journalists, African students, or African readers/listeners/viewers well either." There is a need to introduce curricula that focus on providing critical community–media literacy at universities and colleges as a way to provincialize journalism education (Banda et al., 2010). To further add to the crisis are repressive regimes and, sadly, such environments present challenges for the future of journalism, and journalism education seems to be primarily about finding ways to deal or manoeuvre within the repressive legal environment. For instance, in Zimbabwe, the period from 2000 to 2005 witnessed several legal measures that limited media freedom and freedom of expression (Banda et al., 2010).

Digital Technologies, Journalism, and Media Education

The coming of the internet and information communication technology, in general, has added to the journalism crisis. Do-it-yourself journalism such as blogs, chat rooms, electronic interest groups, and social media among other journalistic practices has shown that journalism is fast succumbing to tech-nological determinism. This, however, has raised questions about the effect of digital media technology on key concepts such as "objectivity, factuality, engagement, accountability, public interest, advocacy, trust, and authentic-ity" (Fourie, 2013: 223). According to Rodney-Gumede (2017), this calls for a redefinition of the profession itself and this is no simple task as there are no simple answers. Now more than ever, key concepts of ethics, sound ideas of news values, and source verification practices as highlighted by Fourie are more important in light of the increased flow of information. "The ability to evaluate sources and the trustworthiness of information is becoming even more vital for the general public to be able to make informed choices about news consumption and which news sources to believe" (Gumede, 2011: 287).

However, the crisis is not unique to present-day journalism only:

> The study of media has always been concerned with the "shock of the new"; with radio in the new sociology of mass communication that began in the USA in the late 1930's; with the very new medium of television in British media studies that began in Birmingham in the 1970's and globally, with the impact of new "social media" in the last decade or so. (Tomaselli et al., 2013: 42)

Thus, "African journalists all need to be conversant with digital technolo-gies information gathering, processing and distribution, and to understand the ethical implications of using these technologies" (Banda et al., 2010: 158). In a networked society, it has thus become even more pertinent that journal-ists not only be conversant with new communication technologies but realize that "information and communication are the most fundamental dimensions of human activity and organisation, a revolutionary change in the material condi-tions of their performance affects the entire realm of human activity" (Castells, 2004: 9). "Networks are becoming the nervous system of our society" affect-ing every part of people's lives (Jan van Dijk, 2006: 2). The media are key in this network society and, as contended by Castells (2004), are the primary source of messages and images today. Journalism education needs to also take into consideration the changing nature of the audience and how to address this new audience and media environment because,

> The media system is characterised by global business concentration, by diversification of audience (including cultural diversification), by techno-logical versatility and channel multiplicity, and by the growing autonomy of an audience that is equipped with the internet and has learned the rules of the game; namely, everything that is a collective mental experience is virtual, but this virtuality is a fundamental dimension of everybody's reality.
>
> (2004: 30)

Thus an African journalist conversant with digital media technologies has necessitated the training of a multi-skilled student who can adapt to this new environment despite the above challenges. However, this has been hampered by the fact that the new skills and technological convergence have seen the industry further shrink and placements in decline as newsrooms have down-sized. The COVID-19 pandemic and the social media infordemic have further affected the media industry and added to the crisis in journalism education today. Teaching the practical/skills aspects in journalism and media studies has become more complex in a socially and physically distanced COVID-19 environment as students cannot be exposed to real-life situations on industrial attachment. Therefore, there is a need to find solutions, which ensure that journalism and media studies education in Zimbabwe rise above the crisis. In other countries, the teaching hospital model in journalism education and training has proffered to curb the decline in quality placements that are in decline and contractions in the industry is a possible solution emerging in the literature (Solkin, 2020). As to whether this is viable or not is what this research seeks to find out and continue this discussion in the light of this COVID-19 and post-COVID-19 environment. Thus, the research unpacks how journalism and media studies' education in Zimbabwe can negotiate these shifts and propose possible future solutions.

Methodology

This research adopts a qualitative research method to collect and analyze data. Specifically, it is an exploratory research exploring the future possibilities of journalism education in Zimbabwe's post-COVID-19 era. Interviews were the main method of data generation. Interviews were mainly suited for this study because they could provide an understanding of people's experiences and perceptions (Heigham & Croker, 2009). These interviews were conducted from August to September 2021. Scholars from both private and public universities in Zimbabwe and media practitioners such as journalists and editors were purposively sampled. Lecturers and professors from universities were interviewed to get a picture of how they were coping with the ever-changing journalism landscape, especially in the COVID-19 scenario. Journalists, editors, and stakeholders provided data on how they viewed journalism education and provided pointers on how training institutions could align themselves with changes in the field. Seventeen interviews were conducted, some were face-to-face while others were done over the telephone or online. This was necessitated due to the restrictions on movement that were still in place during COVID-19. Furthermore, telephone and online platforms also gave quick access to interviewees in faraway places where we could not easily reach due to time and cost constraints. To ensure diversity and inclusivity of the research participants, gender, ethnicity, sexual orientation, and disability were considered. We also used participant observation as we are scholars from this field and are at a public university and thus have first-hand experience. All in all we sought to uncover the state of journalism and media education in the post-COVID-19 times and the future possibilities for the field. The interview data were transcribed and coded into themes using Nvivo software. The themes were presented, analyzed, and discussed in this study.

Teaching Digital Skills and Techniques in Journalism

In Zimbabwe, the institutions that train journalists and the available newsrooms are struggling to cope with the demands of the digital environment. Graduates who are being churned out of journalism institutions are failing to plug in the digital skills gap currently lacking in the Zimbabwean newsroom. The skills they possess while leaving the training schools are in very low demand on the job market because they do not meet the demands of the fast-changing digital newsroom. As in many other industries, large media industrial organizations find their markets taken over by more efficient, targeted start-ups leading to their collapse. It must be clear that the central idea of journalism schooling is that of a professionally oriented program focused on training students for jobs in the newsroom (Becker, 2003). Responding to these issues, a professional journalist at one of the country's leading daily newspapers contends that,

> the ability to navigate the digital web, shoot and edit photographs and videos online is very important when it comes to the skills needed by a modern journalist, but we find these skills lacking in students who come at my workplace on work-related learning and even after finishing school.
> (Personal Interview, August 2021)

It seems there is a significant gap in media and journalism degree education in Zimbabwe when it comes to abilities in digital newsgathering, editing, and presenting the news. The various stakeholders in this subject need to put their heads together and shape the future of journalism education.

The current training curriculum does not address the shortages in digital journalism skills in media houses in Zimbabwe. Digitalization and convergence are reshaping newsrooms and news practices; hence, journalists need to be able to produce and process text, video, and sound in their reporting, but these have remained problematic. The media and journalism training curriculum in Zimbabwe have not fully embraced the digital skills which are essential to online and other new forms of journalism. Admitting to this lack, a Professor of Media and Journalism based at a training institute in Zimbabwe states that "There are gaps in the digital media training category which is important to understand the digital media environment in Zimbabwe and even beyond" (Personal Interview, August 2021, Telephone).

Although the Zimbabwe Council of Higher Education (ZIMCHE) brought in the National Qualification Framework (NQF) and the Minimum Body of Knowledge (MBK), which guides modules that should be taught in each program accredited, this has not solved the challenges of lack of digital skills in media and journalism courses. Unlike in other countries where accreditation rules for journalism courses have encouraged a curriculum with a small core of conceptual courses and an emphasis on reporting, editing, writing, and production courses (Accrediting Council on Education in Journalism and Mass Communications, 2004), ours operating on MBKs tend to focus more on conceptual courses rather than praxis. A journalism lecturer argues that "the MBKs are not enough to solve this challenge we are currently facing because technology is constantly shifting while it takes about three years for a programme to be reviewed" (Personal Interview, September 2021, Telephone). Tying training institutions' curriculum to MBKs denies institutions opportunities to innovate and come up with unique programs that speak to the versatile changes that respond to the ever-changing environment.

The products of the current media and journalism institute have remained incomplete in their approach to the work they are supposed to do in the newsroom. A features editor of a weekly public newspaper contends that,

> I have worked with several students here from different institutes, I have discovered that there are mainly two categories: Good reporters with limited digital skills maybe because of their background and those who are great with digital video but they do not have a nose for news, they cannot write independently and cannot investigate further.
>
> (Personal Interview, September 2021)

Indeed, such students are incompatible with the current trends in media and journalism, students who have gone through the journalism training mill for the 21st century must be versatile. He further claims that

> We have been struggling for so long to have journalists who recognise the importance of time, who break the news every second and every minute on our digital media platforms. However, this has not happened for quite a long time and our journalism training in Zimbabwe seem not to be offering solutions to this. I expect new journalists to come equipped with a lot of digital skills to tackle the current challenges.
>
> (Personal Interview, September 2021)

Training institutions have not been teaching these skills because trainers lack qualifications. One trainer at an institute of higher learning in Harare, argues that "we have not been teaching these skills due to lack of qualified human resource and equipment, we are fully aware that our students must understand digital skills and multimedia storytelling if they're going to be relevant in the 21st-century journalism world" (Personal Interview, September 2021, Harare, Zimbabwe). Further comments from professional journalists show that upcoming journalists would do well with a good liberal education or corresponding life experience and should not get too comfortable with the present because the sands of media and journalism are ever-changing, more than other fields.

A general survey of journalism courses being offered by universities in Zimbabwe indicates that about 90% of lecturers teaching media and journalism in Zimbabwe were trained at the University of Zimbabwe, Midlands State University, and the National University of science and technology with a few coming from an undergraduate program offered by the Zimbabwe Open University. However, they would end up doing their Master's degrees at one of the first three universities named above. Although these institutions were free to incorporate digital skills into their curriculum, most of them did not until the intervention of ZIMCHE with the concept of MBK, which has been described above as not adequate to address the problem of the ever-shifting sands of technology in the Zimbabwean media sphere. Media professionals have always recommended improvements to journalism education that involve hiring more professionals as teachers who can deal with the issue of digital media (Gaunt, 1992). One media editor of an online publication, who passed through Zimbabwean media training experience, argues that,

> During my time at one of the training institutes, the curriculum at the Masters level did not address anything to do with the digital media, our main focus was on theories of the media and other causes which were theoretical. During this time, the most critical skills essential for journalists were the ability to listen, hear what is being said and what is not being said, and the ability to verify and confirm the information. However, things have changed now, journalists need to maintain superiority on a 24/7 news cycle, as well as a critical understanding of the social network. This is so because information now spreads so rapidly online. Therefore, journalism education needs to focus on teaching the fundamentals of storytelling online and mastering the quick pace of modern media reporting.
>
> (Telephone Interview, September 2021)

The emphasis on digital journalism, coding, and programming indicates that digital journalism is here to stay. According to the editor of a weekly community media based in the city of Masvingo, Zimbabwe, media graduates must at least know how the web works and journalism schools must teach "modern journalism." For a long time, students at Midlands State University, University of Zimbabwe, National University of Science and Technology, Zimbabwe Open University, and Great Zimbabwe University were taught both broadcast and print journalism. While this would allow them to specialize and at the same make them better all-around journalists, the "everything shop" approach has been challenged by "modern journalism" and learners now need to be skilled at solving problems and telling stories using digital tools and as part of a team. Interestingly, this gap is being attended to especially on the backdrop of education 5.0 introduced by the government. Here, Zimbabwe's state universities' traditional tripartite mission of teaching, research, and community service has been reviewed to align with the new developments in technology and the government's 2030 vision. The nation's higher and tertiary education sector is now mandated to teach, research, do community serve, as well as innovate and industrialize Zimbabwe.

Those students who will be graduating at the end of four years from now should be equipped with these skills and in media, it is assumed that they are going to be comfortable with the web and the required technology. It is envisioned that these students are going to produce media-related goods and services and be able to create employment. All this should be reflected in the university curriculum currently being reviewed. Some student respondents said that the ability to work with computer languages was important in media. This makes sense because, when students are on campus, they come with all their knowledge of content creation. However, the difference is that this content may be different from journalism content as they will usually be both producers and consumers because they play with digital content and create things though without the purpose of journalism in mind. These types of journalists are, therefore, the most attuned to the technical future of journalism not only in Zimbabwe but across the globe.

Journalism Education in the COVID-19 Era

The coming in of COVID-19 has further necessitated the need to acquire a range of skills essential to navigate this transition and they go far beyond journalism competencies such as writing, editing, and practicing the discipline of verification. The use of digital media such as social media platforms, SMS, and voice calls to formulate teams with citizens so that they may collaborate with professional journalists in writing about events that are happening in their communities is more than critical. This, however, requires training of citizen journalists in aspects like audience engagement, marketing, data journalism, video editing, and basic news writing among several other skills. One editor of a local newspaper based in Masvingo responding to this study said,

> Based on what I know about current challenges in reaching other places to gather news especially in this error of Covid-19, educators may not grasp the importance of multimedia skills or other institutions which train journalists might have a lack of urgency to become 'digital first' in their training … such understandings are contrary to what's happening in newsrooms that I am familiar with, including my own. Our priorities in the newsroom have changed and start with digital-first and the idea of printing is at the end of the line. Besides, the ability to work with HTML and other computer languages is highly prioritised. In fact, due to Covid-19, we have not been printing any copy and we have been sending out e-copies through different online platforms.
>
> (Email response, September 2021)

Although this transition is highly regarded, it affected the business side of the media prompting further questions on the survival strategy of the e-journalism business. A manager of a commercial regional radio station described the challenge this way,

> As we grapple with the issue of reaching our news sources in this Covid-19 era, we also have to be mindful of what it takes to shape a successful digital news and information business creating revenue models that are different from the ones we currently use.
>
> (Telephone Interview, September 2021)

Although there are several business opportunities in digital media because of its reach, there are still few takers of these opportunities because media managers are not educated in these business models. As a result, there is a need for workshops to train these media managers and journalists on the current media business models. There is also a need to hire journalists who understand and accept their role in not just reporting and editing the news but also in increasing consumer engagement and loyalty in digital platforms. Further, there is a need for increased support for the newsroom and advertising department working together on understanding, innovating, and implementing a new business model based on digital media.

Conclusion

Journalism is a capital-intensive profession and so colleges and universities offering these courses should be highly funded by the government so that their curricula move along with the changing times and rapid technological developments. In-service training and outsourcing of well-equipped professionals for the good of our own journalistic practices is more than essential. Training of citizen journalists to bridge the gap between professional and unprofessional news gathers is another way to go. The result is the presence of para-professional journalists who can partly identify and exhibit journalistic ethos. The advent of COVID-19 has exposed a huge chasm between theory and practice in colleges/universities offering media and journalism studies as well as in the field of practice. Inadequacies in journalistic practices that have been highlighted in this chapter that emanate from ill-equipped graduates have resulted in either unavoidable news black holes or rampant unethical journalistic practices characterized by misinformation and disinformation.

Journalism educators in Zimbabwe should expand their conceptions of what constitutes journalism education and how to practice it, taking into consideration the fast evolvement of technology and the emergence of such pandemics as COVID-19, among others. Journalism should be conceived as an act of community where information is gathered by the community itself and disseminated across digitalized platforms as this will help both trainers and trainees respond to the shifting positions catalyzed by digital technologies. These fluctuations offered by the new media technology create opportunities and trials that media and journalism institutes must lead in addressing. Students of journalism must also be trained in relation to the communities they shall be working in as a way of fixing community-centered journalism. Such networked journalism put communities at the center of writing issues that affect them and the professional media rewrite the same stories in a professional way. In the end, we urge that journalism education enable trainers and professionals as well as students to contribute to the construction of a journalistic curriculum which emphasizes journalistic practices that will augment student learning and give them opportunities for innovation and industrialization.

References

Accrediting council on education in journalism and mass communications. (2004). *Journalism and Mass Communications Accreditation.* http://www.acejmc.org/publications /newsletters/.

Ake, C. (1979). *Social Science as Imperialism: A Theory of Political Development.* Ibadan: Ibadan University Press.

Banda, D., Hart, S., & Liu-Gitz, L. (2010). Impact of training peers and children with autism on social skills during center time activities in inclusive classrooms. *Research in Autism Spectrum Disorders* 4(4): 619–625.

Becker, L. B. (2003). Introduction: Developing a sociology of journalism education. In R. Froehlich & C. Holtz-Bacha (Eds.), *Journalism Education in Europe and North America: An International Comparison.* Creskill, NJ: Hampton Press, 1117.

Castells, M. (2004). Informationalism, networks, and the network society: A theoretical blueprint. In M. Castells (Ed.), *The Network Society: A Cross Cultural Perspective.* Chetenham and Northhampton, MA: Edward Elgar Publishing Limited, 1–20.

Gaunt, P. (1992). *Making the Newsmakers: International Handbook on Journalism Training.* Westport, CT: Greenwood Press.

Gumede, V. (2011). The role of public policies and policy makers in Africa: Responding to Global Economic Crisis. In D. R. Lee & M. Ndulo (Eds.), *The Food and Financial Crises in Sub-Saharan Africa: Origins, Impacts and Policy Implications* (pp. 247–263). Wallingford: Centre for Agriculture and Bioscience International.

Hochheimer, J. L. (2001). Journalism education in Africa: From critical pedagogical theory to meaning-based practice. *Critical Arts* 15(1–2): 97–116.

Keith, R. (2009). Interviews. In J. Heigham & A. Robert (Eds.), *Qualitative Research in Applied Linguistics: A Practical Introduction.* London: Palgrave Macmillan, 182–199.

Fourie, J. P. (2013). *Beyond Skills Training: Six Macro Themes in South African Journalism.* Milton Park: Routledge Publishers

Rodney-Gumede, Y. (2017). The impact of social media on journalism. In P. Fourie (Ed.), *Media Studies: Social (New) Media and Mediated Communication Today.* Cape Town: Juta and Company (Pty) Ltd, 267–292.

Solkin, L. (2020). Journalism education in the 21st century: A thematic analysis of the research literature. *Journalism* 23(2): 444–460. https://doi.org/10.1177/1464884920977299.

Tomaselli, K., Mboti, N., & Ronning, H. (2013). South-North perspectives: The development of cultural and media studies in Southern Africa. *Media, Culture & Society* 35(1): 36–43. mcs.sagepub.com.

Van Dijk, J. (2006). *The Network Society: Social Aspects of New Media* (2nd ed.). London, Thousand Oaks, CA and New Dehli: Sage Publications.

Wa Thiongo, N. (1986). *Decolonising the Mind: The Politics of Language in African Literature.* Portsmouth: Heinemann.

Wasserman, H. (2005). Journalism education as transformative praxis. *Ecquid Novi: African Journalism Studies* 26(2): 59–174. https://doi.org/10.1080/02560054.2005.9653328.

Willems, W. (2014). Provincializing hegemonic histories of media and communication studies: Towards a genealogy of epistemic resistance in Africa. *Communication Theory*:1–18. (in press).

4 Communication and New Cultural Order in Zimbabwean Public Health

Reflections from COVID-19

Gift Gwindingwe and Tichaona Zinhumwe

Introduction

The advent of COVID-19 in January 2020 in Zimbabwe marked the birth of various forms of cultural communication and public health patterns and the resultant new cultural order. This chapter takes reflections from COVID-19 to critically discuss the emerging socio-cultural and public health patterns that dominated the lives of Zimbabweans as both the World Health Organization (WHO) and the Zimbabwean government endeavored to manage the spread of COVID-19. The new cultural regulatory signs and the new forms of life patterns that were enforced on people as a way to manage the spread of the pandemic are arguably a manifestation of a new cultural order.

The communal form of life that dominated the rural livelihoods was shredded and revered cultural occasions like funerals and nhimbes (rural cooperatives) were interfered with as large gatherings were criminalized and made taboo. It is against this background that this chapter portends a possibility of the emergence of a new cultural order and new forms of communication that negate existing sociocultural order. This chapter focuses on funeral gatherings and nhimbes as expressions of traditional alternative public sphere among Zimbabweans. The alternative public sphere concept by Fraser (1990) is adopted in this chapter as an expressive platform for deliberative (cultural) democracy amongst the rural folk. The discussion in this chapter centers on the signifying value and the significance of these cultural regulative signs as representative of the traditional public sphere and deliberative (cultural) democracy in Zimbabwe.

Nhimbe refers to a communal rural cooperative that spans from a few hours to a day or two. People in the same village gather at a homestead to do work, have a meal, and drink beer and maheu thereafter (Gombe, 1998, p. 150). Simply put, nhimbe or humwe is "beer party for work" (Standard Shona Dictionary, 1987). Work ranges from cultivating to harvesting crops. In some cases, it involves land preparation, digging up manure or ferrying manure to the fields using ox-drawn scotch carts. It is part of cultural communication when an individual is overwhelmed by tasks at home and "calls" the village for assistance (through the kraal head) where they will work,

DOI: 10.4324/9781003390732-4

eat, and drink amidst fun and uncontrolled talk (Gombe, 1998, p. 151 and Interviews with Chief M1, 12 August 2021; Chief Z, 19 August 2021 and Chief M, 23 August 2021). It is on this platform that many goings-on in villages are publicly discussed without limits. Talk and fun begin from the time people start work to the time of eating and drinking right up to dismissal. All sorts of jokes and discourses are publicly spoken (Gombe, 1998, p. 152). Even the revered of the village are exposed on this forum (Interview with Chief Z 19 August 2021 and Chief C 13 September 2021). Uncontrolled talks can be in groups, depending on issues that interest individuals. It is in this context that we place nhimbe on the same plane with other forms of alternative public sphere, competing or counter-public spheres as Fraser (1992) contends. Unlike Dare, which fits into the Habermasian public sphere and is controlled or dominated or hijacked by opinion leaders or (cultural) superiors of the society (Ncube & Tomaselli, 2019; Fraser, 1992; Price, 1995; Habermas, 1989), nhimbe provides an alternative and unrestricted platform for all and sundry to partake in various cultural and socio-economic discourses of their community, including rebuking leadership for perceived injustices in running the affairs of the community. Nhimbe still resonates with an informal Dare that is both a physical space and a metaphorical symbol (Ncube & Tomaselli, 2019) amongst the Shona people. There is work and entertainment at nhimbe. There is also "search of mutual understanding, reconciliation and solidarity" (Mahoso, 2018 in Ncube & Tomaselli, 2019, p. 39) though in an unstructured way (Chief C, interview on 13 September 2021).

The "democratic and participatory dimensions of the indigenous Shona communication platforms" (Ncube & Tomaselli 2019, p. 39) can be discussed using nhimbe, to advance deliberative democracy at the community level with a major slant on cultural communication. Gombe (1998) points out that nhimbe is a form of cooperative at the village level where each homestead provides three people to do work. With a village comprising at least 30 homesteads, the nhimbe gathering is estimated at a minimum of 90 people. Deliberative democracy "as any practice of democracy that gives deliberation a central place" (Bächtiger et al., 2018, p. 2) is a central feature of the traditional alternative public sphere in the form of nhimbe where all sorts of issues are publicly discussed without fear or favor through song or jokes (Gombe, 1998). This becomes a point of departure from Ncube and Tomaselli's application of Dare which is formal and structural in both set-up and communication channels. Nhimbe serves both as a democratic deliberative platform and a tool for community development (Gombe, 1998). Whilst the bulk of scholars discuss deliberative democracy at the national political level, this chapter deals with the concept at the community level and restricts it to cultural communication, which translates to higher political platforms.

The discussion revolves around the contradictions that arise between the need to uphold cultural practices and to promote internationally upheld public health systems that save lives. Are funeral rites and nhimbe practices not negating the very life-saving measures that the government put in place to curb the spread of COVID-19?

Communication and Ubuntu

Communication in this chapter is conceptualized from the transactional or semiotic school of communication. According to the transaction school, communication is transactional; it is a process in which meaning is created, repaired, and maintained to create sharedness amongst interlocutors (Carey, 2008). The semiotic or transactional school is molded on Newcomb's (1953) model of communication that is also known as the ABX matrix model of communication (Shukla, 2017 and Evangelista & Bacani, 2016). In this model, A and B are communicators and X is a point of mutuality that is supposed to link A and B so that they are in agreement if communication is to be meaningful. If A does not agree with B, then they must strive to establish commonness in X, which is a social environmental factor of convenience for both of them (Evangelista & Bacani, 2016). This field of experience is based on individuals' beliefs, values, and experiences.

In this chapter, communicative cultural regulative signs in the form of funeral gatherings and nhimbes are discussed in relation to the ABX matrix model of communication to unpack how these were shredded and created zones of discomfort amongst communities. The threat posed by COVID-19 is also discussed to assess how it became a zone of commonness that brought A and B together. A can be a subculture, for example, youth and B can be another subculture, for example, the elderly of the society. X is therefore culture.

It is the argument of this chapter that the net effect of cultural communication is social equilibrium, which is rooted in the philosophy of Ubuntu. Ubuntu is when one is involved in meaningful relationships with others and fulfills the reverence that other people may require (Mhlambi, 2020). Mbiti's (1990) philosophical description of Ubuntu that one is what one is because of the existence of others has typical relevance to the understanding of funeral gatherings and nhimbes as expressions of the concept of Ubuntu. In essence, Ubuntu reflects a world view grounded on values of humanness, communality, and interdependence among other values. It shapes the African human identity and this chapter portends that funeral gatherings and nhimbes are some of the cultural regulative signs that hold together communities. A paradigmatic shift in these cultural regulative signs is likely to result in a cultural diversion. This chapter takes the assumption that a disruption of these cultural regulative signs is distortion of the African group identity.

Funeral gatherings are a form of emotional bondage and nhimbes are indicators of community cooperation leading to community development. As argued by Eliastam (2015), Ubuntu has become a basis for morality and (uncodified) public policy. This trajectory has implications for both moral and economic growth. The ABX matrix model of communication as reflected through these non-verbal communication cues has relevance in that it helps to explore the impact of COVID-19 on communication and Ubuntu amongst Zimbabweans. Ubuntu as a social value is not inert but rather an acculturated trait that is nurtured through socialization (Makhudu, 1993). Funeral gatherings and nhimbes are some of the cultural communicative regulative signs that help in the socialization process that nurtures Ubuntu.

The paradox in the preservation of Ubuntu in cultural communication patterns comes with the call to also uphold and respect public health patterns and to respect public health personnel as established in the Public Health Act (2018) (Chapter 15:17, section 17 (1)), which requires the establishment of a Health Centre Committee composed of "representatives of health workers and representatives of the communities in which they operate." Situations like funeral gatherings and nhimbe operated in conflict because the committee that should uphold traditional practices is the same committee that should uphold COVID-19 restrictive measures.

The Alternative Public Sphere and Deliberative (Cultural) Democracy for the Rural Folk

This chapter adopts the concept of alternative public sphere and deliberative democracy to put into perspective the signifying value of funerals and nhimbes as alternative arenas that facilitate deliberative democracy and build on Ubuntu among Africans. A public sphere platform is best represented as Dariro/Dare (Ncube & Tomaselli, 2019). Deliberative democracy is

> grounded in an ideal in which people come together, on the basis of equal status and mutual respect, to discuss the political issues they face and, on the basis of those discussions, decide on the policies that will then affect their lives.
>
> (Bächtiger et al., 2018, p. 2)

Alternative public sphere theory is a reaction by Nancy Fraser (1990) to Jurgen Habermas' (1989) concept of the public sphere. Habermas advanced that it is a forum upon which all and sundry, regardless of race, sex, class, or religion, have access to a platform to partake in rational debates on economic, political, religious, and socio-cultural matters of their societies. Gwindingwe, Alfandika, and Chateuka (2018) argue that the public sphere concept "harbours traits of general accessibility." We relate the concept of the public sphere and deliberative democracy in this chapter because, as argued by Ncube and Tomaselli (2019, p. 38), it

> deals with the media and democracy matrix. The theory is multi-disciplinary and has been used to critique the media, civil society, universities and parliaments.

In the context of this study, we note the inadequacies of the Habermasian public sphere theory and advance the concept of alternative public sphere as put forward by Nancy Fraser (1990). She noted, in her critique of Habermas, that public sphere was not at all inclusive and advocated an alternative space for the excluded classes of society such as women and children and the rest of the marginalized. While in theory Habermas (1962) envisioned a public sphere as grounded on plurality and diversity of ideas, Fraser (1990) noted the exclusionary tendencies of the theory. In real practice, formal platforms are monopolized by opinion leaders and popular figures at the expense of the generality of the society. With such exclusionary tendencies, deliberative democracy, which is "any practice of democracy that gives deliberation a central place," is not feasible (Andre Bächtiger et al., 2018, p. 2). In formal African public sphere, platforms such as the Dare/Dariro, which is "a ubiquitous African circle defined by "call and response" i.e. kushaura nokutsinhira," existed "at the family level, at the community level, at the education and entertainment levels, and at the state level" (Ncube & Tomaselli 2019, pp. 39–40). However, the structural arrangements of a Dare remain rooted in the Habermasian philosophy and do not therefore satisfy the tenets of deliberative democracy.

It is against the background of these limitations of the traditional African public sphere that we advance the Fraserian concept of alternative public sphere. Nhimbes are informal options of making incursions into the realms of deeper societal debates whilst engaging in a community development project such as farming. At nhimbe, there are no restrictions to issues under debate and there are no bureaucratic structures and rules that bar people from partaking in a discussion as might happen at Dare where one speaks after being given the permission. We also affirm that alternative public sphere platforms accord a chance for public opinion to be developed and sustained (Ncube & Tomaselli, 2019).

Discussions on deliberative democracy centered more on broader political discussions (Chambers, 2003, Andre Bächtiger et al., 2018; Schwalisz, 2019). This chapter engages both the alternative public sphere and the deliberative democracy concepts to discuss the relevance of nhimbe and funerals in sustaining communication, fostering cooperation in societies, and promoting public health. Ncube and Toamaselli (2019, p. 39) advance the need to "engage" Western theories to utilize "traditional African communicative platforms in the pre-colonial Shona society of Zimbabwe." Analysis of nhimbe and funeral platforms is done in the context of COVID-19 reflections where these platforms were negatively affected by government policies that sought to fight the pandemic, resulting in major shifts in many cultural communicative patterns. Whilst Dare speaks to a formal platform that engages formal, regulated discussions, nhimbes, and funeral gatherings are alternative communicative platforms upon which emotional bondage and community corporation, leading to development, are developed and sustained. However, with the advent of COVID-19, deliberative democracy practices and ideals may not be suitable/applicable. COVID-19 is such a crisis that instant decisions were needed to sustain the public health system and save the public. By its nature, COVID-19 did not permit people to gather to deliberate on their safety liberally as the ideals of deliberative democracy would permit. At the peak of COVID-19, lockdown restrictions banned gatherings of any nature. The effect at the national level is transferrable to the community level where funerals and cooperatives (nhimbes) were not permissible either. The generally accessible civil platforms in rural communities were rendered inaccessible.

Methodology

The chapter adopts a qualitative research design that is benchmarked on an ethnographic approach to gather data that are subjected to an interpretive analysis to discuss the emerging socio-cultural patterns that permeated the lives of Zimbabweans as both the World Health Organization and the Zimbabwean government endeavored to manage the spread of the coronavirus. Qualitative research "involves taking people's subjective experiences seriously as the essence of what is real for them" (Bryman, 2012; Ncube, 2014, p. 9). The chapter employs both participant and non-participant observation to gather data on the departure from the behavior patterns that held the sociocultural fabric of Zimbabweans. Six funeral gatherings and two nhimbes (communal cooperatives) were purposively sampled as part of cultural communicative patterns that reflect solidarity and Ubuntu amongst Zimbabweans in times of grief and economic community development, respectively. Curfews were also selected as part of a new cultural communicative pattern that ushered in uniform movements and time management. The centrality of the selected three cultural communicative patterns is their overall influence on the philosophy of Ubuntu as a cultural nerve center of Africans in general and Zimbabweans in particular.

Four districts were sampled for accessibility and feasibility reasons and these were Chivi, Masvingo, Mwenezi, and Zaka districts. One chief in each district was selected for interviews. Chiefs are the custodians of culture and their views are deemed very invaluable in this study. Observations were done in three districts, namely Chivi, Masvingo, and Zaka because of the researchers' easy access to these districts. Chiefs' identities were coded C for Chivi; M for Masvingo; M1 for Mwenezi; and Z for Zaka.

Documents were also the source of data. The researcher relied on primary documents such as statutory instruments to support the government's position in enforcing the "new normal." Newspaper articles on the government's response to the ravaging COVID-19 were also used.

Data were analyzed using content analysis under a thematic pattern. The cultural shift from the traditional way of expressing solidarity and Ubuntu to the "New Normal" needed an examination, hence this chapter adopted "an interpretive approach in gathering and discussing the findings of the study" (Ncube, 2014, p. 9) through an interpretive exploration of these cultural communicative signs.

Closure of Front Gates for Society's Free Expression? Funeral Gatherings and Nhimbes under COVID-19

The traditional Shona funeral gatherings are platforms associated with grief and jokes known as Nzveura in Shona. Whilst "colonialism, especially in its last modern phase, dramatically changed the paradigm and practices of communication in African communities" (Bussotti, 2015, p. 206), symbolic communication platforms such as funeral gatherings and nhimbes remained culturally intact, at least in the rural areas. However, the advent of COVID-19 and the ensuing restrictive lockdown measures put the whole cultural practice in disarray. The "collective experience of attending a public" discussion or a debate with the community "creates a commonality within the audience that contrasts with the solitary cultural practice ... that prevails" (Sapiro, 2020, p. 1) at formal gatherings such as Dare. Lockdown measures announced through the government gazette that gatherings of people more than 50 are banned were culturally conflictual. Statutory Instruments 77 and 83 of 2020 banned all forms of gathering as a way to curb COVID-19 and promote public health. Chiefs as custodians of culture found this culturally detrimental. Chief Z, Chief C, and Chief M1 all concurred that banning gatherings stifled community operations because rural societies are guided by the principle of Ubuntu. Chief M1 further argued that lockdown and banning of gatherings or restricting gatherings to numbers not exceeding 30 or 50 is culturally unsustainable, (Interview with Chief M1, 12 August 2021). Gombe (1998) says that at nhimbes, each homestead should send a minimum of three people. Limiting gatherings to 30 or 50 is symbolically annihilating such platforms as nhimbe with the net effect of closing "a front gate for society to be freely expressing themselves towards issues that happen across the country" (Gushendra, 2015, p. 747). Nhimbe is a cultural practice that sustains relationships and togetherness, a unifying cultural factor that defines commonness in communication, a social environmental factor binding a community (Shukla, 2017).

The Zimbabwean government was seized with an emergency disaster in the form of COVID-19, just like in any other part of the world. Sustaining deliberative democracy through traditional festivals such as nhimbe became costly to public health. As argued by Bächtiger et al. (2018, p. 2), "when the time and resources required for extensive deliberation undermine decisive action on a matter of urgent public concern," deliberative democracy ideals may not be sustainable. Chief Z argued in the same line of thought saying that "at least lives were saved and we hope the situation will normalize and people return to their cultural practices" (Interview on 19 August 2021). However, Chief C and Chief M1 shared a pessimistic picture of the aftermath of COVID-19, fearing that certain communities might not revert to their original ways of collaborating in functions that promote community development. The role of festivals in democratizing culture and democratic debates is diminished (Sapiro, 2020).

The four chiefs who were interviewed concurred that nhimbes are a way to unite villagers, to incorporate the marginalized of the society. Banning gatherings would, therefore, further fragment communities and leave out the weaker of the society such as widows. Festivals create a platform that counter structural power relations of the dominant and the dominated, thereby endorsing themselves as genuine alternative public sphere platforms. They provide a local community platform for marginalized voices of the community (Sapiro, 2020). This way, a democratic debate is nourished. However, faced with the ravaging COVID-19 pandemic, the alternative of an alternative public platform was put in place: banning of gatherings except for funerals with limited stipulated numbers. The government took a contingent approach of coming up with "practices that come less close to the deliberative ideal" because "costs in other values of promoting the deliberative ideal seem on reflection too high" (Bächtiger, Dryzek, Mansbridge, and Warren, 2018, p. 3). Avoiding deaths and curbing COVID-19 needed immediate attention. It far outweighed maintaining cultural hegemony. However, it is the intrinsic nature of human beings and strong attachment to particular cultural practices that triggered the dilemma amongst the rural folk. Observations by researchers revealed some kinds of resistance to the call by the government to avoid gatherings. In certain communities in Chivi, nhimbes were still practiced. This was in conflict with government directives and complicated government efforts to curb the COVID-19 pandemic and promote public health.

Cementing Cultural Fabrics: Funeral Gatherings as a Symbol of Ubuntu

Funerals are platforms for communicating shared grief. As people arrive at a funeral gathering, they practice hand shaking as an expression of communicating condolences. Observations have shown that in some cases, people hug each other in consolation, amidst crying. Another symbolic cultural practice that shows togetherness is overnight gatherings as expressive of oneness. There are also graveside speeches on the day of burial. All these rudimentary cultural practices are symbolic of the strong belief in funerals as expressions of Ubuntu. They are practices that cement traditional cultural experiences. Gathering in itself is symbolic as a communication tool.

Chiefs M and M1 concurred in bemoaning the effect of the COVID-19 pandemic, arguing that the practice that cemented Zimbabweans in times of grief has been suspended.

> We wonder how our unity in times of grief at funeral gatherings can be expressed. It is very difficult not to attend a burial in one's village. Absence at a burial is a symbol of deep cruelty and unfeeling for the bereaved. You can be suspected of having bewitched a neighbour.
>
> (Interview with Chief M1 on 12 August 2021)

There are carnivalesque festivals such as Nzveura at funerals where female in-laws make a funeral an alternative public sphere and "their favorite expression medium by showing diverse messages" (Gushendra, 2015, p. 747). Such funeral rites where female in-laws make jokes with male cousins are unavoidable at funeral gatherings. There is also singing and dancing all night, with mourners turning to be merrymakers. All these funeral rites are part of African traditional practices that signify a funeral in Shona culture. A funeral becomes a traditional rite that binds people in society, represented by Newcomb's X, which sustains relationships in communities. In the same vein, upholding public health patterns established at the dawn of COVID-19 paradoxically become another binding factor that brought the community together.

There are contradictions in the current COVID-19-infested conditions. Whilst traditional chiefs strongly believe that some traditional practices must be upheld for the continued good of our culture, some health specialists share different views, especially in the face of the COVID-19 pandemic. Tshili (2021) puts forward that,

> Ubuntu and traditional practices that promote harmony in communities are among social qualities that are causing the rapid spread of the deadly Covid-19.
>
> (*The Chronicle*, 17 July 2021)

Other academic and health experts share the same view as Tshili. Funeral gatherings have been perceived as potential super-spreaders of COVID-19. Certain health experts quoted in *The Chronicle* (17 July 2021) argue that many cultural practices negate efforts to curb COVID-19. For example, body viewing as a funeral rite poses a threat to people's lives as it endangers them by facilitating contact and spreading the virus. Funeral vigils are also in contradiction to social distancing, a measure that helps reduce the spread of the coronavirus. Needless to say, these rites are reflective of the Ubuntu philosophy, which health experts argue can affect people's survival from COVID-19 (*The Chronicle*, 17 July 2021). These views point to the quagmire in which traditional chiefs as custodians of traditional customs find themselves.

Suspension or eradicating the cultural rites in question is tantamount to taking away the Shona people's (cultural) civil liberties. This becomes a philosophical dilemma amongst custodians of the Shona culture.

Conclusion

Nhimbes and funeral gatherings are symbols of both alternative and traditional networked public spheres. Networked public sphere is a "set of practices that members of a society use to communicate about matters they understand to be of public concern and that potentially require collective action or recognition" (Benkler, 2006; Etling et al., 2014, p. 1). Bemkler's (2006) concept of a networked public sphere is in the context of emergent digital platforms. We argue that similarities can be drawn between social media networked platforms and traditional communicative public sphere platforms knitted together by the cultural fabric of a particular people. Cultural practices are in most cases ingrained in communities and an abrupt departure from such practices has some ramifications; people feel culturally dislocated and may want to cling to their practices.

Arguing for the strength of the Habermasian public sphere over traditional African platforms, Ncube and Tomaselli say, "While the idea of Habermas' public sphere is traced in the development of the western capitalist society, African public spaces – Dariro and Dare have always been there" (Ncube & Tomaselli, 2014, p. 42) and that "Dariro has no beginning and no end structure." It is this ubiquitous nature of African traditional communicative platforms that the four purposively sampled chiefs feared would be destroyed if COVID-19 is not contained soon. Nhimbe and funeral gathering as symbolic communicative platforms represented the African traditional networked platforms different from Benkler's (2006) internet-linked platforms. A point of conflation between the two is that there are a "set of practices that members of a society use to communicate about matters they understand to be of public concern and that potentially require collective action or recognition" (Etling et al., 2014, p. 1).

Disrupting these networked traditional platforms that were indices of mutuality and Ubuntu partially failed. Despite jail penalties and fines stipulated in various statutory instruments, villagers found the call of Ubuntu more demanding than the threat of jail sentences or fines. Our observations in Zaka and Chivi districts were that people only paid heed to time limits. Burials in most cases were hurried and done early, unlike at nhimbe where villagers normally dismissed late in the afternoon after meals and beer drink. Practices such as graveside speeches and Nzveura were still observed. Such cultural regulative practices as Nzveura reflected that burials are not all grief as female in-laws would always play fun and demand payment for services like clearing the path that leads to the graveside (Chief Z, Chief M, and Chief C). Chief M1 raised the quagmire that chiefs as custodians of culture found themselves in:

> We aware of government position that funeral gatherings should not exceed a stipulated number. But it is unethical and even inhumane to send away certain individuals upon their arrival at a funeral telling them that the stipulated number has been reached. It is tantamount to accusing them of witchcraft in our culture. At the end of the day, we had to advise the gathering to hurriedly do it.
>
> (Interview with Chief M1, 12 August 2021)

Ncube and Tomaselli have the same line of argument that these traditional public sphere platforms are not merely physical spaces for communication and interaction but represent "the universe of human values, the institutional nature of relations and relationships, which Africans experience only partially through the participation of those individuals who happen to be" in a particular platform (Ncube & Tomaselli, 2019, p. 42). The threat of fragmentation of these ingrained human values and relationships by COVID-19 left chiefs as custodians of culture at crossroads. The discursive nature of these two alternative platforms, the humor and jokes that raise serious community issues and rebuke errand individuals of the village make the African communities closely knit. Social vices were also nipped in the bud through these communicative platforms. Ncube and Tomaselli aver that,

> This occasion was carnivalesque … as participants freely engaged in any kind of talk, mocking those allegedly involved in unacceptable activities such as witchcraft, stealing, gossiping, among others.
>
> (2019, p. 42)

Gombe (1998) also argues that the revered or most feared of the community were also rebuked and reprimanded at such occasions as the nhimbe. We contend that deliberative communicative platforms like nhimbe are a sociocultural therapy that rids a society of social vices in a euphemistic way. Denied of such platforms, the (rural) communities are strained and stretched to the limit. The weakest of the village can be further peripherized and denied voices. Culture is a living being and is not infallible. We contend that it is open to external threats in the form of man-induced calamities as well as natural ones. COVID-19 is a potential threat to the continued existence of certain cultural practices (Chief Z, interview on 19 August 2021).

The nexus between upholding cultural regulatory signs that signify our (traditional) communication systems and moving with the times in a way that manages the contemporary public health patterns as witnessed in the COVID-19 era is quite intriguing. Further research can add both theoretical and methodological value in this area.

References

Bächtiger, A., Dryzek, J. S., Mansbridge, J., & Warren, M. (2018). Deliberative Democracy: An Introduction. In Bächtiger, A., Dryzek, J. S., Mansbridge, J., & Warren, M. (Eds.), *The Oxford Handbook of Deliberative Democracy*. https://doi.org/10.1093/oxfordhb/9780198747369.013.50.

Benkler, Y. (2006). *The Wealth of Networks: How Social Production Transforms Markets and Freedom*. New Haven, CT: Yale University Press.

Bryman, A. (2012). *Social Research Methods*. Oxford: Oxford University Press.

Bussotti, L. (2015). Short Reflections on the History of African Communication. *Historia Comunicación Social, 20*(1), 205–222.

Carrey, J. (2008). *Communication as Culture: Essays on Media and Society* (2nd ed.). London: Routledge.

Chambers, S. (2003). Deliberative Democracy Theory. *Annual Review of Political Science, 6*, 307–326.

Chwalisz, C. (2019). *A New Wave of Deliberative Democracy*. Carnegie Endowment for International Peace.

Eliastam, J. (2015). Exploring Ubuntu Discourse in South Africa: Loss, Liminality and Hope. *Verbum et Ecclesia, 36*(2), 1–8.

Etling, B., Roberts, H., & Faris, R. (2014). Blogs as an Alternative Public Sphere: The Role of Blogs, Mainstream Media, and TV in Russia's Media Ecology. *Berkman: The Berkman Center for Internet & Society*, No. 2014-8, pp. 1–51.

Evangelista, P., & Bacani, D. (2016). Westley and MacLean's Model for Communication Research. https://www.haikudeck.com/westley-and-mcleans-model-for-comm-research-education-presentation-c292d38ca3 (Accessed on August 12, 2021).

Fraser, N. (1990). *Rethinking the Public Sphere: A Contribution to the Critique of Actually Existing Democracy*. Durham, NC: Duke University Press.

Fraser, N. (1992). Rethinking the Public Sphere: A Contribution to the Critique of Actually Existing Democracy, Duke University Press. *Social Text* No. 25/26, pp. 56–80.

Gombe, J. M. (1998). *Tsika DzavaShona*. Harare: College Press.

Gushendra, R. P. (2015). The Role of Graffiti and Mural as Alternative Public Sphere for Society. *PEOPLE: International Journal of Social Sciences, 1*(1), 746–753.

Gwindingwe, G., Alfandika, L., & Chateuka, D. N. (2018). The Tonga People of Northern Zimbabwe: An Encounter with Digital Media. *African Journalism Studies*. https://doi.org/10.1080/23743670.2018.1533487.

Habermas, J. (1989). *The Structural Transformation of the Public Sphere*. Cambridge: Polity Press.

Hall, M. (Ed.). (1987). *Standard Shona Dictionary*. Harare: Literature Bureau.

Habermas, J. (1962). *The Structural Transformation of the Public Sphere*. Cambridge: The MIT Press.

Makhudu, N. (1993). Cultivating a Climate of Co-Operation Through Ubuntu. *Enterprise Magazine, 48*, 40–42.

Mbiti, J. (1990). *African Religions and Philosophy* (2nd ed.). London: Heineman.

Mhlambi, S. (2020). From Rationality to Relationality: Ubuntu as an Ethical and Human Rights Framework for Artificial Intelligence Governance. Car Center Discussion Paper Series, 2020-009.

Ncube, L. (2014). The Beautiful Game? Football, Power, Identities, and Development in Zimbabwe (Unpublished doctoral dissertation). South Africa: University of KwaZulu Natal.

Ncube, L., & Tomaselli, K. G. (2019). 'Watch My Back and I Watch Yours': Beyond Habermas' Public Sphere Concept in Democratic and Participatory Dimensions of Pre-Colonial Shona Society Public Spaces. *Journal of African Media Studies, 11*(1), 35–50.

Price, M. E. (1995). *The Public Sphere and National Identity*. Oxford: Clanderon Press.

Public Health Act (Chapter 15:17) No 11/2018, Veritas: Zimbabwe.

Sapiro, G. (2020). Festivals: Constructing an Alternative Public Sphere. In Tobias Boes, T., Braun, R., & Spiers, E. (Eds.), *World Authorship*. Oxford: Oxford University Press. https://doi.org/10.1093/oxfordhb/9780198819653.013.11.

Shukla, P. (2017). The Newcomb's ABX Model: A Purposive Theory to Decode the Role of Communication in Society. *Techno Group of Institutions*. Available at: The Newcomb's ABX Model -: A Purposive theory to decode the role of communication in society. – POOJA SHUKLA Assistant Professor, TECHNO GROUP OF INSTITUTIONS (wordpress.com)

Statutory Instrument 77 of 2020, Public Health (Covid-19 Prevention, Containment and Treatment) Regulations 2020.

Statutory Instrument 83 of 2020, Public Health (Covid-19 Prevention, Containment and Treatment) Regulations, 2020.

Tshili, N. (2021). Culture of Ubuntu Fan Spread of Covid-19. *The Chronicle*, July 17, 2021. https://www.chronicle.co.zw/culture-of-ubuntu-fans-spread-of-covid-19/.

5 The Dialectics of Language in Zimbabwe's Public Health Communication

Reflections on English as a Lingua Franca in (Post) COVID-19 Era

Esther Mavengano

Introduction

The outbreak of the COVID-19 pandemic brought to the fore the inconsistencies or paradoxes in the postcolonial era. The advent of coronavirus exposed persistent hierarchies entrenched in long-established linguistic traditions that reinforce the self–other conceptualizations of global humanities. The pandemic heightened language-related tensions in postcolonial multilingual contexts like Zimbabwe, which continue to obstruct opportune delivery of public health information in times of health emergencies. It also uncovered the fallacies and deceptive views in the current separatist Anglocentric linguistic ideologies that inform language use in contemporary Zimbabwe. Zimbabwe, being a former British colony with a multilingual sociolinguistic landscape, has to confront the complex challenges of the language politics which have recently resurfaced in public health information delivery. Linguists in the fields of applied linguistics, language policy, and sociolinguistics are tasked to engage in academic reflections on the subjects of language and public communication in contemporary contexts. The onerous task includes imagining progressive language perspectives that would re-define public health communication and the global humanity in the post-COVID-19 era. The general concern about language is raised in a context when the general population is required to understand the novel coronavirus disease in order to dismiss myths and reduce public alarm. Timely dissemination of information to the entire population is one of the necessary control measures during public health crises. Elsewhere, Ingrid, Zhang and Li (2020, p. 503) have observed that:

> [M]multilingual crisis communication has emerged as a global challenge during the COVID-19 pandemic. Global public health communication is characterised by the large-scale exclusion of linguistic minorities from timely and high quality information.

DOI: 10.4324/9781003390732-5

This chapter refocuses a scholarly gaze on the language debate in contemporary Zimbabwe's multilingual context with the intention to break away from Eurocentric language ideologies and linguistic silos that disparage indigenous languages (Mungwini, 2017). The debate about the politics of language provoke the following pragmatic questions that guide the arguments raised in this chapter on rethinking new linguistic perspectives in sync with evolving linguistic communities:

How are the linguistic inequalities and power relations framed and perpetuated in a multilingual present-day Zimbabwe?

How can insights from decolonial and linguistic human rights theorizations provoke rethinking of language ideologies and generate new critical language perspectives for the post-COVID-19 era?

How can the experiences from the COVID-19 pandemic be utilized to challenge linguistic domination and coloniality of being in postcolonial contexts?

What intervening measures can be taken to observe language rights that redefine humanity in the post-COVID-19 era?

Linguistic Human Rights and Decolonial Conceptual Frameworks

This study is located within elaborate interlocking terrain of sociolinguistics, applied linguistics , language policy, and decolonial inquiry that trouble colonial matrixes of power and linguistic frontiers. The study brings into conversation insights from linguistic human rights and evocative articulations of decolonial thinking to foreground the politics of language in public health communication in contemporary Zimbabwe. The theoretical interface of these two analytical paradigms enhances reflections on the intricate politics of language ideologies and language use in the postcolonial African world in general and Zimbabwe in particular. The key proponents of the Linguistic Human Rights Theory are Robert Phillipson and Skutnabb-Kangas (1994; 1997; 1999). Their arguments underline the importance of minority languages. Phillipson and Skutnabb-Kangas (1995) offer salient views about linguistic rights, which they propose are part of the human rights of the speakers of any language. The linguistic human rights framework calls to attention the urgent need to embrace linguistic diversity and the removal of linguistic obstructions. This perspective is reinforced by sociolinguist Canagarajah (1999; 2013) in his translingual theorization. Canagarajah (2013) contends that respecting the linguistic rights of language users is one way of re-humanizing the previously colonized peoples who had been dehumanized and marginalized on the bases of their language and ethnic identities. Certainly, minority groups should have access to public health information disseminated in the languages they understand. Central to linguistic human rights stance is its advocacy for linguistic visibility of the marginalized groups to avoid linguicism. Skutnabb-Kangas (1988: 13) defines linguicism as:

> Ideologies, structures and practices which are used to legitimate, effectuate, regulate and reproduce an unequal division of power and resources between groups which are defined on the basis of language.

Linguicism thus is a term that speaks about othering practices entrenched in the realm of language choice and language use. Although decolonial conversations are multifaceted, their fundamental focus is on how to redefine postcolonial African humanity (Ndlovu-Gatsheni, 2013). This process of becoming is nuanced due to colonial vestiges and emerging power dynamics in the current global arena. Language use provides a provocative site for scholarly scrutiny in postcolonial Africa. This study revisits decolonial sensibilities in debating language ideologies and use in public health communication in present-day Zimbabwe. The current language inquiry is in keeping with the changing sociolinguistic landscapes at both the national and global levels. Walter Mignolo (2000), who is a decolonial theorist, would call for a shift from binary linguistic perspective in order to embrace alternative possibilities of multilingual orientation or "thinking otherwise." This is important in resisting and transgressing linguistic boundaries that speak to the enduring coloniality of being (Mignolo, 2007; 2011). Significantly, rethinking linguistic ideologies is a necessary act of undoing colonial cognitive empires that erect, naturalize, and solidify dichotomies instead of fostering solidarities between peoples from the Global South and the Global North (Maldonado-Torres, Ndlovu-Gatsheni, 2020).

Historical Discursive Contours of Language Ideologies in Zimbabwe

The question of language is always political in nature because languages are not entirely linguistic constructs or simply means of communication but are in actual fact political objects (Mpofu and Salawu, 2018). This makes language subject a polemical one. Zimbabwe is a linguistically diverse society with numerous ethnic groups that speak indigenous languages such as chiShona, isiNdebele, seSotho, Setswana, chiChewa, tshiVenda, and Nambya among others. Yet, Eurocentric monolingual reductionism influences language use in the country (Mumpande, 2020). It is imperative at this juncture to understand the concept of linguistic ideology and its use in this study. Silverstein (1998) defines language ideology as linguistic behavior and belief system that affect speakers' choice and interpretations of communicative interaction. This definition alludes to beliefs about language, which inform attitudes and exert an impact on language use. The language issue in present-day Zimbabwe should be historically situated in order to generate deep reflections since it has been a heated topic for quite some time. Mavengano and Hove (2020) commenting on binaries posit that prevailing language problematics convey the paradox embedded in uncanny resemblances between colonial and postcolonial times. The dissonance in discourses of postcoloniality is indicative of the complexity in narratives of African recovery from colonial disruptions and the convolution of becoming in former colonies like Zimbabwe. Ndlovu-Gatsheni (2015: 15) uses the term "dismemberment" to explain how African people were linguistically and culturally disconnected or uprooted from their roots by adopting colonial cultures. Africans perceived as the wretched of the earth, were pushed to the zones of non-being (Fanon, 1967; Bhabha, 1994) in the structure of hierarchized humanity. Consequently, colonized Africans lost their sense of being and worth. This historical background speaks to the political nature of language debate. The position of English language today in the former Anglophone colonies was crafted during the colonial period (Kachru, 2005; McGroarty, 2008). According to the UNESCO Courier (2000: 20), English is the world's most used language with a population of 1,000,000,000, Portuguese has 200,000,000, and French 125,000,000. Africa has a total of 2,011 living languages, that is, 30% of the world's estimated 6,000 languages (UNESCO, Courier, 2000, p. 20). Ironically Europe, which has a total of 225 languages and constitutes merely 3% of the world's languages, has produced the most widespread languages and dominated the globe linguistically. Matsuda (2003), Kachru (2005), Phillipson (2009), and Canagarajah (2013) commenting on multilingual sensibilities in postcolonial contexts contend that embracing indigenous languages in postcolonial world is a crucial form of contesting linguistic imperialism. Similarly, Grosfoguel (2007, p. 219) established the paradox of the postcolonial world when he argued that:

> [o]ne of the most powerful myths of the twentieth century was the notion that the elimination of colonial administration amounted to the decolonisation of the world. This led to the myth of a postcolonial world. The heterogeneous and multiple global structures put in place over a period of the past 450 years did not evaporate with the juridical-political decolonisation of the periphery over the past 50 years. We continue to live under the same colonial matrix.

The above citation reiterates the problematic terrain of the postcolonial, which is haunted by the tenacity of colonial vestiges. The process of becoming is thus projected as a troubled one since the change from sites of entrapment and hegemonic paradigms to liberal zones is not an easy transition. Decolonial theorists like Ndlovu-Gatsheni (2020) and Mignolo (2000; 2007; 2011) posit that Africans are still burdened by the cognitive empires engrained in the psyche of the postcolonial subjects. Grosfoguel (2007) also stresses this view when he asserts that the coloniality of power articulates continuities of colonial mentalities and practices in often subtle and complex ways. In this chapter, these decolonial sensibilities are utilized to interrogate language ideologies that are projected in the context of COVID-19 in Zimbabwe today.

Chimhundu (1997) and Mungwini (2017) are of the view that the spread of imperial languages, especially English, is one of the most striking and enduring colonial legacies or colonial baggage to borrow from Ngugi (1994). Kadenge and Nkomo (2011) explain that English is Zimbabwe's sole official language and is spoken by the majority of Zimbabweans as a second or third language. The dominance of English in Zimbabwe is historically rooted because the country was a British colony for over a century.

Kadenge and Nkomo (2011) note that in postcolonial Zimbabwe, English retained its central position as an official language in national and international affairs. It is used in all critical facets such as education, economy, politics, and public health. The minority indigenous languages in Zimbabwe remain marginalized (Kadenge and Nkomo, 2011). Commenting on the privileged position of English in postcolonial African contexts, Mumpande (2020, p. 60) notes that:

> [i]n Zimbabwe the first language speakers of English are of low numerical value comprising about one percent of the total population, yet English is an official language due to the political and economic functional value it wields.

This situation reminds us of arguments proffered by Ngugi (1986) in *Decolonising the Mind*, when he posits that marginalization of the African people during colonialism led to linguicides and disempowerment of the speakers of the indigenous languages. In Zimbabwe's postcolonial context, only Shona and Ndebele became national languages, alongside English out of the 16 languages that exist (Chimhundu, 1997). This means minority and immigrant languages are located at the peripheral sites of Zimbabwean society. Bamgbose (2003) posits that the dominance of English and other colonial languages generally prevails in most African countries. This scenario speaks about how the rest of the minority languages and their speakers continue to suffer from invisibility and inaudibility in all essential discourses that take place at the national level as rightly argued by Mutasa (2006). According to Mavengano and Hove (2020), the dominant language ideologies and monolingual linguistic practices in the postcolonial African contexts are deeply embedded in what could be considered as the colonial mortal remains of hegemony that paved way for the exploitation of the degraded other. During the colonial period indigenous languages were degraded, their native speakers were disempowered, and Zimbabwe inherited this colonial legacy that promoted ethnic and linguistic separateness (Chimhundu, 1997). The colonial logic was constructed with the intention to perpetuate a linguistically and politically engrained distinction in society (Gordon, 2000). In other words, language use is still a site that manifests coloniality of power relations as experienced in the prevailing linguistic impediments.

English as a Lingua Franca Paradigm: A Postcolonial Dilemma

While it is ceremoniously acknowledged that Zimbabwe is a polyglot state, it appears that no consorted efforts have been made to put in place essential mechanisms for the effective management of existing languages to ensure there is equal visibility of this linguistic diversity in vital sectors such as the public media, education, national politics, and public health. A dialogic engagement of the currently competing and often-controversial ideas is necessary to address Zimbabwe's linguistic challenges. The issue of English hegemony in Zimbabwe is traceable to its colonial past. The designation of languages and the general perception of their value were mixed up with attempts at the differentiation of races, a situation that created linguistic elitism in the postcolonial era.

Besides the inherited colonial legacy, there are socio-economic and political aspects in the postcolonial era that continue to privilege the use of the English language today. According to Mumpande (2020, p. 19) "until 2002, Zimbabwe's language policy remained discriminatory and significantly influenced by the colonial policy dating back to the 1930s." It is significant to acknowledge that Zimbabwe's multilingual and multi-cultural nature also contributes to the preservation of English as an official language. For some sections of the society, the use of English language is imperative for a nation-building project since indigenous languages such as Shona and Ndebele which were accorded national status and are perceived by these sections as politically divisive and minority linguistic groups remain marginalized (Kadenge and Nkomo, 2011). The current use of indigenous languages in Zimbabwe's public domains such as politics, economy, education, and the media largely reflects the dominance of Shona and Ndebele at the expense of all other minority indigenous communities. Mumpande (2020, p. 11) posits that:

> [m]ore often than not, African governments are struggling with balancing the ever-seething ethnic tensions to which the languages issues are tied. Thus, state governments view the language issues in Africa not only as a highly emotive and potentially destructive issue but also a sleeping dog that is better left to lie undisturbed due to its sensitivity and destructive nature if not properly handled.

The above citation speaks of the intricacies of language problems in postcolonial Africa, which are interlocked with ethnic tensions and the fear of differences. Elsewhere, Tollefson (2000) reinforces the argument for linguistic justice and highlights a paradox in the discourses about the global spread of English language, which is erroneously perceived as related to economic well-being in the current global context. Yet, Tollefson (2000, p. 8) argues that this generalized view of English ignores the reality that the rapid spread of English language has generated "significant social, political, economic, [healthcare inequalities], dogmatic attitudes and binary logics." While stressing the importance of Zimbabwe's indigenous languages, there is a compelling reason to consider the realm of language use in Africa's postcolonial environment as a space of encounter with the cultural pluralities that define the world today. It has to be acknowledged that a number of applied linguists and sociolinguists such as Kachru (1985), Pennycook (1994), and Phillipson (1992) have warned against the dominance of a single language over others and pointed out the messiness of global classification based on monolingual linguistic ideologies in the 21st century. In Zimbabwe, English occupies a prestigious position as it is widely used in the educational, public health, political, science and technology, media, and economic domains (Chimhundu, 1997; Makoni, 2011; Ndlovu, 2013; Chikasha, 2016; Mumpande, 2020). This situation still prevails long after the end of British colonization and despite the fact that Zimbabwe has 16 local languages. Commenting on the controversial issue of language, Nkuna (2013) and Mumpande (2020) state that the language problem in Africa conveys the inherent inability to promulgate language policies that ensure the development and effective use of Africa's indigenous languages.

It is, however, pertinent to consider recent arguments about the new conceptions of English language in postcolonial contexts proffered by sociolinguists like Kachru and Canagarajah. Both Kachru (1985) in the world Englishes paradigm and Canagarajah (2006) in translingual theorization posit that English is no longer the language of native speakers or the inner circle, because there are many Englishes and non-native speakers can claim ownership of such linguistic varieties. This understanding refutes and problematizes rigid artificial linguistic borders and exclusivist perceptions. Most essentially, the widespread use of English is no longer entrenched in European exceptionalism as suggested by Wolff (2017), but rather reflects the (trans)national and porous contact spaces of linguistic borders as evident in translanguaging, transliteration, and translingual practices encoded in Africa's Englishes, which transcend the colonial cartography that mapped current states (Mavengano and Hove, 2020), it can be argued that English has reached an extraordinary number of speakers in the world today (Phillipson, 1992; Pennycook, 1994). The contemporary dispute on language politics and the widespread use of English in postcolonial African societies including Zimbabwe has brought to the fore critical but pugnacious perspectives that demand revisiting the previous conceptions of language vis-à-vis novel functions that arise.

There are numerous factors that have contributed to this linguistic scenario besides the often-overstated experiences of colonization. For instance, the linguistic demands and needs of the current economic and geographical ecologies generate new assemblages. Due to the peripheral position of most of the indigenous languages in Zimbabwe and other African nations, these local varieties are still underdeveloped to carry out effective communicative tasks in the emerging ecologies of the present world. Bamgbose (2003, p. 421) is of the view that the use of English is not a free choice because "there are constraints that make the choice inevitable." This further complicates the language debate in present-day African contexts. Even the native speakers of these languages end up denigrating their own first languages in preference of the dominant linguistic codes of foreign languages (Bamgbose, 2011). The influence of these complex realities cannot be undermined in any discussion of language problematics in contemporary Zimbabwe. The linguistic repertoires and language competencies called upon in the modern day convey a messy and vexing linguistic terrain. Certainly, postcolonial Zimbabweans are at a linguistic crossroads. Clearly, there is dissonance in language policy, linguistic attitudes and practice which together point at the postcolonial paradox (Gordon, 2000; Quijano, 2000; Omorinyi, 2003; McGroarty, 2008; Fofana, 2021). The evolving sociolinguistic landscapes call for a multilingual paradigm, which should be reinforced and encouraged by using both English together with indigenous Zimbabwean languages in a complementary manner that does not denigrate any of these languages in all critical public domains, including health information delivery systems. A case in point is the fact that during the COVID-19 pandemic, penetration of linguistic peripheries was/is important in order to control the spread of the highly infectious disease. The pandemic revealed flaws in public health communication that demanded new paradigms in language management in order to promote complementarity and interconnectedness of the linguistic communities in Zimbabwe. We cannot ignore the fact that there are sections of Zimbabwean society which still find English inaccessible to them, considering that English proficiency is attained through formal education. The dominant use of English language in public health communication ignores the plight of those people who are not educated and are not proficient in English. UNESCO courier (2000) posits that using foreign languages such as English, Portuguese, and French to transmit vital messages in multilingual and multicultural societies that are most found in Africa where the literacy level is about 56% will be counterproductive. This observation has serious implications for Zimbabwe's dominant use of English language to communicate public health messages. This surely takes away the dignity of the speakers of the othered Zimbabwean indigenous languages. This scenario has re-enacted colonial linguistic elitism and social stratification (Wolff, 2017). The information that concerns public health should be easily disseminated and understood across various ethnic, linguistic groups, and socio-economic classes in times of public health crises.

Nkuna (2013, p. 70) condemns African elites in politics and the academia who appear to propose that:

> [c]ompetitiveness and relevance in the global arena is Africa's primary goal and that the most appropriate way to manage globalisation is to significantly increase knowledge of the colonial languages.

Such a perception of globalization and linguistic currency undermines the urgency of Africa's rebirth in the realm of language use in postcolonial contexts. It is thus impetus to critically consider perceptions of globalization in the context of language debate in order to avoid perpetuation of othering linguistic logics. In this case, such views re-inscribe and legitimize linguistic silos, which reproduce inequalities and linguistic-othering practices (Mavengano and Hove, 2020). Ndlovu-Gatsheni (2020) points at the troubling issue of cognitive empires that obscures possible inclusive ideologies. He claims that cognitive empires are deeply entrenched in the African psyche, which continue to naturalize and recreate the center–periphery model of humanity in the global context. In a different context, Nye (2002) has earlier argued against the dominance of English, which he claims is an essential instrument of the soft power exercised through seduction rather than coercion. The current global context further complicates the postcolonial dilemma. It is essential to contemplate how globalization is defined, whose definition or understanding is projected, and in whose language globalization is enacted. Certainly, the present-day linguistic landscape requires new complex spaces for collusion, enriching sharing, difference, interpenetration, hybridization, and reinvention. It appears that globalization is a continuity of the colonization and Eurocentrism in a different guise. This situation needs to be challenged in order to dismantle linguistic dominance and binary linguistic silos that continue to place the previously colonialized people into zones of non-being in the vocabulary of Homi Bhabha (1999).

The Linguistic Binarisms during the COVID-19 Pandemic

As the world grapples with the contagious coronavirus pandemic, also popularly known as COVID-19, it is timely to provide introspection into the lessons drawn from the pandemic in an effort to re-imagine an alternative future. The outbreak of the COVID-19 pandemic came at a time when Zimbabwe's public healthcare system was crippled and it was certainly difficult to handle the enormous task of providing the much-needed health delivery services. It was important to swiftly disseminate the information about the coronavirus disease to the public as a way of reducing the threat of the pandemic. In a different context, Rizwan (2020) notes that in countries where large sections of the population speak various languages, the use of multilingual resources is paramount in fighting coronavirus. The observation is relevant to the Zimbabwean linguistic landscape, which is multi-ethnic and multilingual. It is appropriate to argue that the use of Shona, Ndebele, and English in public health communication makes marginalized minority language speakers more vulnerable in times of both national and global health disasters.

According to Chikasha (2016) and Mumpande (2020), Zimbabwe's constitutional provisions of 2013 legitimately recognizes 16 languages including chiShona, isiNdebele, tshiVenda, Shangani, Kalanga chiTsonga, Ndau, Nambya, English, Sign language, seTswana, Sotho, and Xhosa. Yet Makoni (2011) and Ndlovu (2013) earlier commented that in Zimbabwe language question is reflected in constitutional pronouncements and declarations, but there are no clear guidelines on the implementation of these linguistic policies. The recognition of minority languages in Zimbabwe merely appears in the constitution as politics of rhetoric probably to muffle the linguistic marginal communities. The reality is that even in the education domain where the policy texts state that from Grade 1 to Grade 3 at the primary level pupils are to be taught in their mother tongue, English language still dominates because there are no texts written in indigenous languages to effectively implement the constitutional provisions when teaching subjects such as Mathematics, Science, Religious Education among others. In addition, English language becomes a medium of instruction from Grade 4 to university level. This greatly influences language attitudes since one's access to tertiary education and employability in Zimbabwe requires a pass grade at ordinary level. Bamgbose (2003) has argued in this respect pointing out the flaws of the constitutional declarations without implementation. Furthermore, the positions of other minority indigenous languages are not well-defined except that they are recognized. English is accessible to the educated population in Zimbabwe. Another dimension that seems to be ignored is that of the rural–urban dichotomy in Zimbabwe's sociolinguistic contexts. Most of the old and less-educated people in rural areas are not proficient in English and feel more comfortable with their indigenous languages (Ndlovu, 2013). It is thus quite fundamental to use these languages to communicate vital public health information to reduce misinformation and distortion. It is imperative to seriously consider local linguistic urgency of these peripheral sections of the Zimbabwean society as well as locating the nation within the realities of the global context and recommending harmonizing linguistic perspectives. Certainly, the mutual interaction of these evolving linguistic ecologies is pertinent in current conversations about linguistic challenges in postcolonial Africa in general and Zimbabwe in particular. This approach is meant to foster intricate multilingual repertoires reflective of local and global linguistic solidarities. In other words, there is a need to incorporate European languages such as English into local linguistic ecologies and actively engage in visible egalitarian language practices. Most essentially, linguistic multiplicity is one of the fundamental conditions of (re)connecting and survival of humanity in its diversity in the 21st century. Indeed, there is a need to reconnect the Global South and Global North in the post-COVID-19 era if a new order is to be created and promoted. Certainly, imperial logics left the world broken and, therefore, restoration and rebirth of humanity demand picking up the pieces and stitching them together. In other words, the subject of linguistic ideologies and language use should be re-contextualized to come up with relevant ideas in sync with emerging linguistic ecologies and diverse communicative environments that embrace code-switching, translanguaging, among other pluralingual semiotic strategies.

English language in the 21st century enjoys the international attraction it offers to its non-native speakers which makes it a natural global lingua franca (Canagarajah, 2021). Some of the indigenous African populations abandon their native languages due to linguistic ecologies. Yet, in a different context, Heller and Martin-Jones (2001, p. 3) posit that language is important as one way in which knowledge is constructed and displayed as a resource. This view conveys the significance of embracing indigenous languages in the creation and dissemination of knowledge. In recent years, an increasing body of research has appeared on the present-day sociolinguistic practices that incorporate diverse codes and are predominated by "hybridity, fluidity and diversity" (Canagarajah, 2013, p. 33) as well linguistic transposition. This brings another dimension to sustainability and vitality of the local and non-local languages in the present multilingual contexts. Apparently, these ideas convey complexities related to the language debate, hence scholars need to critically reflect on how to navigate these challenges and re-imagine the linguistic future of the continent in the post-pandemic world. A naïve approach to these problematics will not bring the much-desired transformative ideas. This urgency comes with the realization that decolonization cannot be complete if Africa's indigenous languages continue to be downgraded (Nkuna, 2013). Globalization discourse has dogged the quest for multilingual orientation in Zimbabwe because English is mythologized as the language of the globalized world. This study problematizes the view that Africans should embrace globalization for the advantage of their continent, not some imposed Eurocentric conception of the term globalization (Nkuna, 2013, Ndlovu-Gatsheni, 2020). The challenge is that the discourse of globalization is utilized to perpetuate unfair de jure power and often obscure othering thinking. For instance, it's not clear who gets globalized and into what. It appears getting globalized is again a Eurocentric discourse that imposes English and other European languages on the village people to grapple with the COVID-19 pandemic discourse about the mutations of the coronavirus. Othering thinking is exposed, for instance, when Europe and America claim that the Delta and Omicron variants were first identified in Africa. The implication of this claim suggests that the coronavirus disease grows and mutates in Africa. They then ban flights from leaving Southern Africa. Sadly, African governments accept the embargo flat faced and far-footed. It is troubling that the isolation of Africa is not informed by objective and scientific data that speak to this effect. Paradoxically, the global news agencies, CNN, BBC, and Al Jazeera, record scary figures of Omicron and Delta variant cases in their own European and American spaces. One then wonders how these variants spread so quickly when Africa has been locked out of Heathrow, Detroit, Amsterdam, and Chicago. This ambivalence is a matter of concern and needs to be interrogated since it re-enacts essentialized traditions and myths of thinking and ordering the world.

Shifting from Abyssal Logics to Foster Spaces of Contact for the Post-COVID-19 Era

The foregoing discussion emphasized that traversing the complex sociolinguistic landscapes in contemporary Zimbabwe and the global arena presents challenges that require decisive interventions. What comes out clearly is that the COVID-19 era exposed increased linguistic vulnerabilities and injustices in Zimbabwean society rooted in the domain of language use. The pandemic provided important moments to reflect on the limits of discriminatory and exclusive languaging, especially in time of public health crises when speedy dissemination of pertinent information could save lives. The current language ideologies and linguistic practices privilege the English language at the detriment of minority languages and their speakers in all communicative endeavors in Zimbabwe. This situation alienates and disadvantages minority linguistic groups in Zimbabwe. It has been observed from the foregoing discussion that the complexity within the language debate is influenced by diverse factors, which include the desire to remain relevant in the global arena. Charting pathways out of linguistic alienation and biased ethnic thinking is encouraged. This means that Zimbabwe and Africa in general need to deeply debate language politics and take determined steps towards shifting such linguistic binary thinking in order to invest in the interconnecting multilingual capacities that could foster more transgressive linguistic repertoires and language perspectives that seek to redefine global community in terms of its diversities as rightly suggested by Nkuna (2013) and Ndlovu-Gatsheni (2020). Reflections upon current language ideologies expose the follies entrenched in monological practices. In the post-COVID-19 pandemic era, it is not only necessary to shift from discriminatory linguistic and spatial regimes, but also embrace language practices speak to the multilingual nature of the postcolonial African contexts. Cognizant of the intricacies of the sociolinguistic situation in Zimbabwe and other multilingual African nations, it is imperative to develop more multilingual communication strategies in preparation for future public health demands. Crises are also critical moments of reflection that demand radical change from the status quo, and the COVID-19 pandemic is not an exception in this regard. Certainly, the experiences of the pandemic initiated multi-faceted changes that could redefine humanity. Most importantly, Zimbabweans today should strive to get out of the monological trap and develop complex metacognitive and metalinguistic competencies as survival mechanisms in the 21st century in which interethnic and intercultural solidarity is necessary. In the post-pandemic world, humanity could reconnect and transcend borders and imaginary boundaries. The post-COVID-19 global world envisioned in this study should not be attached to a single linguistic code but rather embrace a humanity with complex linguistic repertoires. This new humanity promotes non-hegemonic and complex language exchange in the utilization of European and African indigenous languages as a welcome plurality that seeks to reflect multiplicities as a new world order. These languages partake in different roles and should complement each other in ways that benefit humanity in its diverse nature. In conclusion, Ndlovu-Gatsheni (2020) rightly notes that COVID-19 pointed to the need to unthink exclusionary logics and generate a new post-COVID-19 moral order premised on social justice, mutual respect, and complementary human relations across trans/national spaces.

Concluding Remarks

It has been established that the subject of language politics is a murky terrain characterized by controversy and ambivalence. In light of the above discussion, a devotion to multilingual or heteroglossic practices is critical to obtain linguistic justice, deconstruct binary logics, and reconstruct new linguistic perspectives. Indigenous languages should be visibly and effectively included in public health communication in order to increase access to health matters and other pertinent sectors. This will ensure that the lives of the different linguistic communities in Zimbabwe are protected. The chapter refocused attention on the language debate in the postcolonial era with the aim to move away from Eurocentric language ideologies, which denigrate indigenous languages and speakers of such languages. Attaining linguistic justice through investing in multilingual repertoires is one way of embracing humankind diversity, challenging abyssal thinking, refuting linguistic imperialism, and re-positioning the global peripheries into an inclusive new global ordering. The chapter quizzed long-standing linguistic ideologies that maintain monocultures of the mind and coloniality of being that largely ignores the imperatives of new becoming in the contemporary world. It reinforced the call for a shift from Cartesian logics and intolerance of difference that continue to place humanity in hierarchical structures that keep the center–periphery schisms intact (Omoniyi, 2003). Separatist thinking continues to shape human relations as reflected in linguistic choice and languaging of important messages in the public health discourses at both the national and international levels. The study noted that although the existing separatist linguistic logics are traceable to Africa's unbroken colonial history, their endurance in the postcolonial environment also mirrors the shortcomings of the local people who should be at the forefront of rehumanizing themselves linguistically. It is thus necessary for Africans to first take deep retrospection and introspection that garners new and vital steps towards re-defining the functional roles of indigenous languages in the time of global health crises.

References

Bamgbose, A. (2003). A recurring decimal: English in language policy and planning. *World Englishes*, 22(4), 419–431.

Bamgbose, A. (2011). African languages today: The challenge of and prospects for empowerment under globalisation. In E. G. Bokamba, R. K. Shosted, and B. T. Ayalew (Eds.), *Selected Proceedings of the 40th Annual Conference on African Linguistics* (pp. 1–14). Somerville: Cascadilla Proceedings Project.

Bhabha, H. K. (1994). *The Location of Culture*. London: Routledge.

Canagarajah, S. (2006). The place of world Englishes in composition: Pluralization continued. *College Composition and Communication*, 57(4), 586–619.

Canagarajah, S. (2013). *Translingual Practice: Global Englishes and Cosmopolitan Relations*. Oxon: Routledge.

Canagarajah, S. (2021). Materialising semiotic repertoires: Challenges in the international analysis of multilingual communication. *International Journal of Multilingualism*, 18(2), 206–225.

Chikasha, J. (2016). Linguistic revitalisation: Tonga in Zimbabwe. PhD Thesis. Johannesburg: University of Johannesburg.

Chimhundu, H. (Ed.). (1997). Language policies in Africa intergovernmental conference on language policies in Africa, Harare, Zimbabwe, 17–21 March 1997. Final Report (Revised), Web Version Edited by Karsten Legere. Harare: UNESCO.

Fanon, F. (1967). *Black Skin, White Masks*. New York: Grove Press.

Fofana, O. M. (2021). Decolonising global health in the time of COVID-19. *Global Public Health*, 16(8–9), 1155–1166.

Gordon, L. (2000). *Existentia Africana: Understanding Africana Existential Thought*. New York: Routledge.

Grosfoguel, R. (2007). The epistemic decolonial turn. *Cultural Studies*, 21(2–3), 211–223.

Heller, M. and Martin-Jones, M. (2001). Introduction: Symbolic domination, education, and linguistic difference. In M. Heller and M. Martin-Jones (Eds.), *Voices of Authority: Educational and Linguistic Difference* (pp. 2–28). London: Ablex Publishing.

Ingrid, P., Zhang, P., and Li, J. (2020). Linguistic diversity in a time of crisis: Language challenges of the COVID-19 pandemic. *Multilingua: Journal of Cross-Cultural and Interlanguage Communication*, 39(5), 503–515.

Kachru, B. B. (1985). Standards, codification and sociolinguistic realism: The English language in the outer circle. In R. Quirk and H. G. Widdowson (Eds.), *English in the World: Teaching and Learning the Language and Literatures* (pp. 11–30). Cambridge: Cambridge University Press.

Kachru, B. B. (2005). *Asian Englishes: Beyond the Canon*. Hong Kong: Hong Kong University Press.

Kadenge, M. and Nkomo, D. (2011). The politics of the English language in Zimbabwe. *Language Matters*, 42(2), 248–263.

Makoni, S. (2011). A critical analysis of the historical and contemporary status of minority languages in Zimbabwe. *Current Issues in Language Planning*, 12(4), 437–455.

Maldonado-Torres, N. (2011). Thinking through the decolonial turn: Post continental interventions in theory, philosophy and critique - An introduction. *Transmodernity: Journal of Peripheral a Cultural Production of LusoHispanic World*, 1(2), 1–23.

Matsuda, P. K. (2003). Proud to be a nonnative English speaker. *TESOL Matters*, 13(4), 15.

Mavengano, E. and Hove, M. L. (2020). The translingual subjects: Shaping identities and deconstructing rainbowism in *One Foreigner's Ordeal*. *Literator*, 41(1), a1691. http://doi.org/10.4102/lit.v41i1.1691.

McGroarty, M. (2008). The political matrix of language ideologies. In B. Spolsky and F. Hult (Eds.), *The Handbook of Educational Linguistics* (pp. 98–112). Maiden, MA: Blackwell.

Mignolo, W. D. (2000). *Local Histories/Global Designs: Coloniality, Subaltern Knowledges and Border Thinking*. Princeton, NJ: Princeton University Press.

Mignolo, W. D. (2007). Introduction coloniality of power and de-colonial thinking. *Cultural Studies*, 21(2–3), 155–167.

Mignolo, W. D. (2011). *The Darker Side of Western Modernity: Global Futures, Decolonial Options*. Durham, NC and London: Duke University Press.

Mpofu, P. and Salawu, A. (2018). Linguistic disenfranchisement, minority resistance and language revitalisation: The contribution of ethnolinguistic online communities in Zimbabwe. *Cogent & Arts*, 5(1), 15517764. https://doi.org/10.1080/23311983.2018.1551764.

Mumpande, I. (2020). The revitalisation of ethnic minority languages in Zimbabwe: The case of the Tonga language. MA Thesis. Pretoria: University of South Africa.

Mungwini, P. (2017). 'African know thyself': Epistemic injustice and the quest for liberative knowledge. *International Journal of African Renaissance Studies – Multi-, Inter- and Transdisciplinarity*, 12(2), 5–18.

Mutasa, D. E. (Ed.). (2006). *African Languages in the 21st Century: The Main Challenges*. Pretoria: Simba Guru Publishers.

Ndlovu, E. (2013). Mother tongue education in official minority language of Zimbabwe: A language management critique. Ph.D Thesis. Bloemfontein: Bloemfontein University of Free State.

Ndlovu-Gatsheni, S. J. (2013). Decoloniality in Africa: A continuity search for a new world order. *The Australasian Review of African Studies*, 36(2), 22–50.

Ndlovu-Gatsheni, S. J. (2015). Decoloniality as the future of Africa. *History Compass*, 13(10), 485–496.

Ndlovu-Gatsheni, S. J. (2020). Geopolitics of power and knowledge in the COVID-19 pandemic: Decolonial reflections on a global crisis. *Journal of Developing Societies*, 36(4), 366–389.

Ngugi wa Thiong'o. (1986). *Decolonising the Mind: The Politics of Languages in African Literature*. Nairobi: James Currey; and Kenya: Heinemann.

Ngugi Wa Thiong'o. (1994). *Decolonising the Mind: The Politics of Language in African Literature*. London: Heinemann.

Nkuna, H. P. (2013). Africa's indigenous languages as the cornerstone of the African Renaissance. *International Journal of Renaissance Studies, Multi-Inter- and Transdisciplinarity*, 8(2), 70–88.

Nye, J. S. Jr. (2002). *The Paradox of American Power Why the World's Only Superpower Can't Go It Alone*. New York: Oxford University Press.

Omoniyi, T. (2003). Local policies and global forces: Multiliteracy and Africa's indigenous 475 languages. *Language Policy*, 2(2), 133–152.

Pennycook, A. (1994). *The Cultural Politics of English as an International Language*. London: Longman.

Phillipson, R. (1992). *Linguistic Imperialism*. Oxford: Oxford University Press.

Phillipson, R. (2009). *Linguistic Imperialism Continued*. Routledge.

Phillipson, R. and Skutnabb-Kangas, T. (1994). English-Panacea or Pandemic? In U. Ammon, K. J. Mattheier, and P. Nelde (Eds.), *Sociolinguistica 8. English Only? in Europa/ in Europe/ en Europe* (pp. 73–87).

Phillipson, R. and Skutnabb-Kangas, T. (1995). Linguistic rights and wrongs. *Applied Linguistics*, 16(4), 483–504.

Phillipson, R. and Skutnabb-Kangas, T. (1997). Linguistic human right and English in Europe. *World Englishes*, 16(2), 27–43

Phillipson, R. and Skutnabb-Kangas, T. (1999). Linguistic rights and wrongs; in Japanese. In Research Group on Linguistic Rights (ed.), *Kotoba e no Kenri (Rights towards Languages)* (pp. 95–128). Tokyo: Sangensya Publishers (translation of Linguistic rights and wrongs from *Applied Linguistics* 16(4), 1995, 483–504).

Quijano, A. (2000). Coloniality of power and Eurocentrism in Latin America. *International Sociology*, 15(2), 215–232.

Rizwan, A. (2020). Multilingual resources key to fighting COVID-19. *Language on the Move*. Advance online publication. https://www.languageonthemove.com/multilingual -resources-keyto-fighting-covid-19/.

Silverstein, M. (1998). The uses and utility of ideology. In B. Shiefflelin, K. Woolard and P. Kroskrity (Eds.), *Language Ideologies: Practice and Theory* (pp. 123–145). Oxford: Oxford University Press.

Skutnabb-Kangas, T. (1988). Multilingualism and the education of minority children. In T. Skutnabb-Kangas and J. Cummins (Eds.), *Minority Education: From Shame to Struggle* (pp. 9–44). Clevedon: Multilingual Matters.

Tollefson, J. W. (2000). Policy and ideology in the spread of English. In J. K. Hall and W. Eggington (Eds.), *The Sociopolitics of English Language Teaching* (pp. 7–21). Clevedon: Multilingual Matters.

UNESCO World Education Report. (2000). The right to education; towards education for all throughout life. https://unesdoc.unesco.org/ark:/48223/pf0000119720.

Wolff, H. E. (2017). Language ideologies and the politics of language in post-colonial Africa. *Stellenbosch Papers in Linguistics Plus*, 51, 1–22. https://doi.org/10.5842/51-0-701.

6 A Language-Policy-Inspired Lesson for the Zimbabwean Post-COVID-19 Era

Isaac Mhute

Introduction

The novel coronavirus SARS-CoV-2, which causes the deadly COVID-19 disease, has been around for over two years now. In addition to the rocketing morbidity and mortality rates it has brought about, the pandemic has dislocated economies and social conditions. For instance, Albarracin (2021) observes that the restrictions imposed by the pandemic have ushered in considerable losses in terms of social contact, jobs, and other elements of people's social networks. Apart from the disruptions made in higher education, Dennis (2020) also notes that the Asian Development Bank estimates that the pandemic could cost the global economy between US$5.8 and US$8.8 trillion. The United Nations Development Program (UNDP) (2020, p. 8) argues as well that "the COVID-19 pandemic may have pushed some 100 million families into extreme poverty, the worst setback in a generation." The World Bank (2020) reiterates that the pandemic has markedly disrupted the global economic system and daily life, sending countries into various degrees of economic recession. It adds that half of the low-income countries were already in economic turmoil and at high risk of debt distress before the pandemic, only to be overwhelmed by the global economic contraction caused by both the pandemic and the health measures used to contain the virus, such as lockdowns as well as the restrictions to movements and economic activities associated with them. Other studies' findings have also raised concerns about the pandemic's impact on mental health (Farkhard & Albarracin, 2020). They have established that the most insidious psychological problems during the pandemic concern inability to regulate oneself from being infected with the SARS-CoV-2 virus. This considerably justifies the UNDP's (2020) assertion that the COVID-19 pandemic is the defining global health crisis of our time and the greatest challenge we have faced since World War II.

The chapter submits that whilst COVID-19's impact on the entire globe is overwhelming, it is being worsened by the fact that other deadly diseases previously declared pandemics, like HIV and AIDS, are still around with real solutions for them yet to be uncovered. Hence, the UNDP's (2020) argument that we are at an unprecedented moment in the history of humankind and the

DOI: 10.4324/9781003390732-6

entire planet, further pointing out that warning lights are flashing red for our societies and the planet, as scientists foresee more deadly diseases approaching. Such a situation is quite alarming making uncovering everlasting solutions for pandemics every continent's logical top priority. In light of the above, the chapter is one of the efforts towards drawing invaluable lessons from the current pandemic in order to inspire a better African approach to such deadly pandemics in the post-COVID-19 era. This is in line with Albarracin's (2021) observation that the pandemic has brought the imperative of producing a rapid and flexible public health response to address rapidly evolving risks.

A look at the global response to the COVID-19 pandemic, just like others such as HIV and AIDS, demonstrates that Africa is yet to make any significant impact. Information on the nature of the virus, the disease, preventive measures, testing machines, as well as the vaccines now in use is all foreign to the continent. In spite of the varying strains being discovered in the continent, there are limited or no substantial efforts to uncover effective local solutions for the pandemic. Rather, efforts in the continent are being made by foreign organizations like the European Union (EU) that have availed $3.6 million to assist Rwanda in upgrading her laboratory capacity, acquiring modern laboratory equipment, and attracting investors to manufacture mRNA COVID-19 vaccines (*Daily Monitor*, 1 July 2021). The same is being done by Aspen Pharmacare, an American organization, which is making efforts to boost its manufacturing capacity for Johnson & Johnson vaccine in South Africa by 200 million doses annually starting January 2022 (Jerving, 2021). Thus, instead of efforts towards coming up with something purely African and inspired by the local strains, foreign organizations are extending their hand in order to make some African countries mere outposts for manufacturing European and American vaccines. The chapter considers this a real confirmation of the aversion of Africans working towards coming up with anything of their own in as far as the fight against the pandemic is concerned. It also demonstrates the need for Africans to get a foreign hand in order to come up with something.

Whilst the vaccines have brought about some relief in the face of COVID-19, just like antiretroviral drugs have done to HIV and AIDS, the chapter argues that there is a need for everlasting solutions for such pandemics. To do this, there is a need for every continent to approach the pandemic from its own angles, as nobody knows exactly where the cure for the deadly disease lies. It stresses that it is very unfortunate that the African continent has comfortably folded its hands hoping for solutions to come from others in response to this as well as any other such alarming pandemics. This is evidenced by African governments' blind faith in foreign efforts against the pandemic. For instance, a number of them were even quicker than the producers of the vaccines in declaring vaccination with foreign vaccines compulsory by making it a requirement for employment retention and freedom of worship, among others, in spite of the coronavirus mRNA "vaccines" being the product of experimental scientific research that has arguably a lot of desired information about them still to be uncovered (Edeling, 2021). The chapter perceives the nature of language policies adopted in the African continent as responsible for this dangerous attitude towards the outside world as well as the approach to the deadly pandemic.

Theoretical Framework

The chapter has been inspired by the cultural dependency theory. Umeogu and Ifeoma (2012) describe cultural dependency as a scenario whereby a country is consciously or unconsciously forced to thrive or depend on another for her needs. Whilst proponents of the theory appreciate the need for exchanges between countries for the sake of formal education, civilization, and modernization, cultural dependency theory focuses on instances where there happens to be overdependency leading to abuse and mental enslavement. Thus, it invariably puts pressure on some societies to adopt the culture, values, beliefs, and lifestyles of others, since culture is summarily seen as the totality of a people's way of life (Umeogu & Ifeoma, 2012) as it is carried by their languages. For instance, whereas people now talk of every country's membership in the global village, villagers have an uneven playground with some accorded more importance than others through languages adopted for international communication. The chapter perceives the current approach to the COVID-19 pandemic, and other global responsibilities, as basically being dictated by the countries that have been promoted within the global village through the recognition of their ideologies advanced by the adopted language policies. It perceives these countries as readily pressurizing their so-called dependents to look to them, as they are unprepared to consider anything from them, in spite of the fact that nobody knows exactly where the real solution lies. As such, the dependents have accepted their language-policy-inspired fate, folded their hands, and completely entrusted the responsibility for this and other such vital tasks for the first world countries to accomplish. They have been made to willingly accept their enslavement as logical and the only noble thing to do resulting in blind faith in whatever outcome from them.

African Language Policies as Promoters of Cultural Dependency

Language and culture are inseparable as every culture is carried by a language. As such, destroying a language is tantamount to destroying the culture and tradition associated with it. This is properly captured by Wa Thiong'o (2017) who observes that the promotion of a language also comes with the rise in status of the culture it carries, since every language is a soul of its respective culture. Reiterating to the observation, Okunna (1999) talks of cultural syncronization as a situation whereby a people's culture is eliminated resulting in loss of identity and the need for a new one. To fill this vacuum for a culture and identity, the people thus become synchronous with the culture that led to the elimination of their original one. This means the emergence of an immense respect for the traditional wisdom or indigenous knowledge systems typical of that culture. One easy way through which a language could be promoted or destroyed is through language planning. Through it, a society's future could be harnessed by forcibly destroying respect in its own culture to ensure it remains within the clutches intended by the proponents of the ideologies behind the adopted language policies. The power of this effect is hereby likened to some kind of "mind controlling activity," which Flores (2018) describes as a reductive process in which a man is reduced to an animal or machine. The language policies of most African countries (most of which are former mother powers' legacies) are hereby considered to be acting like techniques skillfully designed to suppress the will of the countries by making them dependent on what is dictated by the native speakers of the languages they have adopted. Therefore, their center has been transferred for repositioning in the countries whose languages and cultures they have promoted at the expense of their own. This makes everything suggested or done by native speakers of the adopted languages appear as their own. This confirms Wa Thiong'o's (2017) perception of language on its own as having the capacity to keep Africans in some full-fledged slavery if not prioritized for placement at the center of the decolonization process. According to Mapara (2017), the situation is made worse by the fact that the education that Zimbabweans, just like almost every African state, continue to receive does not promote appreciation of their own countries' heritage but that of the West. For example, school quizzes focus on western knowledge and not indigenous knowledge and cultures.

The current chapter argues that slavery and colonization in Africa have reached such disastrous levels that they are dangerously affecting even the way in which the countries respond to fatal pandemics like COVID-19 that are threatening to extinguish humanity. As indicated earlier on, there is full, if not blind, trust in everything that comes from foreign nations whose languages and cultures have been promoted through adopted policies. This is resulting in risking of local lives as some of the medicines are still in the trial stage with their efficacy and nature of side effects yet to be fully ascertained. This is properly captured by Edeling (2021) who argues that the pandemic's harmful effects are being aggravated by official African COVID-19 narratives that seem in blind faith to echo the official narratives of the World Health Organization (WHO), Food and Drug Administration (FDA), Centre for Disease Control (CDC), as well as European, American, Canadian, and Australian governments, inter alia. He indicates that blind faith is, for instance, in aspects whose nature is yet to be ascertained like whether the experimental coronavirus mRNA "vaccines" are safe and effective or how long immunity from them may last. This is quite alarming in light of Mestrovic's (2021) report that, according to the Israeli Ministry of Health, by the end of April (2021), a total of 397 people fully vaccinated (with the 94–95% effective Pfizer/BioNTech's BNT162b2 and Moderna's mRNA–1273 vaccines) were hospitalized with the severe acute respiratory syndrome coronavirus 2 (SARS-CoV-2) with 90 of them succumbing to it.

Direction of African Scientists and Researchers' Focus

As specified by cultural dependency theory, African scientists are proving to have been fully captured by foreign institutions. Instead of pursuing promising local initiatives to combat local coronavirus strains, they are busy pursuing foreign-funded agendas and testing foreign medical combinations using COVID-19 patients within the continent. For instance, Drugs for Neglected Diseases initiative (DNDi) (2020) reports of the ANTICOV study (the so-called largest clinical trial in Africa) to identify and treat COVID-19 mild and moderate cases before they become severe to prevent spikes in hospitalization. In a trial that started in September 2020 and funded by European organizations such as the German Federal Ministry and Research, ANTICOV was testing, in 13 African countries, a new potential treatment that combines antiparasitic nitazoxanide and the inhaled corticosteroid ciclesonide. It was a collaborative effort by many African scientific leaders and organizations and the trial was reviewed with support from the African Vaccine Regulatory Forum (ALVAREF), a platform established by WHO in 2006, which is mandated to expedite clinical trial reviews for COVID-19. Though the trial did not yield the best expected results, a second trial, funded by the European Union, was following, among others (DNDi, 2020). Thus, the effort that focused on trying combinations of foreign medicines within the continent, rather than on generating new local ones inspired by the local coronavirus strains, readily received overwhelming support from local scientists, researchers, and governments. This confirms Mapara's (2017) observation that research in African institutions of higher learning seeks to confirm and validate western knowledge and not indigenous one adding that where research has been done on indigenous knowledge systems, researchers do not want to confirm it but to do what Masoga (2002, p. 3) calls "boundary jumping," which is not ethically proper.

The chapter perceives overwhelming participation in efforts like DNDi as clear evidence of lacking originality on the part of local scientists, researchers, and governments. They demonstrate an insatiable need for foreign leadership and foreign funding to pursue foreign ideas in order to do something against such deadly pandemics. This is a typical demonstration of the dependency syndrome rampant in the continent that emerged from the adopted language policies. It shows how much the foreign organizations are taking advantage of the syndrome to test their own medicines within the continent using local scientists. This is a dangerous attitude towards the foreign organizations and their efforts considering that African citizens are being used as guinea pigs for vaccines and medicines, some of which are proving to have deadly side effects. For instance, Botswana was reported by the *News24* of 12 April 2021 as probing the death of two people who took AstraZeneca shot in the country at the same time South Africa was reported to have halted the rollout of Johnson & Johnson vaccine after six US women developed unusual blood clots with low platelets after receiving the dose (www.aa.com>africa). Both developments only surfaced way after the vaccines had already been offered to a considerable number of Africans. This calls for an urgent reversal of the impacts of the adopted language policies that have bred so much dangerous trust and belief in foreign organizations as big brothers even in such sensitive matters.

Opportunities Being Ignored by African Scientists and Researchers

The chapter asserts that the major challenge is that African initiatives showing considerable potential to make an international impact against the local strains seem to attract no attention from first-world countries. This is basically because they do not expect anything serious from the continent and, therefore, still share the perception observed by Nhemachena et al. (2020) that colonialists erroneously assumed that Africans were indistinct from animals and lacked autonomy, sovereignty, human essence, morality, and dignity. Consequently, the potential initiatives are going unnoticed by local scientists and researchers as they seem to only respect initiatives and developments approved by foreigners, whose lifestyles and judgments they now blindly appreciate, courtesy of the adopted language policies. A good example is that of April 2020 when, at a time the COVID-19 pandemic was proliferating and the scientific researchers were racing towards finding even a short-term solution for it, Madagascar's president, Andry Rajoelina, announced a plant-based tonic he claimed could prevent as well as cure the novel virus (Atabong, 2020). The remedy, which was an African formula and named COVID-Organics, had been proven effective in the country but instead of seriously examining the discovery scientifically, health personnel were quick to warn against the use of such traditional herbs as some could have undesired side effects. This was confirmed by Cachia (2020) who notes that, whilst scientific tests on the efficacy were still to be done, the United Nations' health body quickly urged skepticism over such claimed cures for COVID-19 whilst the United States CDC said, "There is no scientific evidence that any of these proposed remedies can prevent or cure the illness caused by COVID-19." This brought the talks about the discovery to an end.

It is of considerable concern for the chapter that, instead of readily collaborating to establish the efficacy of the local initiative on the local strains, African scientists and researchers were not moved and as such remained silent. This was a good opportunity that could have inspired collaborative scientific research efforts towards a local cure for the disease or at least for the reduction of the impact of some of its effects. Rather, they were not perturbed, which goes on to demonstrate how effectively the language policies have promoted foreign countries as the model in Africa. They have been blindly accepted as the assessors and judges for any global efforts as their utterance was enough to declare Madagascar's major effort useless and unworthy of any continental scientific attention. This contrasts so well with the DNDi trials that readily received attention and voluntary participation of scientists from around 15 African countries, just because it was a foreign initiative and, though the first one did not yield the best result, more efforts were scheduled to build on it in a bid to improve the outcome. This explains the logic behind African governments that readily enforce vaccination of their citizens with foreign vaccines, some of which are still in the trial stage and proving to be risky, way after many have already received them.

In Zimbabwe as well, desperate reactions saw a revisit to the indigenous knowledge system (also known as indigenous technical science by Mapara (2017)) to make use of traditional herbs like *zumbani* (*Lippia javanica*) in bailing out a considerable number of citizens (Moyo, 2021), especially those who could not afford the hospital intensive medical care required for combating effects of the virus infection, way after many such had already succumbed to it. It was only after such discoveries that the herbs bounced back from being popularly condemned as useless, barbaric, evil, and associated with witchcraft to being nicely packaged for placement on even the most prestigious supermarkets' shelves in the country. Some COVID-19 Zimbabwean patients (e.g. Nyson and Gertrude Mhaka) have testified how they were healed, courtesy of *zumbani* (Moyo, 2021). Maroyi (2017) confirms the wide range of *zumbani's* healing activities including anticancer, antipoetic, and antidiabetic effects but is quick to indicate that scientists are yet to evaluate the safety and clinical value of its main crude as well as pure compounds and to clarify their mechanisms of action. This confirms Mapara's (2017) argument that most local scholars are at the forefront of not accepting indigenous knowledge systems by pointing out that they need to be validated. They do so even when they understand that the standards of validation are foreign and do not fit into the indigenous way of doing things.

Just like the Madagascar case alluded to earlier, such developments in Zimbabwe never attained any of the first-world countries' attention and, as such, never inspired any local efforts towards a proper solution for the pandemic. In such a continent with a lot of high-profile scientists and researchers, who showed considerable interest in uncovering a solution for the pandemic during the DNDi trials (DNDi, 2020), such developments could have received considerable attention as they highlighted the potential of the medicinal properties of flora and fauna that are possessed by local communities (Mapara, 2017). The scientists could have probably made a global impact along those lines as advised by Singh (2011) that Zimbabweans should utilize the available knowledge as an opportunity to innovate and develop new technologies based on and informed by indigenous knowledge systems. The chapter considers this a clear demonstration of the level of dependency syndrome in the continent, courtesy of the language policies in use. It proves how much the local scientists and researchers have been put under clutches by foreign countries. This is in line with Mapara's (2017) argument that Zimbabweans in particular and Africans in general have no faith in themselves due to the development of a rabid consumer culture. They have thus been blinded by their insatiable love and hunger for foreign commodities (Hattingh, Russo, Sun-Basorun and Van Wamelen, 2012).

Similar scenarios are transpiring across the African continent. For instance, Xinhua (2021) reports on how traders often run out of the local medicinal spices like ginger, garlic, and many others which Zambians use in making concoctions for successfully treating flu-like illnesses including COVID-19. Traders like Naomi Kakoma and Doreen Nyoya confirm the news and explain how the concoctions are made as well as how much they successfully combat illnesses and boost immune systems. In a situation where COVID-19 has proven to be placing the elderly and those with underlying conditions who are immunocompromised at high risk, such discoveries could have been received with great joy. Local researchers and scientists could have logically initiated efforts to promote research on such as a way of combating the disease. Logical efforts would have included scientific research on the medicinal properties for combating flu-like diseases and the immune-enhancing ones. This could surely enhance the fight against the pandemic by availing alternatives to foreign ones, some of which have become unbearably expensive for common Africans apart from demonstrating considerable side effects. The chapter perceives such ignorance as resulting from a shift of belief in everything that is related to local languages, cultures, and traditional knowledge systems. The language policies have, thus, made the governments, scientists, and researchers believe fully in foreign approaches and answers for all problems, a habit that might place people at unnecessary risks from foreign medicines and vaccines when solutions to the pandemic could be uncovered locally.

Lessons for the Post-COVID-19 Era

The period people are living in does not afford to take chances. First, there is the UNDP's (2020) observation alluded to earlier, that people are at an unprecedented moment in the history of humankind and the entire planet further indicating that warning lights are flashing red for societies and the entire planet, as scientists foresee more deadly diseases approaching, which require a proper approach to such deadly pandemics. As such, continental intellectuals must eradicate their language-policy-inspired dependency syndrome, reclaim their responsibilities, and rise up to the demands of the situation as the approaching diseases might deny foreigners an opportunity to bail others out just like COVID-19 is making it almost difficult to avail enough vaccines for everyone. This is also the best thing to do in light of the diseases that often take different strains in varying circumstances. Second, people often hear of coronavirus, just like HIV/AIDS, as man-made biological weapons intended to facilitate the achievement of different selfish personal goals (*The Connexion French News and Views*, 17 August 2021). Furthermore, the vaccines being availed are proving to have compromised efficacies (Mestrovic, 2021). These alleged conspiracies (no matter the truth behind them) must inspire Africans towards understanding that the dependency syndrome they have as a result of the adopted language policies might endanger the entire continent's well-being. In light of this, the current approach in the continent, of blindly trusting everything said or produced by foreigners without proper analysis, has to be revised in the post-COVID-19 era, as some proposed cures may prove worse than the illnesses themselves (Edeling, 2021). To ensure this, governments must revise their approach to reality by revisiting their language policies with the motive of replacing them with those that promote local ideologies. If it proves too late to revise the language policies, they must at least consider putting in place measures for mitigating the effects of the promotion of foreign languages in their societies. These would ensure the restoration of the lost respect for local cultures and their traditional knowledge systems as starting points for better approaches to all the challenges that might be encountered in the post-COVID-19 era.

Conclusion

The chapter demonstrates the difficult situation the entire world is in courtesy of the deadly diseases piling up without proper solutions. It argues that the African continent is dangerously dependent upon efforts in other continents, which it blindly trusts without proper examination, considering the alleged conspiracies about the origins of diseases. The attitude is hereby linked to the language policies adopted within the continent, which advance the ideologies of foreigners at the expense of the local ones. As such, the chapter demonstrates the preparedness of the local governments, scientists, and researchers to support anything foreign at the same time ignoring anything local unless it gains foreign endorsement. This calls for a need to stop trusting foreigners blindly as this might place the lives of many at risk especially now that some people have developed unbelievably evil intentions. There is, therefore, a call for a revisit of the current approach to issues in order to eradicate the dependency syndrome and to achieve this, it is advised that countries should at least mitigate the effects of the foreign ideologies advanced by language policies adopted in the continent. The move would restore the traditional thirst for self-respect and desire to be self-reliant, which have the potential to bail out the entire world from some of the pandemics bedeviling it.

References

Albarracin, D. (2021). A research agenda for the post-COVID-19 world: Theory and research in social psychology. *Asian Journal of Psychology*, *24*(1), 10–17.

Atabong, A.B. (2020). How Pan-African media helped Madagascar advance its claim of a COVID-19 'miracle cure' as a form of medical diplomacy. *Africaportal*. https://www.africaportal.org/publications. Accessed on 14/04/2021.

Cachia, A. (2020). Madagascar vows to 'change the history of the entire world' as it carries out tests on mystery plant it claims can cure coronavirus. https://www.dailymail.co.uk/news/article-8204131/Plant-remedy-virus-tested-says-Madagascar-leader.html. Accessed on 14/04/2021.

Daily Monitor. (2021, 1 July). Rwanda signs $3.6m deal with EU to upgrade labs for COVID jab production. www.monitor.co.ug>news. Accessed on 11/08/2021.

Dennis, M.J. (2020). The impact of COVID-19 on the world economy and higher education. *Enrollment Management Report, 24*(9), 3–14.

DNDi. (2020). Largest clinical trial in Africa for people with mild COVID-19 to test new drug combination. www.dndi.org>press-releases. Accessed on 14/08/2021.

Edeling, J.H. (2021). COVID-19 pandemic health and economic crises: Open letter to president Ramaphosa. www.emlct.com>index.php. Accessed on 18/08/2021.

Farkhard, B.F., & Albarracin, D. (2020). Insights on the implications of COVID-19 mitigation measures for mental health. *Economics and Human Biology, 40*, 16–28.

Flores, D.S. (2018). Transhumanism: The big fraud-towards digital slavery. *International Physical Medicine & Rehabilitation Journal, 3*(5), 1–12.

Hattingh, D., Russo, B., Sun-Basorun, A., & Van Wamelen, A. (2012). *The Rise of the African Consumer: A Report from McKinsey's Africa Consumer Insights Center*. New York: McKinsey and Company.

Jerving, S. (2021). South Africa's Aspen to boost COVID-19 vaccine manufacturing, says AU. www.devex.com. Accessed on 11/08/2021.

Mapara, J. (2017). Binarism as a recipe for lukewarm research into indigenous knowledge systems in Zimbabwe. In P. Ngulube (Ed.), *Handbook of Research on Theoretical Perspectives on Indigenous Knowledge Systems in Developing Countries*. (pp. 1–21). Hershey, PA: IGI Global.

Maroyi, A. (2017). Lippia javanica (Burm.f.) Spreng.: Traditional and commercial uses and phytochemical uses and pharmacological significance in the African and Indian subcontinent. www.ncbi.nlm.nih.gov. Accessed on 14/08/2021.

Masoga, M.A. (2002). Contesting space and time: Intellectual property rights and the indigenous knowledge systems research in South African universities. Paper presented at the International Symposium CODESRIA/ILLINOIS under the theme: African Universities in the 21st Century.

Mestrovic, T. (2021). Israeli study of breakthrough infections following full BNT-Pfizer vaccination, 0% immunocompromised. In *News Medical Life Sciences*. www.news-medical.net. Accessed on 17/08/2021.

Moyo, J. (2021). Zimbabweans pin hopes on woody shrub to beat COVID-19. www.aa.com.tr>africa>zimbababwe. Accessed on 08/04/2021.

News 24. (2021, 12 April). www.news24.com>news. Accessed on 14/04/2021.

Nhemachena, A., Hlabangane, N., & Kaundjua, M.B. (2020). Rationality or hospitality in twenty first century research? Big data, internet of things and the resilience of coloniality on Africa, modern Africa *Politics, History and Society, 8*(1), 105–139.

Okunna, S. (1999). *Introduction to Mass Communication.* Enugu: New Generation Books.

Singh, P.R. (2011). Consumer culture and postmodernism. *Consumer Culture and Postmodernism in Postmodern Openings, 5*(5), 55–88.

The Connexion French News and Views, 17 August 2021. www.connexionfrance.com Accessed on 18/08/2021.

The World Bank. (2020). *Confronting the Economic and Financial Challenges of COVID-19: A Conversation with World Bank Group President David Malpass.* www.worldbank.org. Accessed on 08/04/2021.

Umeogu, B., & Ifeoma, O. (2012). Cultural dependency: A philosophical insight. *Open Journal of Philosophy, 2*(2), 123–127.

UNDP. (2020). *Human Development Reports.* New York: UNDP.

Wa Thiong'o, N. (2017). Public lecture. A call for preservation and inclusion of African languages in learning institutions. www.nepad.org>news. Accessed on 14/10/20.

Xinhua. (2021). Zambian Traders benefiting from medicinal spices during COVID-19 pandemic. *Global Times*, 05 July, 2021. www.globaltimes.cn. Accessed on 14/08/2021.

7 Language Change beyond the COVID-19 Pandemic

The Case of Shona Language

Mika Nyoni and Tsitsi Nyoni

Introduction

The COVID-19 pandemic has dictated a global "new normal" as far as human behavior is concerned, and this shift in behavior includes a shift in language use. Beyond the pandemic, languages would have acquired or reassigned existing linguistic resources to grapple with the new reality on the ground. In short, the chapter submits that Shona as a language will not remain the same beyond the pandemic as its repertoire needs to change to accommodate the new environment. As the "operating environment" changes, languages need to change in order to remain relevant. The chapter thus makes an analysis of the impact of the COVID-19 pandemic on the Shona language, a language spoken natively by approximately 75% of Zimbabweans (Chimhundu, 1997). The chapter explores the sociolinguistic factors that enhance and shape the word-building processes in such environments that include need and function, superstratum influence, and the "principle of ease."

Language use/discourse gathered shows various morphological processes at play as language users attempt to linguistically "contain" the pandemic that has become part of their lives. Culture, according to Macionis (2012: 54), entails "the ways of thinking, the ways of acting, and the material objects that together form a people's way of life." COVID-19 has entered our lives and become part of our way of life. It has entered and become part of the 21st-century culture. Since language is not only a part of a people's way of living but also one of the conveyors of that culture, we thought it prudent to unpack the linguistic apparatus that the Shona of Zimbabwe has and use it to "talk" about the life-changing pandemic. Many governments and supranational organizations such as World Health Organization are talking about a new normal, which suggests a new cultural trajectory. Culture has to do with the lived experiences that have to be carried by an adoptive and adaptive linguistic apparatus. In future the pandemic might be reduced to a containable disease where people will need just a jab or two or pills to get inoculated at a certain age, but they are likely to live with it and inevitably assign linguistic resources in the form of expressions to "contain" it. Language as a carrier of the culture has to adapt to an ever-changing cultural terrain through various

DOI: 10.4324/9781003390732-7

morphological processes such as initialism, abbreviation, clipping, blending, neologism, and borrowing.

Anticipated Contribution to Society and Scholarship

Language is a carrier of culture and attitudes and by studying it one can deduce the speakers of that language's values and world view. COVID-19 has become part and parcel of our lives. The impact of COVID-19 on Shona has thus become of interest to researchers because it is a pandemic of unprecedented proportions, which at one time threatened to wipe out the whole global population. Given this impact, scholars from different disciplines cannot afford to ignore this pandemic; particularly its ramifications in all spheres of life. It has revolutionized the way we look at even those things we yesteryear took for granted. From studying linguistic items such as those collected and analyzed in this research, we can gauge the level of tolerance, knowledge about the disease the speakers of the language might have, and craft intervention strategies, if necessary, to destigmatize the disease. The linguist can, as in the case of this research, collect and analyze such language items and note various morphological processes at work.

Background

This section of the chapter briefly looks at the origin and impact of the COVID-19 pandemic as this is the stimulus that triggered the linguistic changes that motivated the construction of this chapter. In a very short span of time the epidemic graduated into a pandemic touching all corners of the world. Since homo sapiens are endowed with language, they express their experiences mainly through this medium. Since the aforesaid experiences are everchanging, language has to be realigned through various word-building processes to enunciate the nuances of the novel experiences.

The coronavirus disease (COVID-19) is a highly transmittable and pathogenic viral infection caused by severe acute respiratory syndrome coronavirus 2 (SARS-CoV-2), which emerged in Wuhan, China, and spread around the world in a very short span of time (Zhong et al. 2003; Li et al. 2020; Wang et al. 2020; Holshue et al. 2020). Coronaviruses belong to the Coronaviridae family in the Nidovirales order. Corona represents crown-like spikes on the outer surface of the virus; thus, it was named a coronavirus (Lu et al., 2020).

At the end of 2019, Wuhan, a region in China, experienced an outbreak of a new coronavirus that resulted in about 2,000 deaths and about 70,000 infections within the first two months of its detection. This new virus was named the Wuhan coronavirus or 2019 novel coronavirus (2019-nCov) by Chinese researchers. The International Committee on Taxonomy of Viruses (ICTV) named the virus SARS-CoV-2 and the disease COVID-19 (Gorbalenya et al. 2020; Muhammad et al. 2020).

Within two years of detection of the coronavirus, the devastation astronomically climbed to 235,611,921 cases and 4,809,532 worldwide deaths with

Africa contributing 8,370,243 cases and 212,068 deaths (European Centre for Disease Prevention and Control, October 2021).

In its second volume report entitled "How COVID-19 Is Changing the World: A Statistical Perspective Volume II Committee for the Coordination of Statistical Activities" the United Nations Department of Economic and Social Affairs (UN DESA) warns that "The information contained herein is even grimmer than in the first volume, confirming the unprecedented impact of the pandemic on the economic and social fabric of our societies" (UN DESA, 2020, p. 3). The report goes on to show a grim picture of the plummeting of global foreign direct investment and global manufacturing output. It goes on to show how the pandemic, in a period of just about a year, plunged about 100 million people into extreme poverty and rendered up to 155 million jobless in the first quarter of 2020 (UN DESA, 2020).

Zimbabwe was not spared. By 7 October 2021, Zimbabwe had 131,129 recorded cases and 4,627 deaths (European Centre for Disease Prevention and Control, 2021).

The UN paints an even grimmer picture when they describe the pandemic as more than a health issue:

> In an attempt to understand the potential impact of the pandemic on Zimbabwe, it is instructive to note that although it is primarily a health crisis, it nonetheless has far-reaching public governance, socio-political and economic ramifications.
>
> (United Nations Zimbabwe, 2020, p. 10)

The above statistics paint a grim picture of the state of the pandemic and its impact on the society the research is focused on. The pandemic took lives, condemned some to poverty and joblessness due to company closures, and fueled gender-based violence, led to juvenile delinquency, deprived humanity of a free life, among others. This grim scenario finds import in the language used as shall be shown in the analysis.

It is against this background that this chapter gathered lexical items pertaining to COVID-19 in different public spaces in Zimbabwe that include radio stations, newspapers, social media, and public places such as marketplaces, learning institutions, and public transport. The study is confined to a few selected words that were recorded during the COVID-19 pandemic. The COVID-19 pandemic has had so much widespread and multifaceted impact on people's lives globally, however, this chapter will only focus on just one aspect, namely linguistic change.

Brief Literature Review

Trask (1997, p. 25) notes that "every language that is spoken as a mother tongue is changing constantly in pronunciation, in grammar, and in vocabulary. There is no such thing as a living language, which fails to change."

Similarly Keith and Shuttleworth (2006, p. 219) posit that "Caterpillars change into butterflies, tadpoles into frogs and winter into spring. Change is an essential part of life. Without change, life ceases. *Language too must change, if it is to remain alive*" [Emphasis added].

Michigan State University is currently studying how COVID-19 is affecting language change in real time in a project led by Prof. S. Wagner, who observes that:

> We know from numerous studies of 20th century speech from different communities around the world that the second World War was a big inflection point for language change ... Historically major events like natural disasters and war have proven to have big impacts on language.
> (Popiolek, 2020 https://msutoday.msu.edu)

What is clear from her submission is that people's experiences, particularly those that affect many have an impact on the languages spoken. The recent and ongoing COVID-19 multifaceted experience cannot go uncaptured by the linguistic repertoires we use as human beings to "talk" about our experiences. Fox cited in Mahlberg and Brookes (2021, p. 441) has this to say on illnesses particularly life-changing epidemics and pandemics and their relationship with language:

> Illness cannot be just illness for the simple reason that human culture is constituted in language ... and that health and illness, being things which fundamentally concern humans and hence need to be "explained," enter into language and are constituted in language regardless of whether or not they have some independent reality in nature.
> (Fox cited in Mahlberg and Brookes, 2021, p. 441)

Khotimah, Laksono, Suharton, Pairin, and Darni (2021) researching on linguistic expression in Indonesian online media coverage in the era of COVID-19 note that new lexical items have been coined as well as reassigned words to deal with the new health and linguistic emergence. Ahmed and Islam (2020) provide a corpus-based analysis of the influence of COVID-19 on the lexical features of English in Pakistan. Their study notes an exponential rise in the use of new words and acronyms as well as a rise in prominence of previously "inactive" words.

Kupolati, Adebileje, and Adeleke (2021) explore lexical innovations and variation in the lexemes of Nigerian English formed during the COVID-19 pandemic. Their conclusion is that the pandemic significantly influenced Nigerian English from both the acrolectal and basilectal angles. Mweri (2021) analyses how English language in Kenya has been able to adapt to the changes that COVID-19 occasioned, what he terms the "corona vocabulary" (Mweri, 2021, p. 36).

Nyoni et al. (2012) posit that change is an irresistible and inevitable law of nature that affects both living and non-living things on earth of which language is a part. This is a common feature of languages that they do not remain static but adapt to the environment in which they are spoken. What it implies here is that, even language has to change in order to fit the environment in which it is used (Keith & Shuttleworth, 2006; Trask, 1997). Shona is no exception, since it also has the propensity to change like any other language (Poole, 1999; Wardhaugh, 1998; McMahon, 1996). The change can be seen in pronunciation, grammar, terminology, and semantics (Machakanja & Machakanja, 2004; Crystal, 1992; Malmkjaer, 2010). The change also involves several linguistic processes such as borrowing, coinage, phonoligization, and semantic broadening among others. In a diglossic linguistic situation like the one prevailing in Zimbabwe, where borrowing is involved, it has mainly been from English (H) to Shona. Where there have been semantic shifts, words may retain their denotative meaning but have also been extended to mean other things in the context of whatever new environment that has emerged. This has been the case of Shona in the wake of new developments and the COVID-19 pandemic is no exception. Thus, there is a need to explore how this change has come in, in the Shona language. In a related research on HIV and AIDS pandemic and its influence on Shona language, Nyoni et al. (2012) established that the advent of the pandemic resulted in a significant linguistic change to fill in a gap that had been created by the new phenomenon. The researchers have not come across any research that has been done on how the COVID-19 pandemic has impacted the Shona language. Therefore, this research seeks to fill the gap in the Zimbabwean speech community.

Theoretical Framework: Systemic Functional Approach

Systemic Functional Grammar (SFG) is a form of grammatical description founded by Michael Alexander Kirkwood Halliday. It is part of a social semiotic approach to language called Systemic Functional Linguistics. The term "systemic" suggests the view of language as "a network of systems, or interrelated sets of options for making meaning" (Halliday, 1994, p. 15), while the "functional" component emphasizes the primary role of language as a vehicle to enable message transaction. Thus, what he refers to as the "multidimensional architecture" of language "reflects the multidimensional nature of human experience and interpersonal relations" (Halliday, 2004, p. 29). Halliday posits that language is primarily used to express meanings and perform various functions in different contexts and situations of our daily lives. These variables help to explain how individuals' use of language is predominantly dependent upon metafunctions, namely, the ideational, interpersonal, and textual (Halliday & Matthiessen, 2004; Eggins, 2004). The first refers to language's ability to carry and convey the nuances of human experience, the second embodies the ability of language to negotiate social roles and attitudes while the textual function refs to the internal organization and communicative nature of a text to create discourse. The SFG goes beyond just looking at how language is organized (grammar) by explaining and describing this linguistic infrastructure as made up of "meaning-making resources" (Halliday & Matthiessen, 2004) we use as "homo significans" (Chandler, 2007, p. 13) to achieve communicative goals. He further submits that every linguistic choice a user of a language makes is systematic, and the reason one says something in a certain way is the result of a choice that may be conscious or unconscious. Such choices are made from a set of systems containing structures but not confined to these allowing users unlimited ways of creating meaning (Bloor & Bloor, 2004), while our experiences of the world, of text types, and socially and culturally bounded situations, help build up our schemata of these systems. Van Dijk (1977) explains how these experiences enable us to distinguish between different genres of texts (spoken or written) by their patterns of linguistic choices and to notice when choices are inappropriate. The SFG is, thus, a study of meaning construction through systems of lexicogrammatical choices that serve functions within social and cultural contexts.

The four main theoretical claims of Systemic Functional Grammar about language are that:

i.   language use is functional;
ii. language function is to make meanings;
iii. the aforesaid meanings are influenced by the social and cultural context in which they are exchanged; and
iv. the whole process of using language is a semiotic process, a process of making meanings by choosing.

These tenets will guide the analysis of the chosen linguistic items that describe COVID-19 as a disease as well as related matters.

Various Ways of Word Formation

Languages have three major ways of extending their vocabulary namely, deriving new words from existing words and word parts, borrowing from other languages, as well as "creating"
new words from scratch (Finegan, 2008). The following section briefly describes some of the ways in which a language's repertoire is expanded.

1. **Affixation** involves forming words by adding morphemes at the beginning (prefixation), in the middle (infixation), or at the end (suffixation) of a base. The three can be illustrated by making a morphological analysis of the word "informational."

form	inform	informational
	in + form	in + form +-ation+al
(base)	(prefix + base)	(prefix + base + infix +suffix)

2. **Compounding**

   New words can be formed by stringing together words to create a combination of words, for example, redhot, eagle-eyed, ice-cold, crystal-clear, fishing-rod, eavesdrop, etc. The lexical items that constitute the compound have positional mobility when used in sentences since they are independent words.

3. **Acronyms**

   These are words derived from the initials of several words e.g. *radar* from radio detecting and ranging, *laser* from light amplification by stimulated emission of radiation. The shortenings are pronounced as words unlike initialisms or abbreviations that are pronounced as sequences of letters.

4. **Clippings**

   Clipping involves using words in shortened form by cutting off some of the syllables. It can be at the beginning, middle, or end of a word. An example is the word "phone" for the longer version "telephone."

5. **Blends**

   Blending occurs when two words are clipped and then conjoined; for example, "motel" from "motorist" and "hotel."

6. **Borrowing**

   Involves taking words from other languages. Globalization makes this practice inevitable through ease of travel and interaction whether physically and virtually of people from different linguistic backgrounds making the adstratum influence inevitable where linguistic borrowing across cultural and linguistic boundaries is observed.

7. **Backformation** involves the reduction of a word often by shortening the original word.

   It can involve the formation of new words by subtracting a part.

8. **Conversion** involves converting a word from one grammatical category to another without any changes to its form. This word formation process is also called functional shift or category change.

9. **Words derived from names**

   Words can be derived from the names of people in the process called eponymy. A word like "nichodemuously" is an example.

A Note on Data Gathering

This research falls in the ambit of the interpretivist paradigm and uses the qualitative approach or methodology. According to Creswell (2014, p. 3), this approach aims at "exploring and understanding the meaning individuals or groups ascribe to a social or human problem." The design is qualitative content analysis, which uses Systemic Functional Approach in the analysis of the gathered linguistic items. According to Ary, Jacobs, Sorensen, and Razavieh (2010, p. 29), content analysis "focuses on analyzing and interpreting recorded material to learn about human behavior. The material may be public records, textbooks, letters, films, tapes, diaries, themes, reports, or other documents."

Data were gathered from radio news bulletins and discussions/awareness programs, jingles in Shona aired on Zimbabwe Television, and national and community radios that included, Radio Zimbabwe, National FM, Star FM, Ya FM, and Hevoi FM. Posters stuck in public spaces such as shops, workplaces, schools, clinics, and churches also provided the raw material for the research, that is, the observed novel linguistic uses motivated by the COVID-19 pandemic. In addition, the researchers observed language use *in situ* in public spaces particularly markets, public transport, and institutions of learning. The period of data gathering stretched from January 2020 to October 2021.

Social media was extensively used to disseminate information during the pandemic, and hence the researchers thought it prudent to use this source of discourse as well. Social media was used among group members to discuss issues including COVID-19.

Social media included unsolicited voice notes and videos from all over the world that were shared, with some containing supposed mitigatory measures against the pandemic. Several millions of Zimbabweans are in the diaspora and many of these belong to various social media groups, particularly WhatsApp, and use such platforms to share "information" on the pandemic. From these, pieces of discourse on the pandemic in the language concerned were gathered and analyzed. It is now a norm to belong to social media groups. One can belong to as many as ten groups that may include various religious, work, "hobby," parents' association, commodities and services, residents, teaching/ learning, as well as old students' association groups. Social media platforms are playing key roles in communication especially during lockdown environments when most of the data analyzed in this research were gathered. As Nyoni (2020) points out, social media are becoming more and more the rendezvous where interactants/interlocutors from all over the world meet unfettered by geographical limitations. The social media forum is not just a meeting place but a platform for the exchange of at best information and at worst infodemics. It is a platform that no social scientist can afford to ignore. For the language researcher it is a platform where he/she experiences language-in-use (synchronically), how language is actually used as opposed to the diachronic stance.

Objectives of the Study

i. Identify linguistic expressions which are used by the Shona to describe COVID-19 and related issues.
ii. Classify such expressions in terms of the grammatical categories they belong to.
iii. Attempt an analysis of Shona linguistic expressions. which describe COVID-19 in terms of their classes with the view to deducing the Shona speakers' attitudes towards COVID-19 as reflected in their language.

iv. Sensitize stakeholders on the linguistic scenario as it relates to the pandemic so that intervention strategies are mounted.

Analysis of Linguistic Items Gathered

This section analyses a selection of linguistic items collected. The expressions were collected from:

i. Shona news from radio and television
ii. COVID-19 awareness jingles from Zimbabwe Television and radio
iii. Talk shows on radio and television on COVID-19
iv. Interactions with language users in public places such as markets and public transport
v. Social media groups particularly WhatsApp

During the period in question media and social media were inundated with material related to the pandemic. At one time no news broadcast would be complete without updates on the pandemic or simply an appeal to stick to COVID-19 protocols. The linguistic items are discussed under word-building categories. However, some of them belong to more than one as shall be shown in the discussion that follows.

Compounding

Dzihwamupengo

The word *dzihwamupengo/dzibwamupengo* (literal translation – mad flu/mad disease) is a complex nominal construction formed by compounding two nouns. The nouns are *dzihwa* (cl.5), which in its denotative form means mucus, and *mupengo* (mad person) (cl.1) (Mpofu et al., 2004; Chimhundu, 2001). *Dzihwa* in semantic extension terms also refers to the common cold associated with the cold winter season. In fact, "in some contexts, *dzihwa/dzihwa* can also be used to refer to an illness that has taken long for one to recover from as in, "Dzihwa *rakura*" (literal translation: "The illness has become serious"). It can also be used to refer to a disease that affects many people at the same time reaching pandemic levels. In this case *dzihwa* is synonymous with *hosha* (cl.9) and *denda* (cl.5) all meaning a disease that affects and even kills many people as is the case of COVID-19. The disease is behaving like a mad person (*mupengo*) who is unpredictable and out of control. It is a pandemic that is difficult to comprehend and is unpredictable. By terming it *dzihwamupengo* (mad disease), COVID-19 is personified. Combining *dzihwa* (cl.5), which belongs to a class of nouns to do with frightening things, for example, *gudo* (baboon), bere (hyena); nauseating things for example *doto* (chicken dropping), *dzihwa* (mucus), and people whose behavior is unbecoming, for example, *gomana* (huge and intimidating male), and *mupengo* (cl.1), which belongs to a class of nouns denoting human beings, gives COVID-19 human qualities and hence it is behaving like a mad person. The new cold is different hence its description as "mad." The word *mupengo* reflects the speech community's prejudices towards mental illness. The term is usually used to describe a person who suffers from mental illness particularly those who are violent. The pandemic is not only mad and therefore violent but is personified to show its power over ordinary people. The traditional Zimbabwean society believes that a person suffering from mental illness is possessed with evil spirits. When possessed one has supernatural powers that can easily overpower ordinary people who do not have assistance from spirits residing in them. The cold is not the ordinary type hence the term *dzihwa* is an understatement. This cold appears to be harmless initially but proves to be mad as time passes. This progression is in sync with our reading of the word – we start with *dzihwa* and move on to *mupengo* the latter marking an unexpected adversative turn. It is difficult to comprehend, it is unpredictable, it is cruel, among many other behaviors. Like a roaming mad person, the pandemic can cause untold suffering and harm. It can affect anyone, anywhere just like a mad person can do as he/she roams around.

Borrowing

"COVID" and "mask"

The terms "COVID" and "mask" have been borrowed by the Shona language from English, which is a language the former is in contact with and which is also of wider communication. The former acts as the donor language here because the disease got to Africa months after its initial detection in China and travelled to Europe and other continents. By the time it came to Africa it had already been named. The term "COVID" is clipped. The full term is "COVID-19," which can be taken as a blend of "COVID 2019" with "20" clipped. This may have been done for ease of articulation. The researchers noted that the younger users tended to use the borrowed versions while the older and the radio stations dedicated to broadcasting in indigenous languages especially during bulletins tended to use the nativized and phonologized versions *masiki* and *kovhidhi*. The latter may have been doing this in order to be more accessible to communities they were mandated to serve. *Kovhidhi* [kovɪdɪ] for Covid [kovɪd] and *masiki* [masɪkɪ] for mask [mask] are phonologized terms from the source to the target language. The terms have been adapted to fit into the Shona sound system and orthography. According to Hock and Joseph (2009, p. 247) loans are "nativized thus integrating them into the linguistic structure of the borrowing language." Thus, they have become acceptable as part of the Shona vocabulary when it comes to discussions or references to the COVID-19 pandemic.

Borrowed and Nativized

Korona *(corona)*

The word *korona* (corona) like *masiki* and *kovhidhi* discussed above is also a borrowed and nativized term for the virus. This is done at the orthographical level. "Korona" is a loan from "crown" in English, which in Shona is used for the same referent. It means crown as worn by kings and queens and conjures images of power, luxury, and nobility. However, in the context of the COVID-19 pandemic, the term *korona* for the virus is derived from the shape of the virus which looks like the thorny plant known as the crown of thorns, Christ plant, or Christ thorn (euphoria milii), which is native to Madagascar (Ombrello, 2021). As a biblical allusion, the plant has the shape of the crown of thorns that the Jews placed on Jesus' head when they nailed him to the cross (Matthew 27: 29; Mark 15: 17; John 19: 2). Danzey (2021) asserts that a crown is a symbol of royalty and honor, but for Jesus the crown of thorns was created with opposite intent. She argues that it was aimed at humiliating and dishonoring Him, to cause Him pain, and make Him bleed. For the corona plant, apart from the prickly thorns, the sap irritates the skin and can be toxic if ever ingested (John Riga cited by Danzey, 2021). Thus, when used with reference to COVID-19, one understands why; due to the excruciating pain that one infected by the virus goes through. The use of the term *korona* especially in a largely Christian Zimbabwean community, therefore, conjures up feelings of pain and suffering – a paradoxical crown of suffering. This resonates well with the indifference and pessimism that often accompany authorities' efforts to control the spread of the coronavirus through control of people's behavior.

Jebwa

This word is from the English word "jab." It is phonologized to *jebha* to suit the linguistic climate of the recipient language, Shona, before the passive extension is applied to change it to *jebwa*. This word is an example of the results of languages in contact. The word *jebha* is a verb that means "to prick with a surgical needle in order to inoculate" while *jebwa* is a passive verb that means to have been injected as in:

- "*Ndajebwa*" (I have been vaccinated/injected)
- "*Vakajebwa*" (Those who have been vaccinated/The vaccinated.)

Semantically Broadened Items

Chisekete

This is a device used to cover the mouth of an animal to prevent it from grazing or eating crops while on the span. *Chisekete* is therefore associated with animals yoked up and hence restricted in their freedom. *Chisekete* is a metaphor for control, restriction akin to imprisonment, and pain. Its use is meant to show how humanity has been reduced to powerless animals. While *chisekete* seems to control and constrain people the practice of masking up also "masks" the virus to prevent it from free flowing. Therefore, *chisekete* while worn by the people is also in a way "worn" by the then-disabled virus. When perceived from a deeper level it is a convenient inconvenience that humanity needs to embrace for its own good.

Junga

The word *junga* originally meant to pierce with a sharp or pointed object. Originally the meaning carried a negative meaning as the aim is to cause pain. The word *junga* during COVID-19 has assumed an ameliorative disposition. It now refers to being pricked or jabbed in order to be prevented from severe illness. The prick is an insignificant sacrifice in order to prevent a bigger catastrophe. The use of the word and its derivative may cause the listener to think about the pain associated with the original "jab," but in this case it is a necessary pain to bear. In a way the word may be said to have undergone some ameliorative metamorphosis in the COVID-19 discourse.

Madaranganwa *(Social and Physical Distancing)*

Language change during the pandemic came in the form of what is termed semantic broadening (Yule, 2017; Fromkin et al., 2017) for concepts and behaviors that were viewed as new in the context of the pandemic. For example, one of the World Health Organization (WHO) guidelines for preventing the spread of COVID-19 is social and physical distancing. According to WHO, the aim of social and physical distancing is slowing the spread of disease by stopping chains of transmission and preventing new ones from appearing https://www.who.int/emergencies/diseases/novel). Physical distancing has to do with physically distancing oneself from others by keeping a distance of at least 1 meter while social distancing has to do with staying at home, limiting travel, avoiding crowded places, and using no-contact greetings as much as possible to help prevent the spread of COVID-19 (https://www.hopkinsmedicine.org). It is physical and social distancing for which *madaranganwa* (spaced) came into use. In its denotative form, *daranganwa* (spaced grain) refers to a maize cob whose grains are spaced due to poor fertility, or poor synchronization of tasseling and silking or high temperature resulting in drying of the silk (*rebvu*) before full fertilization. However, in the context of the COVID-19 pandemic, the term has been subjected to semantic shifting resulting in broadening of its meaning as reflected in the following examples:

- "*Mirai madaranganwa*" (Stand apart/Maintain social distance while standing.)
- "*Garai madaranganwa*" (Sit apart/Maintain social distance while sitting).
- "*Ngatiitei madaranganwa*" (Let us be apart/Let us maintain social distancing).

However, it should be noted here that language users do not differentiate between social and physical distancing. Both are referred to as social distancing. In both cases though, the idea of being separate from others is key for curbing the spread of COVID-19. Thus, *madaranganwa* with its broadened meaning has become part of the Shona linguistic topography post-COVID-19.

Narrowing

The mask is also referred to as *chikovhidhi* (Class 7) as an item for use brought about because of COVID-19. The argument is that it is because of COVID-19 that people have to put on masks. It is common to hear statements like:

- *"Pane amboona chikovhidhi changu here?"* ("Has anyone seen my mask?")
- *"Nditambidzewo chikovhidhi changu."* ("Please pass my mask to me.")
- *"Ndadonhedza chikovhidhi changu."* ("I have dropped my mask.")

The context, that is, the COVID-19 era makes it understandable that *chikovhidi* is a mask.

Translations

Zvivharo zvepamuromo

The researchers observed a vendor referring to his wares as *zvivharo zvepamuromo* literally meaning "mouth lids." The informal sector seems to be fertile ground for new lexical items (Nyoni & Nyoni, 2013). This is the vendors' metalinguistic strategy to lure potential customers through the language medium. In the characterization by the vendor, we detect a bemoaning tone at how humanity was silenced by the pandemic. He seemed to be laughing at himself and fellow human beings on how the pandemic has deflated their ego as the super creature sophisticated and armed with technology to solve about every problem only to be vanquished and silenced by a "flu." Another version of the Shona term is *zvivharamuromo*, which literally means "things to close the mouth." The coined word is a compound word comprising "to close" and "mouth." However, the two terms reflect a lack of knowledge on the prevention of the coronavirus as the term only refers to the covering of the mouth excluding the nose. The diminutive prefix "zvi-" which is the plural form of "*chi-*" suggests that these are small things that close the mouth. They are small in size yet they are important in preserving lives.

There is a pun with *vharamuromo* as well as *vhuramuromo*. The word *vharamuromo* echoes the well-known cultural practice *vhuramuromo* meaning "open the mouth," which is a payment the groom's family makes to "unlock" the bride's father's mouth to kick start the marriage negotiations. The thinking is that the father-in-law is so important that he has to be paid to start to speak. The pun or wordplay on opening and closing of the mouth is characteristic of vendors who engage in wordplay to mesmerize customers with their words to sell their wares. The closure of the mouth as suggested by the term *vharamuromo* that is used to describe face masks might refer to being dumbfounded or speechless as a result of the manner in which the world was ravaged by the pandemic in a short span of time. However, speaking can still be done with a closed mouth about how the pandemic has left humanity at a loss for words.

Conclusion

The chapter showed that the COVID-19 pandemic has effected change in the Shona language through the borrowing of lexical items from English to fill a gap in its linguistic requirements and through a multiplicity of endogenous word-building processes. It also asserts that the whole word-building exercise has been facilitated by some sociolinguistic factors inherent in the Shona speech community, which help to color the pandemic's perception. The research shows that Shona as a language has not remained static in the advent of changes going on in the environment in which it is used. Thus, the advent of the COVID-19 pandemic has resulted in the expansion, in most cases, of the Shona language lexicon as the speakers try to make sense of how the virus came into their world, how they perceive it, and how they should act in its wake. The morphological processes have been occasioned by the need to fill in a linguistic gap created by the novel situation the language users find themselves in.

References

Ahmed, A., & Islam, M. (2020). Influence of COVID-19 on the lexical features of English in Pakistan. *Linguistics and Literature Review*, 6(2), 69–82.

Ary, D., Jacobs, L.C., Sorensen, C., & Razavieh, A. (2010). *Introduction to Research in Education*.Wadsworth: Belmont.

Bloor, T., & Bloor, M. (2004). *The Functional Analysis of English*. London: Hod.

Chandler, D. (2007). *Semiotics: The Basics*. London: Routledge.

Chimhundu, H. (1997). *Keynote Address at 'The Inter-Governmental Conference on Linguistic Policies in Africa'*. Harare.

Chimhundu, H. (2001). *Duramazwi Guru reChishona*. Harare: College Press.

Creswell, J.W. (2014). *Research Design: Qualitative, Quantitative, and Mixed Methods Approaches*. Los Angeles: SAGE Publications, Inc.

Crystal, D. (1992). *The Cambridge Encyclopedia of Language*. Cambridge: Cambridge University Press.

Danzey, E. (2021). What is the meaning behind Jesus' crown of thorns? crosswalk.com (Accessed 12/10/21). https://www.bing.com/search?q=Danzey%2C+E.

Van Dijk, T.A. (1977). *Text and Context: Explorations in the Semantics and Pragmatics of Discourse*. London and New York: Longman.Eggins, S. (2004). *An Introduction to Systemic Functional Linguistics*. London and New York: Continuum.

European Centre for Disease Prevention and Control. (2021). Covid 19 situation update worldwide, as of week 10. Updated 7 October 2021.

Finegan, E. (2008). *Language: Its Structure and Use*. New York: Harcourt Brace College Publishers.

Fromkin, V., Rodman, R., & Hyams, N. (2017). *An Introduction to Language*. Wadsworth: Cengage Learning.

Gorbalenya, A.E., Baker, S.C., Baric, R.S., de Groot, R.J., Drosten, C., Gulyaeva, A.A., et al. (2020, February 11). Severe acute respiratory syndrome-related coronavirus: The species and its viruses—A statement of the coronavirus study group bioRxiv. https://doi .org/10.1101/2020.02.07.937862.

Halliday, M., & Matthiessen, C. (2004). *An Introduction to Functional Grammar* (3rd ed.). London: Arnold.

Halliday, M.A.K. (1994). *Introduction to Functional Grammar.* London: Edward Arnold.

Halliday, M.A.K. (2004). On the "architecture" of human language. In M.A.K. Halliday, & J.J. Webster (Eds.), *On Language and Linguistics (Vol. 3, The Collected Works of M.A.K. Halliday)* (pp. 18–49). London: London University Press.

Hock, H.H., & Joseph, B.D. (2009). *Language History, Language Change, and Language Relationship: An Introduction to Historical and Comparative Linguistics.* Berlin:Walter de Gruyter GmbH & Co.

Holshue, M.L., DeBolt, C., Lindquist, S., Lofy, K.H., Wiesman, J., Bruce, H., et al. (2020, January 31). First case of 2019 novel coronavirus in the United States. *The New England Journal of Medicine.* https://doi.org/10.1056/NEJMoa2001191.

Keith, G., & Shuttleworth, J. (2006). *Living Language.* London: Hodder and Stroughton.

Khotimah, K., Laksono, K., Suhartono, S., Pairin, U., & Darni, D. (2021). The ecological impact of the covid-19 pandemic infodemic discourse in social media: Ecolinguistic perspectives. *Procedia of Social Sciences and Humanities,* 1, 117–128. https://doi.org/10 .21070/pssh.v1i.31.

Kupolati, O. Adebileje, A., & Adeleke, A. (2021). "Someone has been coronated" Nigerian English lexical innovations in the COVID-19 pandemic. *Cogent Arts & Humanities,* 8, 1. https://doi.org/10.1080/23311983.2021.1947559.

Li, Q., Guan, X., Wu, P., Wang, X., Zhou, L., Tong, Y., et al. (2020). Early transmission dynamics in Wuhan, China, of novel coronavirus-infected pneumonia. *The New England Journal of Medicine.* https://doi.org/10.1056/NEJMoa2001316.

Lu, H., Stratton, C.W., & Tang, Y.W. (2020). Outbreak of pneumonia of unknown etiology in Wuhan China: The mystery and the miracle. *Journal of Medical Virology.* https://doi.org/10.1002/jmv.25678.

Machakanja, I.T. and Machakanja, P. (2004). *A Workbook on Basic Linguistics.* Mutare: Africa University.

Macionis, J.J. (2012). *Sociology.* Boston: Pearson.

Mahlberg, M., & Brookes, G. (2021). Language and Covid-19:Corpus linguistics and the social reality of the pandemic. *International Journal of Corpus Linguistics,* 26(4), 441–443.

Malmkjaer, K. (Ed.). (2010). *The Linguistics Encyclopedia.* London: Routledge.

Muhammad, S., Khan, S., Kazmi, A., Bashir, N., & Siddique, R. (2020). COVID-19 infection: Origin, transmission, and characteristics of human coronaviruses. *Journal of Advanced Research,* 24. https://doi.org/10.1016/j.jare.2020.03.005.

Mpofu, N., Chimhundu, H., Mangoya, E., & Chabata, E. (2004). *Duramazwi Reurapi Neutano.* Gweru: Mambo Press.

Mweri, J.G. (2021). Corona virus disease (COVID-19) Neologisms. Linguistics and Literature studies 9(1), 36–47.

Nyoni, M. (2020). Images of Covid-19 in selected socially mediated WhatsApp messages shared in Zimbabwe. *Journal of New Vision in Educational Research Special Covid,* 1(2).

Nyoni, M., Grand, N., & Nyoni, T. (2012). Beyond The Humour: A Newspaper Cartoon as Socio-Politico-Economic Commentary: The Case of *'Wasu'* of the *Manica Post in Zimbabwe. Greener Journal of Social Sciences,* 2, 179–190. 10.15580/ GJSS.2012.6.102512152.

Nyoni, M., & Nyoni,T. (2013). Vuya uhodhe! Unpacking the form and content of informal traders' advertisements: A submission from the railway siding market expedition in Masvingo. *Greener Journal of Social Sciences*, 3(5), 220–231.

Ombrello, T. (2021). *Crown of thorns plant of the week* (Accessed 11/10/2021). https://www.bing.com/search?q=Ombrello%2C+T.(2021)+Crown+of+Thorns+Plant+of+the+Week.

Poole, S.C. (1999). *An Introduction to Linguistics*. New York: Palgrave.

Popiolek, K. (2020). Researchers study how COVID pandemic is affecting language change. MUS Today. (Accessed 15/11/2020). https://msutoday.msu.edu//news/202/researchers-study-how-how-covid-pandemic-is-affecting-language-change/.

Trask, R.L. (1997). *A Student's Dictionary of Language and Linguistics*. London: Arnold.

UN DESA. (2020). *How COVID-19 Is Changing the World: A Statistical Perspective Volume II*. New York: United Nations Department of Economic and Social Affairs (UN DESA).

United Nations. (2020). *Immediate Socio-Economic Response to Covid-19 in Zimbabwe: A Framework for Integrated Policy Analysis and Support*. Harare: United Nations Zimbabwe.

Wang, C.P., Horby, W., Hayden, F.G., & Gao, G.F. (2020). A novel coronavirus outbreak of global health concern. *Lancet*, 395(10223), 470–473. https://doi.org/10.1016/S0140-6736(20)30185-9.

Wardhaugh, R. (1998). *Sociolinguistics: An Introduction*. Oxford: Blackwell Publishers, Ltd.

Yule, G. (2010). *The Study of Language: An Introduction*. Cambridge: Cambridge University Press.

Yule, G. (2017). *The Study of Language* (6th ed.). Cambridge: Cambridge University Press.

Zhong, N., Zheng, B., Li, Y., Poon, L., Xie, Z., Chan, K., et al. (2003). Epidemiology and cause of severe acute respiratory syndrome (SARS) in Guangdong, People's Republic of China. *The Lancet*, 362(9393), 1353–1358.

8 COVID-19 Related Communications on Zimbabwean Online Health Communities

A Netnographic Study

Shupikai Kembo

Introduction

The coronavirus disease of 2019 (COVID-19) was declared a global pandemic in March 2020 (Basch et al., 2020, p. 1089). Due to the COVID-19 pandemic, there has been an exponential increase in social media usage. This increase has been attributed to the public trying to understand the disease, maintain social ties, and seek information and support (Isaias et al., 2021, p. 121). The surge in social media usage has also resulted in the proliferation of COVID-19 virtual/ online communities. Social media platforms such as Facebook enable the formation of virtual communities where members share and discuss topical issues.

For this study, virtual community and online community shall be used interchangeably. Online/virtual communities are defined in this study as the use of internet-based platforms to bring together a group of individuals with shared interests (Green et al., 2020). Virtual communities transcend geographical constraints to allow people in different locations to connect, discuss, and share information and receive or give support (Green et al., 2020). Although there are various virtual communities, this study is based on virtual health communities, which are online communities specifically constituted for different health-related issues such as the COVID-19 pandemic.

Despite the value and promise that Online Health Communities (OHCs) hold with regard to engaging people in a variety of health issues, research on virtual health communities in developing countries, such as Zimbabwe, is still in its infancy. There is a dearth of studies that analyze the impact and contributions of OHCs to public health. Thus, this study seeks to address this gap and contribute to existing knowledge that has been provided from the perspective of developed nations. Given the COVID-19-induced lockdowns and the recommendations to reduce physical interactions and keep physical distances, several COVID-19-related virtual communities have been constituted by Zimbabweans to deal with issues related to the pandemic. It is in these communities that Zimbabweans have received information about the disease, found comfort, and received support when affected or infected by the virus. The study teases out and analyses the major thematic issues discussed

DOI: 10.4324/9781003390732-8

in these online communities. It applies the uses and gratifications theory to understand the goals and motivations behind Zimbabweans joining COVID-19-related virtual communities and draws conclusions related to whether individuals managed to obtain gratifications from joining these COVID-19-related communities.

The Role of Virtual/Online Communities in Public Health

The growth in internet usage witnessed in the past decade has triggered the proliferation of virtual health communities, which have been used for health communications and marketing, health education, and for support (Horrell et al., 2019; Zhou, 2020). Virtual health communities can either be open or closed forums. Whereas open virtual health communities are accessible to everyone and open to everyone to join, closed online health communities require prospective members to request to join and administrators of the communities will either approve or dismiss the request (Green et al., 2020).

People are increasingly using online communities for finding solutions to their health problems through posting their symptoms, seeking advice, and support (Tacco et al., 2018; Naveh and Bronstein, 2019). Research has shown that individuals join health-related online communities to get information and support (Zigron and Bronstein, 2018; Horrell et al., 2019; Green et al., 2020). Support comes in different forms, ranging from emotional, social, etc. (Green et al., 2020). Regarding information, virtual health communities facilitate the sharing of health information (Green et al., 2020). It has been a common trend that once an individual is diagnosed with a disease, they go online to find out more about the disease and learn how to manage it from others who are in the same situation. Virtual health communities are also well positioned to provide emotional support. Emotional support is the expression of concern and care; empathy and sympathy; encouragement, security, and affection to an individual (Tacco et al., 2018). It has been established that empathy from other members of online health communities can aid the healing process by lowering the level of distress and raising optimism (Khanpour et al., 2017; Horrell et al., 2019; Zhou, 2020).

The OHCs are also a source of social support. Results from Naveh and Bronstein (2019) found that OHCs were sources of social support for pregnant diabetic women. Given that diabetic women face constant health challenges during pregnancy, interaction and supportive relationships found in virtual communities for pregnant diabetic women assisted these women in better managing their complex health situation (Naveh and Bronstein, 2019). For those suffering from chronic ailments, virtual health communities are valuable sources of medical information and support. In virtual communities, chronic patients get information on how to manage the disease and those who reside in rural locations or who are restricted to their homes can get social support without having to travel long distances, as is required in face-to-face support groups (Zigron and Bronstein, 2018; Green et al., 2020). Results from a study by Green et al. (2020) demonstrated that people with chronic illnesses appreciated the opportunity to support and share their stories with others in similar circumstances in online communities.

Apart from social support it has been noted that participation in online health communities has the potential to positively influence preventive health care. Online health groups may encourage participants to adopt healthy habits by supporting behavior change (Tacco et al., 2018). This is because people trust information that is shared by peers (Willis, 2018). In OHCs, community members regard themselves as peers. Additionally, online communities provide users with a safe and private space where they can engage without fear of being judged or being recognized (Porteous, 2021). Users can seek support and advice on personal or sensitive matters, either anonymously or under their names (Porteous, 2021). The ability to conceal part or their full identity gives users the confidence to reveal information they might not feel comfortable disclosing in person, express their complaints, ask questions, and discuss behaviors they would prefer others not to know, about treatments or daily coping habits (Zigron and Bronstein, 2018).

Theoretical Framework – Uses and Gratification Theory

The Uses and Gratifications Theory (U&GT) was coined in the 1940s by Katz and Blumler (Kasirye, 2021). The U&GT is used to understand why individuals use different sorts of media, the needs and goals behind the use, and the benefits gained from using the different media (Vinney, 2021). Key assumptions of this theory are that media use is goal-directed or motivated, and people use media to satisfy their needs and desires (Kircaburun and Alhabash, 2020). Individuals actively seek out the best-suited media to satisfy these desires and needs (Zhang and Zhou, 2020). These needs and desires include getting knowledge and information, affective needs, and social interaction (Zhang and Zhou, 2020). Social media have become one of the most-sort-after media to gratify different needs. Thus, this study applies the U&GT as a framework to understand why Zimbabweans joined COVID-19-related virtual communities on Facebook. It was also used to assess whether the gratifications that were initially sought before joining the communities were subsequently obtained by these individuals after becoming members of the groups.

Methodology – A Netnography Strategy of Enquiry

The researcher adopted an exploratory approach to the study utilizing netnography as a strategy of enquiry. Netnography seeks to understand the cultural experiences that encompass and are reflected within traces, practices, networks, and systems of social media (Kozinets, 2020, p. 19). Given that the study at hand is on Facebook-based virtual communities, netnography became the strategy of choice to address the research questions. The research questions were: What are the major COVID-19-related thematic issues discussed in these virtual communities? What were the goals and motivations behind Zimbabweans joining COVID-19-related virtual communities? Were the needs of Zimbabweans who joined COVID-19-related virtual communities fulfilled? Netnography provides a specific set of approaches and processes that need to be followed when conducting online research as discussed in the next subsection (Kozinets, 2018, 2020, p. 19).

Entrée

Entrée is the first step when conducting netnographic studies. This stage involves general planning of the research, the identification of suitable online sites, as well as gaining access to the research sites (Jong, 2018). Two types of online environments can be studied; open environments where content is free and accessible to anyone and closed groups where content can be accessed upon a user's registration and approval by administrators (Addeo et al., 2019, p. 20). For this study, the researcher searched for COVID-19-related groups for Zimbabweans on Facebook and the search yielded three groups. She realized she was already a member of one of the groups. Since one group was public, she simply joined. She then requested to join the remaining group. Of the three groups, one was open while two were closed/private. Before collecting data, the researcher reached out to the administrators of the two closed groups to seek permission to carry out the research. A detailed discussion is provided under ethical considerations.

Data Collection

Data were collected from the three groups from 1 August 2020 to 30 June 2021. The researcher opted for a longitudinal approach to immerse herself in the communities and get a deep on-the-ground appreciation of the members' experiences and perceptions towards the information they were receiving in the groups. Data in netnographic studies can be collected from multiple sources although the main sources of information are online environments (Kozinets, 2018). For this study, data were collected through observation and interviews as explained below.

• *Observation*

Observations come in two forms: participant or passive observation. Related to passive observation, the researcher simply observes without taking part in the activities being observed or activities of the online community (Asongu, 2018, p. 78). In contrast, participant-observers can interact with other community members, practice group activities, and exchange ideas or information. However, in some cases, participation is not just confined to actively posting messages in the online community but can also include reading through and interacting with posted online material over time and understanding the various interactions, be it archived texts, informational web pages, interviews, or any other means (Kozinets, 2018). Thus, for this study, the researcher was a participant-observer in that she read through and interacted with posts in real-time and regularly in the three groups. She took screenshots and snips of relevant posts and archived them for analysis.

* **Interviews**

In netnographic studies, interviews are a form of elicited data. Elicited data are data that are elicited or co-created through the netnographer's online and social media communications (Jong, 2018; Kozinets, 2018). In simple terms, this is the information that the netnographer educes from other community members in the form of engagements such as interviews. For the current study, the researcher purposively selected ten individuals who posted or reacted to posts shared in the groups and conducted virtual interviews using the Google meet platform and WhatsApp calls. The interviews lasted an average of 45 minutes.

Data Analysis

To address the research questions the researcher used thematic analysis. Thematic analysis is a qualitative descriptive approach for finding, analyzing, and reporting patterns (themes) within data (Scharp and Sanders, 2019, p. 117). The researcher developed codes from the archived data and interview transcripts and salient themes were extrapolated. These themes are presented under the section "Results and Analysis."

Ethical Considerations

Ethics in research fall into two main categories, that is, procedural ethics and ethics in practice (Reid et al., 2018). Procedural ethics involves seeking approval from the relevant authorities to undertake research justifying the study and commitment to adherence to ethical standards, before the commencement of the study (Shaw et al., 2019). The researcher requested permission to conduct her study from the administrators of the two closed groups. Permission was granted on these conditions; the researcher was allowed to observe the groups but was prohibited from disclosing the name of the groups, the researcher was also requested to ensure that all the information was anonymized before it could be used in the write-up.

For the third group, because it was public and open, the researcher did not request permission to conduct her research. According to Cilliers and Viljoen (2021), posts to publicly accessible forums or sites are not private and are not protected by privacy laws. However, care was still taken to ensure confidentiality through anonymization, and de-identification of data extracted from the group. Ethics in practice refers to the everyday situational and unanticipated ethical issues that occur when researching (Shaw et al., 2019). These include issues such as informed consent, privacy, confidentiality, and a commitment to collecting and presenting accurate findings (McKenna and Gray, 2018). The researcher sought informed consent for the interviews and all the information was anonymized to ensure privacy and confidentiality.

Results and Analysis

The results of the study are presented and analyzed under the broad themes below.

Major COVID-19-Related Thematic Issues
Discussed in These Virtual Communities

A thorough examination of the issues that were discussed in the three Facebook OHCs (hereafter referred to as OHC1, OHC2, and OHC3) revealed that the topics fell into six main categories. These were COVID-19 daily updates, COVID-19 prevention tips, COVID-19 myths busting, coping mechanisms, COVID-19 vaccines, and mobilizing resources for those infected and affected by the pandemic. Related to the daily updates, it was noted that situational reports from the Ministry of Health and Child Care (MoHCC), Zimbabwe, were shared daily in OHC1. In OHC2 the daily updates were not shared frequently. As for OHC3, it was noted that no updates were ever shared during the period under study. It was observed that the daily updates contained statistics on new infections, deaths, recoveries, etc. However, because sometimes the ministry's situational reports were barely readable, OHC1 administrators provided a summary of the report, which helped community members to get an appreciation of the information contained therein. It was observed that this happened throughout the period under study. Situational reports that were shared in the community were always accompanied by a summary of the key information that was contained in the report. This was commended and appreciated by community members. In contrast, in OHC2, the situational report from the ministry was shared in the group without any accompanying information.

COVID-19 prevention and protection tips were also shared in all three communities albeit to different degrees. It was observed that in OHC1 messages on prevention and protection were shared at regular intervals during the period under study. In OHC2 prevention and protection information was shared here and there, whereas in OHC3 the information was seldom shared. Related to the formats of the posts, it was noted that the information was shared in the form of either infographics or plain text. Infographics with information on how to stay safe and prevent the spread of COVID-19 from credible health organizations such as the World Health Organization (WHO) were shared in the groups.

Plain text posts aimed at encouraging members to protect themselves and prevent the spread of the virus were also shared in the communities as demonstrated below:

"Handwashing is one of the most effective ways to protect yourselves and others, not just from Covid-19 but from other viruses too. Wash them regularly for 20 seconds with soap and water.

Let's remember to always

- *mask up*
- *sanitize*
- *maintain physical distance*
- *avoid unnecessary movement*
- *avoid crowded places*

#letsbesafe#" **(A post shared in OHC1)**

In addition to sharing prevention and protection measures, there were also discussions on coping mechanisms in the event of being infected by the virus or a member of the household being infected. In one of the groups, members who had recovered from COVID-19 were invited to share their experiences on how they managed to recover from the disease. It was observed from the comments that other members appreciated these discussions as there were a lot of insights on what to do after testing positive, the medication and home remedies to do as well as how to cope with the anxiety of testing positive. Some of the members who heeded the call to share their COVID-19 recovery experiences had this to say:

"I used to steam a lot, took paracetamol and ibuprofen every 6 hrs to bring down the temp, managed to get antibiotics cause the coughing was becoming too much plus every night I used to sleep on my tummy that really helped. Not forgetting praying. I prayed for healing and God answered."

In another group, one member shared this with other members:

"1. Covid haidi anxiety. There were days andaifunga the close people vakashaya or see statuses. Haa breathing would become a struggle. Bed haigumike uchitadza kurara zvese nekutya.

2. Natural remedies plus mapiritsi prescribed from pharmacists and chiremba.

3. Garlic raw onion ginger, zumbani, lemon, salt gargling. Kutsengachaizvo not zvekumboisa mumvura. Imwe onion wonamira pachest nemusocks.

4. Steam paunonzwa kuremerwa

5. Fluids hobho nekudya. Ukasadya you feel weak hauzigone fight unonzwa sewakufaurunzara."

In summary, the member was informing other members that there was no need to get anxious after contracting COVID-19. She also encouraged others to take the medication prescribed by medical personnel as well as to do home remedies such as taking herbs, steaming, and taking a lot of fluids. It was observed that most of the issues discussed with regard to coping were centered on home remedies, taking medication, and having a positive state of mind.

The issue of COVID-19 vaccines and vaccination was also extensively discussed especially in the OHC1. There was a myriad of posts that centered on the provision of information on vaccination as well as calls to action in the form of persuasive messages for people to get vaccinated. Posts such as the ones below were shared in the group to persuade and appeal to members to get vaccinated.

> *"As more vaccines come into the country, we need more of them in people's arms not fridges. Its vaccination, and not vaccines, that saves lives!"*
> *"Get vaccinated to protect yourself, your family, your community and the health system."*
> *"Just a reminder! People who look like you and speak like you are also vaccinating!"*

In response to such posts, members pointed out that there was a need for the experts in the group to educate members and convince them about the importance of getting vaccinated given the proliferation of myths, fake news, and misinformation about the COVID-19 vaccines. It was also noted that members of OHC1 who were vaccinated were also invited to share their experiences as a way of debunking some of the misconceptions about vaccines.

> *"Calling on all Zimbabweans who have been vaccinated in Zim so far to share their experiences. Its good that others learn from us!"*

It was noted that several people heeded the call as evidenced by the more than 900 comments from members who were sharing their vaccination experiences. From the comments, it was observed that most of the members reported that they had not experienced any side effects and they were satisfied with the vaccines. When the Vice President of Zimbabwe was inoculated, the news was shared and discussed at length in the group. While the move for the Vice President to be publicly inoculated was meant to inspire confidence in the vaccine, the opposite was observed from the comments:

> *"Its difficult to trust a system and a group of people who have previously demonstrated to have limited concern for our general welfare. Is he receiving the real vaccine? We don't know. Do i trust my government as well as the Chinese generosity? No. If they had used real money to pay for the vaccine maybe i would personally think there is no hidden agenda. I was team vaccine but since the Chinese donation Im not getting the jab. No thank you."*

Related to the other two communities OHC2 and OCH3 it was noted that in OHC2 discussions were mainly centered on if one could get vaccinated if they had previously been infected, how long after recovery one had to wait to get their vaccine, which vaccine was the best, and the chances of re-infection if one was vaccinated after previously contracting the disease. However, for

OHC3 no discussions on vaccines were observed during the period under study.

Although there were posts that encouraged members to shun fake news or to desist from spreading unverified information, it was observed that for the duration of the period under study, nothing much was discussed regarding coronavirus fake news and misinformation in OHC1. However, members were always discouraged from spreading unverified information in general. In the second community, it was noted that posts on home remedies that were not scientifically proven were rife. Posts such as the one below were shared by both ordinary community members and administrators:

> "Covid buster- 1/4 cup grated onion, 1/4 cup grated ginger, 1/4 cup grated garlic, Tablespoon turmeric, Tablespoon cinnamon, Cayenne pepper, 1/4 cup apple cider vinegar or lemon. Blend these together and eat spoonfuls regularly. It opens airwaves and expels mucus which blocks the lungs and interferes with gases exchange that take place in the lungs."

Regarding the issue of mobilizing resources for those affected and infected by COVID-19, it was noted that the issue was never shared or discussed in OHC1 and OHC2. Calls to donate were mainly shared in OHC3. It was also in OHC3 that information on donations that were received was shared. From the discussion above, it is shown that several topics were shared and discussed in these online health communities. To get an appreciation of whether the topics discussed above were of any consequence to members, there is a need to discuss the motivations that compelled individuals to join these online health communities. A discussion on whether these topics managed to satisfy the needs of members is also provided.

Goals and Motivations Behind Zimbabweans Joining COVID-19-related Virtual Communities

While some joined the groups a few weeks or months after they were created, others only joined the groups during the second wave that was experienced in early 2021. In respect of the goals and motivations that impelled Zimbabweans to join COVID-19-related online communities, it was discovered that the major factors were informational, emotional, and social support needs. Since the coronavirus was a novel virus that was associated with a lot of uncertainty, all ten interviewees revealed that they joined the COVID-19 virtual groups to get information and understand more about the disease. The information sought was in the form of updates on new positive cases, deaths, recoveries, hot spots; prevention and protective measures; vaccines, and other COVID-19-related news. The information from the daily updates gave them an appreciation of the rate at which the disease was spreading in the country.

"When the first positive case of COVID-19 was reported I panicked. I was so scared given what was happening in the developed countries where so many people getting infected and dying. So, I joined the group to get more information about the disease to allay my fears." **Interviewee 1**

One participant pointed out that getting information on the hot spots helped her make informed decisions regarding visiting areas that were classified as hot spots. Due to the rate at which the disease infected and killed many people in other countries, one of the participants revealed that he joined the group to get testimonials from those who had recovered, to get assurance that more people were recovering than dying from the disease in the country.

"Getting testimonials from real people who had recovered instead of just a number assured me that more people were recovering than dying in the country."

Interviewee 2

Participants also revealed that they joined the online health communities so that they could get information on what they could do to protect themselves from contracting the virus. Information was shared in some of the groups on how to mitigate the spread of the virus through preventative measures such as wearing masks, frequently washing hands with soap or sanitizing hands, physical distancing, avoiding crowded places, coughing into the elbow, etc. Additionally, some of the interviewees informed the researcher that they had joined one of the groups after learning that the administrators were medical experts who only shared scientifically proven information. Therefore, individuals joined this group because they believed that they would get credible information in an environment that was characterized by an infodemic and uncertainty.

In addition to fulfilling informational needs, some of the participants informed the researcher that they joined the groups to get support while they were suffering from COVID-19 and offer support after they had recovered. One of the participants revealed that after he tested positive for COVID-19 in January 2020, he panicked as he thought he would die. He was encouraged by a friend to join two COVID-19 online communities for Zimbabwe. From there, he managed to get tips on how to manage the disease and cope with the stress and anxiety that came with testing positive. He further explained that some of the home remedies he got from one of the groups assisted him even though they were not scientifically proven that they could cure COVID-19. He went on to reveal that after his recovery he offered emotional support to those who shared in the group that they were affected or infected by the coronavirus.

Another participant informed the researcher that she had joined the group after her husband contracted the virus. She revealed that the family had suffered from anxiety and stress due to stigmatization by the community. However, after joining one of the groups she managed to get emotional and social support. Fellow community members would check virtually on the family from time to time while the family was under quarantine. Still on the issue of support, some participants informed the researcher that they joined one of the groups to seek support in terms of resources. The participant revealed that he was not formally employed, and the COVID-19-induced lockdowns had adversely affected his livelihood. He joined one of the groups after he was advised by a friend to seek help. However, the participant pointed out that he did not receive much help in terms of the resources he sought from other members of the community. He may not have received much assistance from the community maybe because the other members were also struggling financially due to Zimbabwe's economic situation as well as COVID-19's effects on national economies worldwide.

COVID-19 Online Communities and Gratification Sought Versus Gratification Obtained

Concerning the issue of whether the needs that motivated Zimbabweans to join COVID-19-related online health communities were fulfilled, it was discovered that the needs of the majority were gratified. As previously discussed, the major compelling factors for joining these groups were informational and the need for support. From interviews with group members and the observations, it was noted that members in the different groups managed to get the information they sought. Related to members in OHC1, it was noted that members would get updates daily on new cases, deaths, recoveries, hot spots, etc. In addition, as the government began rolling out the COVID-19 vaccination program, statistics of those vaccinated were also shared in the group. It was also noted that the need for credible information was gratified especially by OHC1. It was observed that OHC1 had medical experts who only shared factual information from credible public health organizations such as MoHCC and WHO.

Moreover, information shared and discussed in the group enabled members to be kept abreast of the trajectory of the disease globally. Members in these groups accessed COVID-19-related issues and developments not only in Zimbabwe but also from the continent and the globe. However, it was observed that the other two groups did not share or discuss much on statistical updates but information on other COVID-19-related issues was shared and discussed. It was observed that informational needs were also gratified through the prevention and protection information that was shared and discussed. Some members reported that they had joined the groups to get information that would enable them to protect themselves and prevent the spread of the disease. Therefore, the fact that such information was shared and discussed demonstrates that the needs of those who were seeking this kind of information were gratified.

Even though most of the participants expressed satisfaction with the way the OHC1 shared information, a few individuals reported discontent with the way

OHC1's posts were mainly on statistics at the expense of other COVID-19-related topics. It was observed that for the period under study, statistics were shared in the group daily whereas other issues were not as frequently shared and discussed. This gave some members the impression that the main business of the group was just to share statistics and not an array of COVID-19-related topics. Related to OHC2 and OHC3 some interviewees expressed disappointment with the way they also concentrated on a few COVID-19-related issues such as mobilizing resources (in the case of OHC3) or discussing COVID-19 home remedies. The interviewees informed members that they felt these two communities neglected other COVID-19-related pertinent issues.

Concerning support, most of the participants informed the researcher that they were satisfied with the level of support and encouragement that they received in the group. Some reported that when they tested positive for the coronavirus, they panicked and suffered from anxiety. The communities helped them deal with the anxiety and some of the effects. Members of OHC2 reported that they felt they were not alone on the road to recovery as other members would constantly send them direct messages checking on how they were feeling and faring. Some of the respondents reported that the home remedies that were shared in the groups assisted them to deal with symptoms such as loss of appetite. Despite the majority expressing gratification in respect of the support they received from the group, a few individuals particularly members of OHC1 stated that they were not entirely satisfied when it came to getting support or giving support. One of the respondents had this to say:

> *"When I joined the group, I expected a lot of discussions on coping with the disease. I also expected to get advice on how to handle a situation where some family members were infected while others were not. I also expected to be given the opportunity to share my experiences after I had recovered. Sadly, these kinds of discussions were seldom there."*

Discussion

This study aimed at examining the communications and discussions on COVID-19-related OHCs for Zimbabweans, to explore the motivations behind Zimbabweans joining these COVID-19-related OHCs, and to assess if the needs that compelled these individuals to join these groups were gratified. Results suggest that OHCs play a critical role in the circulation of information. It was observed that various COVID-19-related topics were discussed in these groups ranging from COVID-19 daily statistics, prevention, protection, and management, coping mechanisms, COVID-19 vaccines, etc. These results also confirm the findings by Horrell et al. (2019), Tacco et al. (2018), and Green et al. (2020) that OHCs are a critical source of health information.

Results from this study also show that individuals seek certain media to fulfill certain needs. Participants chose COVID-19-related OHCs in particular because they wanted to satisfy certain COVID-19-related needs. Regarding the motivations that impelled participants to join these COVID-19 OHCs, results showed that individuals became members of these groups due to informational needs and emotional support. As previously discussed, participants needed information on COVID-19 statistics, information on preventive and protective measures to take, COVID-19 management and coping mechanisms, etc. These same results were also noted by Zigron and Bronstein (2018) who found that participants on different online forums sought informational support. Findings from this study also demonstrated that individuals join OHCs to get emotional support from others in the same situation as them. This resonates with the findings of Khanpour et al. (2017) who found that empathy from other members of OHCs helped to lower distress and anxiety and raised optimism. However, although most of the participants indicated gratification with the information and the support they received, some indicated that their needs were not met.

The OHCs also have the potential to positively influence individuals to adopt healthy habits (Tacco et al., 2018) such as getting vaccinated, wearing masks, physical distancing in public spaces, frequently washing hands with soap, or sanitizing hands and surfaces. This is because people trust information that is shared by peers (Willis, 2018). Although the OHC1 had experts it was noted that most of the members were individuals who considered themselves peers. Thus, some members took the advice that was shared because they believed the information to be true since it was coming from people who were on the same level as themselves. With regard to the other two OHCs, it was noted that all members considered themselves peers who could share information freely. Although it cannot be proven that members adopted certain positive behaviors due to discussions in the groups, some comments indicated positive reception of the messages that encouraged certain recommended behaviors.

Conclusion

This study examined the COVID-19-related communication in OHCs for Zimbabweans on Facebook. The empirical results show that several COVID-19-related topics were discussed in these OHCs. Furthermore, the motivations behind individuals joining OHCs were explored. The study assessed whether members' needs were gratified, and results indicated that to a greater extent the needs of members were gratified. This research advances the previous literature on the role that OHCs play in public health by giving insights from the perspective of a developing country. Given the exponential growth in internet and social media usage in developing countries, there is a need for public health officials to seriously consider utilizing OHCs as vehicles for health communications and marketing interventions. The OHCs can play a critical role in information dissemination and persuasion. Additionally, OHCs have great potential in crises as they allow for the rapid dissemination of critical information, especially when people are in lockdowns in different and sometimes remote places around the globe.

References

Addeo, F., Delli, A. D., Esposito, M., and Ylenia, B. M. (2019). Doing Social Research on Online Communities: The Benefits of Netnography, *Athens Journal of Social Sciences*, 7(1), 9–38. doi: 10.30958/ajss.7-1-1.

Asongu, N. (2018). *Tuberculosis Awareness Created Through Facebook: A Case Study Approach of TB Proof South Africa's Facebook Page.* University of South Africa.

Basch, C. H., Kecojevic, A., and Wagner, V. H. (2020). Coverage of the COVID-19 Pandemic in the Online Versions of Highly Circulated U.S. Daily Newspapers, *Journal of Community Health*, 45(6), 1089–1097. doi: 10.1007/s10900-020-00913-w.

Cilliers, L., and Viljoen, K. (2021). A Framework of Ethical Issues to Consider When Conducting Internet-Based Research, *South African Journal of Information Management*, 23(1), a1215.

Green, B. M., Van Horn, K. T., Gupte, K., Evans, M., Hayes, S., and Bhowmick, A. (2020). Assessment of Adaptive Engagement and Support Model for People with Chronic Health Conditions in Online Health Communities: Combined Content Analysis, *Journal of Medical Internet Research*, 22(7), 1–15. doi: 10.2196/17338.

Horrell, L. N., Lazard, A. J., Bhowmick, A., Hayes, S., Mees, S., and Valle, C. G. (2019). Attracting Users to Online Health Communities: Analysis of lungCancer.net's Facebook Advertisement Campaign Data, *Journal of Medical Internet Research*, 21(11), 1–7. doi: 10.2196/14421.

Isaias, P., Miranda, P., and Pifano, S. (2021). Framing Social Media and Web-Based Communities within the COVID-19 Pandemic: Enduring Social Isolation and Subsequent Deconfinement, *International Journal of Web Based Communities*, 17(2), 120–134. doi: 10.1504/IJWBC.2021.114450.

Jong, S. T. (2018). Netnography: Researching Online Populations, in: Liamputtong, P. (ed.), *Handbook of Research Methods in Health Social Sciences*, pp. 1–17. doi: 10.1007/978-981-10-2779-6_17-2.

Kasirye, F. (2021). The Importance of Needs in Uses and Gratification Theory, *Advance* (Preprint). doi: 10.31124/advance.14681667.v1.

Khanpour, H., Caragea, C., and Biyani, P. (2017). Identifying Empathetic Messages in Online Health Communities, *Proceedings of the 8th International Joint Conference on Natural Language Processing*, pp. 246–251. Available at: https://csn.cancer.org.

Kircaburun, K., and Alhabash, S. (2020). Uses and Gratifications of Problematic Social Media Use Among University Students: A Simultaneous Examination of the Big Five of Personality Traits, Social Media Platforms, and Social Media Use Motives, *International Journal of Mental Health and Addiction*, 18(3), 525–547.

Kozinets, R. V. (2018). Netnography for Management and Business Research, in: Cassell, C., Cunliffe, A. L., and Grandy, G. (eds.), *The SAGE Handbook of Qualitative Business and Management Research Methods: Methods and Challenges*, pp. 384–397. SAGE Publications Ltd. doi: 10.4135/9781526430236.

Kozinets, R. V. (2020). *Netnography: The Essential Guide to Qualitative Social Media Research* (3rd ed.). SAGE Publications, Inc.

McKenna, L., and Gray, R. (2018). The Importance of Ethics in Research Publications, *Collegian*, 25(2), 147–148. doi: 10.1016/j.colegn.2018.02.006.

Naveh, S., and Bronstein, J. (2019). Sense Making in Complex Health Situations Inform: Virtual Health Communities as Sources of Information and Emotional Support, *Journal of Information Management*, 71(6), 789–805. doi: 10.1108/AJIM-02-2019-0049.

Porteous, J. L. (2021). *Anonymous, Healthy and Male: Social Media Assists Men to Join Together in Supportive Online Communities.* Curtin University.

Reid, A., Brown, J. M., Smith, J. M., Cope, A. C., and Jamieson, S. (2018). Ethical Dilemmas and Reflexivity in Qualitative Research, *Perspectives on Medical Education*, 7, 69–75.

Scharp, K. M., and Sanders, M. L. (2019). What Is a Theme? Teaching Thematic Analysis in Qualitative Communication Research Methods, *Communication Teacher*, 33(2), 117–121. doi: 10.1080/17404622.2018.1536794.

Shaw, R., Howe, J., Beazer, J., and Carr, T. (2019). Ethics and Positionality in Qualitative Research with Vulnerable and Marginal Groups. *Qualitative Research*, 1–17. doi: 10.1177/1468794119841839.

Tacco, F. M. de S., Sanchez, O., Connolly, R., and Compeau, D. (2018). An Examination of the Antecedents of Trust in Facebook Online Health Communities, *Twenty-Sixth European Conference on Information Systems (ECIS2018)*.

Vinney, C. (2021). Uses and Gratification. ThoughtCo. https://www.thoughtco.com/uses-and-gratifications-theory-4628333 (Accessed on 18-10-2021).

Willis, E. (2018). The Power of Peers: Applying User-Generated Content to Health Behaviors "Off-line", *Qualitative Health Research*, 28(13), 2081–2093. doi: 10.1177/1049732318786704.

Zhang, X., and Zhou, S. (2020). Sharing Health Risk Messages on Social Media: Effects of Fear Appeal Message and Image Promotion, *Cyberpsychology*, 14(2). doi: 10.5817/CP2020-2-4.

Zhou, T. (2020). Understanding Users' Participation in Online Health Communities : A Social Capital Perspective, *Information Development*, 36(3), 403–413. doi: 10.1177/0266666919864620.

Zigron, S., and Bronstein, J. (2018). "Help Is Where You Find It": The Role of Weak Ties Networks as Sources of Information and Support in Virtual Health Communities, *Journal of the Association for Information Science and Technology*. doi: 10.1002/asi.24106.

9 Ndebele Funeral Rites and COVID-19

Deciphering Public Health in Spirituality

Sambulo Ndlovu

Introduction

The COVID-19 pandemic has been and continues to be a human catastrophe. Sridhar et al. (2021) posit that COVID-19 has been among the most devastating scourges affecting the health and well-being of humans since World War II. Guner et al. (2020, p. 571) concur and point out that "on January 30, 2020, the World Health Organization (WHO) declared COVID-19 outbreak a public health emergency of international concern and by March 2020 it was characterised as a pandemic." Pandemics are highly communicable and the fatalities are high. While modern public health advises people to be careful when handling bodies of people who die from pandemics, in Nguni spirituality each death is treated as a highly contagious misfortune that should be contained before it spreads to other people in the family and the community (Ndlovu, 2013). Each death is treated as a possible source for pandemics hence the public-health-inclined funeral rites. Pandemics require more community participation if they are to be overcome, making them domains for public rather than clinical health.

The Centre for Disease Control (CDC) Foundation (2021) describes public health professionals as those who try to prevent problems from happening or recurring through implementing educational programs, recommending policies, administering services, and conducting research, in contrast to clinical professionals like doctors and nurses, who focus primarily on treating individuals after they become sick or injured. Ndebele funeral rites incorporate elements of public health to curb the spread of diseases and death. The rites, practiced as part of Ndebele religion and spirituality, facilitate the implementation of physical public health rituals such as isolation, sanitization, and shielding. According to Elibol (2021) social distancing, case isolation, and shielding have been widely used to limit community-level transmission of COVID-19 to protect vulnerable groups. This chapter argues that Ndebele funeral rites, although performed in the context of spirituality, incorporate public health measures to curb the spread of communicable diseases during funeral wakes. While it is easy to identify the Ndebele culture of *Ubuntu* which encourages togetherness and communalism (Mabovula, 2011), as a super-spreader

DOI: 10.4324/9781003390732-9

institution when it comes to COVID-19, practical application of the spiritual taboos and services during Ndebele funerals actually enforce the very measures the WHO and public health practitioners recommend for the prevention of the spread of COVID-19.

The aim of the study was to analyze the protective and preventive value of Ndebele funeral rites in the fight against communicable diseases including COVID-19. The study was motivated by the fact that funerals, especially African ones, have been identified as super-spreader events for COVID-19, yet Ndebele culture has always placed more caution on disease control during funerals. The objectives of the study were to identify Ndebele funeral rites and compare them to the WHO public health preventive measures against the spread of COVID-19. Data analysis is done thematically to answer these research questions:

1. What measures are taken during Ndebele funerals to prevent disease or misfortune?
2. Are these measures comparable or compatible with COVID-19 preventive measures?

Literature Review and Theory

This section reviews relevant literature for the data and its analysis. As the chapter addresses COVID-19 in the context of Ndebele funeral IKS the domains of African religion, public health, and the coronaviruses are important concepts. The chapter engages the theory of IKS discussed in this section.

Ndebele Religion

Ndebele cosmology is based on spirituality and this world view is shared by many African aggregates. There are debates as to the appropriateness of the term African religion or even traditional African religion because of the different forms of belief systems across the continent. However, Idang (2015) postulates that while different African cultures may perform religious rites differently, their core belief systems and values are similar. They all hold a moral sense of justice and truth and the knowledge of the existence of good and evil (Umoh, 2005). Above all, the underlying characteristic of African spirituality, which is central to the arguments in this chapter, is its applicability in all aspects of life. Idang (2015, p. 104) avows that "Religion in African societies seems to be the fulcrum around which every activity revolves. Hence religious values are not toyed with [...] African religious values seem to permeate every facet of the life of the African and the African believes that anything can be imbued with spiritual significance."

Ndebele religion embodies moral, religious, environmental, and social values meant to manage people and the environment. Ndebele funerals are characterized by robust social values that regulate both the bereaved and their mourners. Idang (2015, p. 103) posits that "Social values can simply be seen as those beliefs and practices that are practised by any particular society. The society has a way of dictating the beliefs and practices that are performed either routinely by its members or performed whenever the occasion demands." Funerals are occasions that demand the exercise of certain values and these prevent, among other things, the spread of diseases. Moyo (2018) opines that the Ndebele conduct their funerals in a somber atmosphere because to them dying is perishing (*ukubhubha*) or sinking (*ukutshona*). While they believe in the continuation of life after death, death is an unpleasant "pandemic" which has to be avoided and prevented as much as possible. The somberness of Ndebele funerals includes a certain level of reverence, which excludes singing, dancing, shaking hands, and talking volubly. The funerals also involve the observance of isolation and cleansing taboos (Sibanda, 1998; Nyathi, 2001; Mpofu, 2011). Suffice it to note that Christianity, especially Pentecostalism, has revolutionized the conduct of Ndebele funerals. It has introduced singing and dancing. Moyo (2018) argues that the dancing and carnival in Pentecostal funerals derive from the fact that they believe that at death one goes to heaven. He further notes that there are some Christian churches that do not allow dancing at funerals and Ndebele people now belong to a variety of churches and funerals, especially in urban areas are now a hybrid of tradition and Christianity.

The conduct of funerals is one aspect of Ndebele cosmology, which is governed by spirituality; the Ndebele cultural milieu is spiritual (Nyathi, 2005). In his analysis of Ndebele religion, Nyathi (2001, p. 4) concurs that "It becomes very difficult, in fact, impossible, to isolate religion from other aspects of Ndebele culture." Mbiti (1990) describes African religion as functional in its approach; it is tailored to address physical problems using spiritual value systems. Religion facilitates the policing of people to make sure they do not violate social, environmental, and physical constraints. African religion serves a practical function to regulate society including the conduct of funerals.

One good example of the practical function of African religion is the taboo system. Ndlovu (2020) instantiates that taboos combine cultural knowledge, religion, and psychology to protect and groom. He gives, as an example, the taboo whereby children are prohibited by taboo to sit on the road as they will develop boils. The enforcement of the taboo is spiritual, yet the regulation of physical harm from cars and strangers is achieved. Life is religious in African cosmology. Mbiti (2015) avers that for the African, religion is a way of life. The domains of public and clinical health are also practiced within the realms of African religion. Afrika (1993) terms this approach, African holistic health science. He further notes that this holistic health approach requires the usage of highly developed psychic and spiritual energy; he laments that most of this spiritualized health science has been distorted and acculturated by colonialism and current global colonialities. This chapter seeks to bring to light the acculturated holistic public health measures practiced as spiritual funeral rites in Ndebele culture. While death in the Ndebele belief system is the gateway to the spirit world, it is actually treated with suspicion and this suspicion leads to measures that amount to public health. The public health elements within Ndebele funeral rites are effective in preventing communicable diseases including COVID-19. The public health measures in Ndebele funeral rites involve ritual cleansing, isolation, norms of interaction during a funeral wake, and handling the dead body.

COVID-19

The COVID-19 virus is the seventh of the coronaviruses. Su et al. (2016) avow that six coronavirus species are known to cause disease in humans; of the six, four (Z29E; OC43; NL63; HKU1) are prevalent and cause mild flue. Cui, Li, and Shi (2019) further state that the other two, Severe Acute Respiratory Syndrome Coronavirus (SARS-CoV) and Middle East Respiratory Syndrome Coronavirus (MERS-CoV) originate from animals and sometimes cause fatal illness. These were the six known coronaviruses before the discovery of the seventh and deadliest of them all in December 2019 when patients linked to the Wuhan seafood and wet animal market in China presented with novel pneumonia symptoms. The isolated coronavirus was named 2019-nCoV (Zhu et al., 2020). The disease has had negative effects on public health globally due to its rapid spread and mutation. Deceukelaire and Bodini (2020) observe that in less than two months the disease had spread from China to over a hundred countries. The disease mutates as it spreads creating different and more dangerous strains (Sridhar et al., 2021). The disease is more catastrophic in people who are already managing some illnesses or conditions such as hypertension, diabetes, and asthma (Elibol, 2021). Nhari et al. (2020) link COVID-19 fatalities to other endemic diseases such as tuberculosis, HIV, and AIDS in Zimbabwe. The disease is also difficult to manage as it presents with different symptoms in different people. However, Elibol (2021) identifies the following as the common symptoms: sore throat, cough, nasal congestion, post-natal discharge, gingivitis, loss of smell, loss of hearing, loss of taste, septic shock, and multi-organ failure. Because of its rapid spread and mutations, it has affected Ndebele people and their institutions including funerals. However, this chapter argues that Ndebele funeral rites have always anticipated disease transmission during funerals where people encounter death and gather in numbers (Sibanda, 1998).

Public Health and COVID-19

It has been established that infected people can spread the virus through aerosol droplets from their bodies especially through the mouth when talking, coughing, sneezing, and through the nose too. The virus can also survive on surfaces and people can get it through contact with such surfaces. Tabatabaeizadeh (2021) avers that the virus spreads between people in close contact, a meter or less apart through droplets. It can be transmitted by touching your eyes, nose, and mouth after touching a contaminated surface. Supermarkets have also been identified as high-contamination areas. Han, Zhang, He, and Jia (2021) note that frozen and refrigerated foods, as well as commonly touched surfaces such as shared tongs, handles of bakery and refrigerated cabinets, shopping baskets, and payment terminals have an elevated risk of contamination with COVID-19. Ndebele funerals also involve people gathering and touching many surfaces and tools as part of the funeral and burial procedures. People use picks and shovels in turns as they dig the grave and when they cover it, they also use knives and plates in food preparation and serving, respectively. Highly communicable diseases such as COVID-19 can spread easily in such gatherings.

Due to the rapid spread of COVID-19 and the rise in fatalities, governments and the World Health Organization (WHO) have put in place public health measures to control the spread of COVID-19. Guner, Hasanoglu, and Aktas (2020) identify the WHO prevention and control measures in the community as handwashing, isolation, personal protective equipment, social distancing, school, and workplace measures that include closures. They further state that the WHO recommends cleaning and disinfection of high-touch areas such as bedsides, tables, and door handles; these are to be done together with increased testing capacities. Nouvellet et al. (2021) establish that reduced mobility is a key preventive measure against COVID-19. Governments have been implementing national and partial lockdowns to reduce population mobilities as a preventive measure. The carnival that characterizes some funerals in Zimbabwe, for example, the Pentecostal Christian church funerals (Moyo, 2018), has also been curbed as it increases the aerosol transmission of COVID-19. The wearing of face masks in public areas has been made mandatory and in cases of close contact during talk shows and singing, people wear face shields to guard against mouth droplets from fellow interlocutors or singers. Public buildings have sanitizers by their entrances and some people carry their own hand sanitizers. Houses and vehicles are fumigated, this includes hearses and caskets. All these preventive measures can be gleaned from traditional Ndebele funeral rites, which use spiritual emphasis to promote public health.

Indigenous Knowledge Systems (IKS)

This chapter engages IKS as a theory that espouses the utilitarian value of Ndebele funeral rites and taboos in the prevention of COVID-19 and other communicable diseases. The term IKS and its subterms come with their own controversies in terms of colonial and decolonial semanticization. However, the term IKS has gained currency as a meta-linguistic label for the knowledge systems of autochthones. The IKS is the sum total of the survival skills of autochthones within their cultural milieu. Death and disease pose a threat to people and they galvanize their ways of knowing to prevent these. Barnhardt and Kawagley (2005) state that IKS is a matter of survival or extinction. Aikenhead and Ogawa (2007) make the observation that IKS translates to ways of living or ways of being whereby knowledge and the knower are intimately interconnected. It is the quest to become wiser so as to live in harmony with nature and each other. Cajete (2000) defines IKS as the process of coming to know. As African religion is functional in its practice IKS is also subsumed in religion. Idang (2015, p. 103) confirms that "some social values, especially in African society, cannot exactly be separated from religious, moral, political values and so on." Social management through religion has proven to be more effective in community mobilization. Hens (2006, p. 25) argues that "maintenance of rules based on tradition is stronger and more community owned than government rules."

Through coloniality of knowledge and successive years of colonialism, western science has managed to undermine IKS to the point of attempting to replace it. African religion, which is the vehicle of most African IKS, was mutilated by colonialism and the Abrahamic religions and this affected African IKS as well. Dei (1994, p. 4) posits that "there is a long history of Euro-American dominance of what constitutes valid knowledge and how such knowledge should be produced and disseminated internally and internationally." Western science gradually replaced IKS in Africa due to its alliance to colonial power. Briggs (2005, p. 102) postulates that the ostracization of IKS as a way of knowing is based on the view that "western science is seen to be open, systematic and objective, dependent very much on being a detached center of rationality and intelligence, whereas indigenous knowledge is seen to be closed, parochial, un-intellectual, primitive and emotional." However, Battiste (2005, p. 2) establishes that:

> Indigenous scholars discovered that indigenous knowledge is far more than the binary opposite of western knowledge. As a concept indigenous knowledge benchmarks the limitations of Eurocentric theory, its methodology, evidence, and conclusions re-conceptualises the resilience and self-reliance of indigenous peoples, and underscores the importance of their own philosophies, heritages, and educational processes.

IKS has been proven to work even in regulating modern societies in the areas of disease control and environmental conservation. Agrawal (2002, p. 288) indicates that "Some databases catalogue 'best practices,' highlighting successful efforts by various indigenous peoples or local communities to address problems related to environmental conservation, health, education, or agriculture." The conduct of Ndebele funerals addresses among other issues, public health concerns. Barnhardt and Kawagley (2005, p. 9) note "a significant 'paradigm shift' in which indigenous knowledge and ways of knowing are recognised as complex knowledge systems with an adaptive integrity of their own." Muyambo and Maposa (2014) for example, vindicate the adaptive integrity of the Ndau taboo system in south eastern Zimbabwe to conserve water resources. Hens (2006) concurs as he describes the contribution of IKS in biodiversity conservation and management in Ghana. The taboos and rituals performed during Ndebele funerals also have an IKS value which is comparable to the WHO COVID-19 preventive measures.

Research Methodology

The study is an African socioreligious approach to death and burial; it employs qualitative research methodology, which, according to Holloway (1997) and

Blanche and Durrheim (1999) offers rich descriptive reports of the individuals' perceptions, attitudes, beliefs, views and feelings, as well as the meanings and interpretations given to events and experiences. It is also grounded in the lived experiences of the participants in the study. Most of the data were collected through document analysis. The study deployed document analysis (Patton, 2002) as some Ndebele funeral rites were collected from books, journals, and newspaper opinion columns on Ndebele funerals. Participant observations of Ndebele funerals in the districts of Silobela, Nkayi, Zhombe, Lower Gwelo, and Mangwe were also sources of data on the conduct of Ndebele funerals. Intuitive knowledge of the treatment of death and sickness in Ndebele was also a source of data as the researcher is an adult who grew up in the practice of Ndebele culture and IKS. Unstructured interviews with purposively sampled interviewees were also used to explain some of the rituals. Aronson's (1994) thematic analysis is engaged as a method for data collection and analysis, here the data are categorized thematically so as to facilitate for comparison between WHO COVID-19 preventive measures and the public health IK in Ndebele funeral rites.

Findings and Discussion

The findings are presented and discussed thematically according to the COVID-19 preventive measures of social distancing, quarantine, sanitizing, temperature/weather, and testing.

Social distancing

The WHO recommendations on social distancing require people to be at least one and half meters apart in public places (Tabatabaeizadeh, 2021). This distance is to make sure that as people speak, droplets from their mouths do not reach the next person. The droplets are also prevented from becoming aerosol by wearing face masks and at times face shields; people are also advised to cough or sneeze into their elbows. Handshakes are not encouraged as hands are easily contaminated with the virus, hence people use elbows for greetings (if it is necessary to have contact greetings). Large gatherings are discouraged including large numbers of people during funerals. All these global public health social-distancing measures are not new to the conduct of Ndebele funerals.

In Ndebele culture it is considered taboo to shake hands when consoling each other (Moyo, 2018; Sibanda, 1998, Mpofu, 2011). The practice of shaking hands is a cultural borrowing which Ndebele people detest; this was evidenced by the unanimous disdain of the practice by interviewees. On two funeral occasions, Ndebele elders refused to shake the hand of the researcher arguing that doing so was against Ndebele culture. The belief is that when you shake hands you spread *umnyama* (the misfortune of death); what a fitting IKS for the public health control of viruses and germs spreading! In terms of crowd control around the dead body, only close relatives are allowed near the corpse.

Also, few female relatives are allowed in the hut that houses the corpse (Mpofu, 2013). This way, people are socially distant from the corpse which may harbor communicable viruses. They are also socially distanced from those who have been close to the dead person during their sickness.

Ndebele funerals are solemn occasions and carnival activities are tabooed (Moyo, 2018). Observations and interview data show that it is expected of mourners in Ndebele custom not to raise their faces (*ukuthwala amehlo*), the general expected posture is to look down. When looking down, the mouth spray as one talks is directed downward and not to other people and this reduces the aerosol spread of COVID-19 as well. Singing and dancing in gatherings increase the risk of COVID-19 spreading through droplets. Suffice it to say that Ndebele custom does not allow dancing and singing during funeral wakes. Dancing, or any kind of merrymaking, is not accepted in Ndebele funeral wakes because this is a sad and solemn occasion (Mpofu, 2013; Sibanda, 1998; Nyathi, 2001). While other people look down in silence to respect the dead and the solemnity of the occasion, the widowed persons especially women are expected to cover their faces (Mpofu, 2013). On why widowers do not cover their faces during the funeral wake of their wives, one interviewee indicated that women are caregivers and they nurse their husbands, parents, children, and this way they can remain with the *umnyama* (misfortune), hence the face covering. On the other hand, men do not nurse their wives and hence they may not need to prevent the spreading of the *umnyama* by a face covering. Magwaza (2006) states that before and at the burial the wife of the deceased would be easily spotted by a large animal skin over her head concealing her from the public eye; nowadays they use blankets. The covering acts as a face mask to prevent droplets from reaching other people given that the widow was close to the sickness. The widow's mouth is covered so that she does not spread *umnyama* to others just as the face mask and shield prevent the aerosol spread of COVID-19.

Besides limiting the number of people in the hut with the corpse, social distancing in Ndebele funerals also involves controlling the numbers of people who attend the burial. Ndebele cosmology is grounded on Ubuntu, which emphasizes communalism (Mabovula, 2011). The people who live together can help each other in the unfortunate occurrence of death. They do not have to wait for the deceased's relatives who come from distant lands, the immediate community takes the place of the family according to the Ubuntu philosophy. The conduct of Ndebele funerals is such that people coming from afar are excluded from the burial. Mpofu writing in the Southern Eye Newspaper of August 20, 2013, points out that:

> Usually when death occurs today, burial would take place the next day if it is in rural areas. This is because there is a problem of how to preserve the body against decomposition and of course the traditional fear and discomfort of keeping a dead person around. By the next day most of the relatives would have arrived. If not, those who cannot make it will miss the burial,

but will still come to perform the traditional "throwing a stone" (*ukuphosa ilitshe*) on the grave.

The rite of *ukuphosa ilitshe* is as important as burying someone and hence people cannot wait for relatives coming from distant lands as they can always do their own burial after. This ensures that those people traveling from far places do not expose the whole community to possible infection by viruses from other areas. Travelers are classified as high-risk people, which is why national lockdowns affect traveling. The provision of the rite of *ukuphosa ilitshe* serves as a crowd-control IKS and this enforces social distancing during Ndebele funerals.

Quarantine

Isolation of sick people and those who have had contact with sick people is common practice in the fight against COVID-19. Some travelers are required to undergo mandatory quarantine at designated centers or at home because the WHO advises this isolation as a method of preventing the spread to others; this is the essence of public health. In Ndebele spirituality, bereaved people and their home are believed to be harbingers of death and the whole community should be protected from contracting this misfortune. Ndlovu (2013) postulates that when death occurs in a home, the home and its people have a black cloud hanging over them. Just like COVID-19, this black cloud can be passed on to others, hence quarantine is part of Ndebele funeral rites.

When death occurs in a home, children are quickly removed from the home to a relative's home (Ndlovu, 2020). This is to make sure that they do not remain exposed to further misfortune. At a practical level, children may not be able to observe the solemnity of funerals for this way, they may be exposed and expose others to disease given that children interact more. The children are quarantined in a relative's home because they carry the death misfortune hence, they can only be isolated at a home which carries the same misfortune too. This way, all people who were exposed to the disease that killed their relative are quarantined so as to prevent the spread of death to the community. It is taboo for the bereaved family to be seen in public, children are isolated from school and adults avoid going to work or gatherings. This process is called *ukuzila* (respecting their dead relative) (Ndlovu, Ndlovu, and Ncube, 1995). As the bereaved undergo the process of *ukuzila* they spare the community from possible COVID-19 transmission, that is if the cause of death was COVID-19. Grieving people also wear distinctive clothing or black badges; these identify them as grieving and people are expected to be socially distant from them. Those women who sit in the hut with the corpse are also targeted for quarantine; they move back into the hut and remain together for a week without active interaction with other people. Three interviewees indicated that the hut itself is actually isolated after burial and the mourners shift to another hut. The isolation is extended to the clothes, tools, and utensils of the diseased, which are packed and isolated for a long time and viruses like COVID-19 cannot survive long isolation periods on surfaces.

Sanitizing

Apart from social distancing and quarantine, the other very important COVID-19 preventive measure is sanitizing. People wash their hands with soap and sanitize with chemical sanitizers, they also fumigate houses, cars, corpses, caskets, offices, and churches. The essence of sanitizing is to kill COVID-19 or to wash it away. In Ndebele, spirituality death is *umnyama* that can be spread to other people if there is no ritual cleansing (Nyathi, 2001) and this works just like the sanitizing done to curb the spread of COVID-19.

Handwashing is encouraged and public health officials run educational programs on proper handwashing. The washing can be done using detergents or chemical sanitizers that kill COVID-19. The WHO and various public health actors have been running campaigns on how people should wash their hands. The linguistic landscape is full of posters demonstrating how people should wash their hands. Ndebele spirituality has always incorporated ritual handwashing for all mourners after burial. Mpofu writing in the Southern Eye Newspaper of September 13, 2013, confirms that as mourners troop back to the homestead after burial:

> Just outside the homestead there are dishes of water (or buckets or calabashes) and the water contains leaves of certain herbs (mainly *umsuzwane*) which have been soaked. All mourners are required by custom to wash their hands to ward off bad luck cast upon them by handling or working on the corpse. Some people even wash their faces as well. Also, this is to exorcise evil spirits stalking the place of death. This ceremonial medicine is called *intelezi*.

The ritual of handwashing after burial is corroborated by interview data and observations over the years. Tree leaves which are soaked in the hand-washing water are from *umhlonhlo* tree. Suffice it to note that *umsuzwane* (*Lippia javanica*) has become popular in the fight against COVID-19 in Zimbabwe. It is used for steaming and as drinking medicine. The herb has also been commercialized as the popular brand *uzumbani*, which includes the *uzumbani* tea (Bhebhe, Chipurura, and Muchuweti, 2015). *Umsuzwane* is also used as a mosquito repellent, and I can say with the benefit of experience that its strong scent does repel mosquitoes and this prevents malaria. The *mhlonhlo* herb has a pungent choking smell and it is most likely effective in killing germs and viruses. A chemical investigation of these two herbs is one of those urgent researches so as to establish their chemical properties. The ritual cleansing is extended to all those who carry out the burial and to the tools. Ranger (2004, p. 114) avows that "Those who carried out the burial had to be purified with herbs and the digging tools ritually cleansed." The tools are actually piled and left for seven days thereafter, there is a cleansing ceremony whereby the tools and the home are cleansed using herbs. Tools are high-touch surfaces and are easily contaminated with COVID-19 hence people are not supposed to take their digging tools with them after the burial. The tools are left behind for seven days and can only be collected after the *amanzi* cleansing ceremony. During the *amanzi* cleansing ceremony the tools are washed (*ukugezisa*) using herbs to cleanse them of death misfortune.

The cleansing by the healer is also extended to the hut or house that housed the dead body. The hut is temporarily vacated and is ceremonially cleansed by being sprinkled with medicines and for some families, certain aromatic herbs are burned (*ukuthunqisela*). The medicine man may walk all over the homestead sprinkling the herbs or smoking incense (Mpofu, 2013; Nyathi, 2001). I have witnessed funerals whereby the medicine man sprinkles his *muti* on all people who get back into the home after the burial, thereafter he or she sprinkles the whole home. COVID-19 prevention involves the disinfection of houses, homes, and cars, and this has always been the practice in Ndebele funerals. Cars that leave the home after the burial *ziyageziswa* (they are cleansed) so that they do not carry death with them to wherever they came from. The utensils that the dead person has been using are cleansed and buried with them, their clothes are cleansed and stored only to be opened after a period that can be up to a year. The preoccupation with sanitizing and cleansing in Ndebele funerals is to protect the community from the death that has robbed them of one of their own; this is public health enforced through spirituality.

Warmth and Testing

It has been established that the spread of COVID-19 is related to temperature. It spreads faster in low temperatures and is slowed by high temperatures (Notari, 2021). The WHO also encourages increased testing capacity as a way of preventing the spread of the virus. Ndebele funeral rites emphasize on maintaining warmth at the bereaved homestead and that people consult on the cause of death before or after the funeral.

High temperatures slow down the virus. Notari (2021) establishes a correlation between low temperatures and the rapid spread of COVID-19. He found the spread to be slower at high temperatures. When someone dies in Ndebele culture, men make a big fire in the deceased's homestead, the fire is particularly important at night during the night vigil when temperatures go down. Mourners are kept warm by the big bonfire making sure temperatures are high. High temperatures have been proven to slow down the rate of spread of COVID-19. After the burial, the family engages in testing to establish the cause of death so as to prevent it from happening again (Ndlovu, Ndlovu and Ncube, 1995). Mpofu writing in the Southern Eye Newspaper of September 13, 2013, notes that:

> The last action is *ukuyabonisa* which is a visit to a traditional spiritual seer (not witchdoctor) to consult about the cause of death of the deceased.

The strong belief among the Ndebele people is that all death is a result of a spell of an evil enemy. The dead person is always bewitched (*uloyiwe*). The question that the family will ask themselves is; *uthethwe yini?* (what took them?)/*udliwe yini?* (what ate them?)/*ubulelwe ngubani?* (what killed them?).

Corpses are now tested for COVID-19 to establish the cause of death and advise people on how to handle the corpse for their own protection (Griffin, 2021). The ritual of *ukuphalala* (to consult on the cause of death) is a form of testing so that the community can be aware of the cause of death and prevent further deaths from the same cause. Testing for COVID-19 even on corpses is public health practice and engaging a seer to establish the cause of death in Ndebele funeral rites fulfills the WHO testing requirement.

Conclusion

The effects of COVID-19 have disrupted social life and culture, especially in Africa, where the cultural practice is tied to the philosophy of Ubuntu where people depend on each other. African funerals and weddings have been identified as COVID-19 super-spreader events and governments have sought to regulate these gatherings. However, a closer analysis of Ndebele funeral rites exposes the IKS of public health embedded in the spiritual rites. The conduct of Ndebele funerals incorporates the key COVID-19 preventive measures emphasized in public health. The culture discourages handshakes during funerals just as the WHO advises people to avoid handshakes to curb the spread of the virus. Funerals are somber events where people do not sing or talk loudly, which also limits the chances of aerosol transmission of the virus. Those who were close to the deceased during sickness cover their heads and mouths and this acts as personal protective wear just like face masks and shields. Strong herbs are soaked in water and are used to wash hands and in the cleansing of the home and tools, these are instances of sanitizing and fumigation. The bereaved are expected to isolate from the community, school, and work so as not to spread their bad luck to others. Isolation is also one of the key WHO measures in the fight against COVID-19. The funeral rites also allow for relatives coming from distant lands to come after the burial and still take part in the burial by placing their stones on the grave, this controls crowd numbers and mobility. Mourners are kept warm and after the burial the family consults on the cause of death so as to protect others from a similar death.

References

Afrika, L. O. (1993). *Afrikan holistic health*. New York: A and B Publishers Group.

Agrawal, A. (2002). Indigenous knowledge and the politics of classification. *International Social Science Journal, 54*(173), 287–297.

Aikenhead, G. S., & Ogawa, M. (2007). Indigenous knowledge and science revisited. *Cultural Studies of Science Education*, 2(3), 539–620.

Aronson, J. (1994). A pragmatic view of thematic analysis. *The Qualitative Report*, 2, 1–3.

Barnhardt, R., & Kawagley, O. A. (2005). Indigenous knowledge systems and Alaska Native ways of knowing. *Anthropology and Education Quarterly*, 36(1), 8–23.

Battiste, M. (2005). *Indigenous knowledge: Foundations for first nations*. Saskatoon: Purish Publishing.

Bhebhe, M., Chipurura, B., & Muchuweti, M. (2015). Determination and comparison of phenolic compound content and antioxidant activity of selected local Zimbabwean herbal teas with exotic Aspalathus linearis. *South African Journal of Botany*, 100, 213–218.

Blanche, M. S., & Durrheim, K. (1999). *Research in practice: Applied methods for social science*. Cape Town: University of Cape Town.

Briggs, J. (2005). The use of indigenous knowledge in development: Problems and challenges. *Progress in Development Studies*, 5(2), 99–114.

Cajete, G. A. (2000). *Native science: Natural laws of interdependence*. Santa Fe: Clear Light.

Cui, J., Li, F., & Shi, Z. L. (2019). Origin and evolution of pathogenic coronaviruses. *Nature Reviews in Microbiology*, 17(3), 181–192.

Centre for Disease Control Foundation. (2021). What is public health? https://www.cdcfoundation.org/what-public-health.

De Ceukelaire, W., & Bodini, C. (2020). We need strong public health care to contain the global corona pandemic. *International Journal of Health Services: Planning, Administration, Evaluation*, 50(3), 276–277.

Dei, G. J. (1994). Afrocentricity: A Cornerstone of pedagogy. *Anthropology and Education Quarterly*, 25(1), 3–28.

Elibol, E. (2021). Otolaryngological symptoms in COVID-19. *European Archives of Oto-Rhino-Laryngology*, 278(4), 1233–1236.

Griffin, K. J. (2021). Autopsy in the time of COVID. *Diagnostic Histopathology*, 27(3), 134–137.

Güner, H. R., Hasanoğlu, İ., & Aktaş, F. (2020). COVID-19: Prevention and control measures in community. *Turkish Journal of Medical Sciences*, 50(SI–1), 571–577.

Han, J., Zhang, X., He, S., & Jia, P. (2021). Can the coronavirus disease be transmitted from food? A review of evidence, risks, policies and knowledge gaps. *Environmental Chemistry Letters*, 19(1), 5–16.

Hens, L. (2006). Indigenous knowledge and biodiversity conservation and management in Ghana. *Journal of Human Ecology*, 20(1), 21–30.

Holloway, I. (1997). *Basic concepts for qualitative research*. London: Blackwell.

Idang, G. E. (2015). African culture and values. *Phronimon*, 16(2), 97–111.

Mabovula, N. N. (2011). The erosion of African communal values: A reappraisal of the African Ubuntu philosophy. *Inkanyiso: Journal of Humanities and Social Sciences*, 3(1), 38–47.

Magwaza, T. S. C. (2006). Age and status identification through the traditional dress of Zulu women. *Southern African Journal for Folklore Studies*, 16(2), 103–115.

Mbiti, J. S. (1990). *African religions & philosophy*. Portsmouth: Heinemann.

Mbiti, J. S. (2015). *Introduction to African religion*. Long Grove: Waveland Press.

Moyo, C. (2018). Dance and song as grieving: Examining the role of (Pentecosatal?) Christianity in shifting Ndebele people's perceptions on grieving. *Pharos Journal of Theology*, 99(1), 1–10.

Mpofu, I. (2013a). Death, burial in Ndebele culture part 3. Southern eye, August 30, 2013. https://www.southerneye.co.zw/2013/08/30/death-burial-ndebele-culture/.

Mpofu, I. (2013b). Death, burial in Ndebele culture part 4. Southern eye, September 13, 2013. https://www.southerneye.co.zw/2013/09/13/death-burial-ndebele-part-4 -burial/.

Mpofu, I. N. (2011). *Sithini IsiNdebele?* Harare: Radiant Publishing Company.

Muyambo, T., & Maposa, R. S. (2014). Linking culture and water technology in Zimbabwe: Reflections on Ndau experiences and implications for climate change. *Journal of African Studies and Development, 6*(2), 22–28.

Ndlovu, C. D. (2013). *The mourning cultural practices amongst the Zulu-speaking widows of the KwaNyuswa community: A feminist perspective* (Doctoral dissertation). University of KwaZulu Natal. https://ukzn-dspace.ukzn.ac.za/handle/10413/11374.

Ndlovu, S. (2020). Child development through Ndebele taboos: Motivation to blend the indigenous and the exotic. *Inkanyiso, 12*(1), 36–55.

Ndlovu, T. M., Ndlovu, D. N., & Ncube, B. S. (1995). *Imikhuba Lamasiko AmaNdebele.* Gweru: Mambo Press.

Nhari, L. G., Dzobo, M., Chitungo, I., Denhere, K., Musuka, G., & Dzinamarira, T. (2020). Implementing effective TB prevention and treatment programmes in the COVID-19 era in Zimbabwe: A call for innovative differentiated service delivery models. *Public Health in Practice, 1*, 100058. https://doi.org/10.1016/j.puhip.2020 .100058.

Notari, A. (2021). Temperature dependence of COVID-19 transmission. *Science of the Total Environment, 763*, 144390. https://doi.org/10.1016/j.scitotenv.2020.144390.

Nouvellet, P., Bhatia, S., Cori, A., Ainslie, K. E., Baguelin, M., Bhatt, S., Boonyasiri, A., Brazeau, N. F., Cattarino, L., Cooper, L. V., Coupland, H., Cucunuba, Z. M., Cuomo-Dannenburg, G., Dighe, A., Djaafara, B. A., Dorigatti, I., Eales, O. D., van Elsland, S. L., Nascimento, F. F., FitzJohn, R. G., Gaythorpe, K. A. M., Geidelberg, L., Green, W. D., Hamlet, A., Hauck, K., Hinsley, W., Imai, N., Jeffrey, B., Knock, E., Laydon, D. J., Lees, J. A., Mangal, T., Mellan, T. A., Nedjati-Gilani, G., Parag, K. V., Pons-Salort, M., Ragonnet-Cronin, M., Riley, S., Unwin, H. J. T., Verity, R., Vollmer, M. A. C., Volz, E., Walker, P. G. T., Walters, C. E., Wang, H., Watson, O. J., Whittaker, C., Whittles, L. K., Xi, X., Ferguson, N. M., & Donnelly, C. A. (2021). Reduction in mobility and COVID-19 transmission. *Nature Communications, 12*(1), 1–9.

Nyathi, P. (2001). *Traditional Ceremonies of Amandebele.* Gweru: Mambo Press.

Nyathi, P. (2005). *Zimbabwe's cultural heritage.* Oxford: African Books Collective.

Patton, M. Q. (2002). *Qualitative research and evaluation methods.* London: Sage Publications.

Ranger, T. (2004). Dignifying death: The politics of burial in Bulawayo. *Journal of Religion in Africa, 34*(1/2), 110–144. Retrieved August 22, 2021, from http://www.jstor.org/ stable/1581483.

Sibanda, J. (1998). *Isikithi.* Harare: College Press Publishers.

Sridhar, A., Yağan, O., Eletreby, R., Levin, S. A., Plotkin, J. B., & Poor, H. V. (2021, June). Leveraging a multiple-strain model with mutations in analyzing the spread of COVID-19. In *ICASSP 2021–2021 IEEE international conference on acoustics, speech and signal processing (ICASSP)* (pp. 8163–8167).New York: IEEE.

Su, S., Wong, G., Shi, W., Liu, J., Lai, A. C., Zhou, J., Liu, W., Bi, Y., & Gao, G. F. (2016). Epidemiology, genetic recombination, and pathogenesis of coronaviruses. *Trends in Microbiology, 24*(6), 490–502.

Tabatabaeizadeh, S. A. (2021). Airborne transmission of COVID-19 and the role of face mask to prevent it: A systematic review and meta-analysis. *European Journal of Medical Research, 26*(1), 1–6.

Umoh, J. O. (2005). *Elements of sociology of religion.* Ikot Ekpene: Iwoh Publishers.

Zhu, N., Zhang, D., Wang, W., Li, X., Yang, B., Song, J., Zhao, X., Huang, B., Shi, W., Lu, R., Niu, P., Zhan, F., Ma, X., Wang, D., Xu, W., Wu, G., Gao, G. F., & Tan, W. (2020). A novel coronavirus from patients with pneumonia in China, 2019. *New England Journal of Medicine*, 382(8):727–733.

10 Securitization of COVID-19 and the Imagination of Post-COVID-19 Burial Ceremonies in Kenya and Zimbabwe

Loreen Maseno and Sibanda Fortune

Introduction

The years 2020 and 2021 will go down in history as the most tragic period in the second decade of the new millennium as the novel coronavirus (COVID-19) pandemic resulted in death and untold suffering the world over (Sibanda et al. 2022:1). Through this pandemic, the world "stood still," instilled fear, caused trauma, and suffered unexpected losses in diverse ways. Initially perceived as a health emergency, COVID-19 pandemic revealed itself to be a multifaceted crisis, which raised questions that could not be answered in a mono-dimensional way (Hampton & Thiesen 2021:1; Michaud 2021:66). The virus was non-discriminatory as it affected people across varied groups regardless of one's ethnic, racial, religious, gender, or sexual orientations in different geographical regions. Emerging in December 2019 in Wuhan, China, COVID-19 quickly spread across the world such that by March 2020, it was recognized as a global pandemic (Pentaris 2022). As it spread across the globe, individuals and communities faced the tragic loss of human life and affected the ways of grieving and mourning according to tradition handed over from one generation to the next. Therefore, death, loss, grief, and related burials experienced in the context of COVID-19 in sub-Saharan Africa, with particular reference to Kenya and Zimbabwe, evoke many unanswered questions from a religious perspective. Apparently, governments imposed restrictions in order to tackle the spread of the virus, but placed those affected in a quandary. As Pentaris (2022:3) rightly observes, "The inability to be near a loved one who is dying, or travel to attend a funeral, pay respects, and say goodbyes, has left many grievers in a helpless state." In a related way we ask: But how has COVID-19 been securitized by the state and what impact has this had on burial ceremonies in Kenya and Zimbabwe?

The overall objective of this chapter is to critically examine the existential threat and measures through which the Health Ministries prescribed the conduct of burial ceremonies in both Kenya and Zimbabwe under COVID-19 pandemic. The chapter posits that the securitization of COVID-19 pandemic triggered a re-imagination of post-COVID-19 burial ceremonies in Kenya and

DOI: 10.4324/9781003390732-10

Zimbabwe. The research grapples with the question: How has policy or securitization responded to the coronavirus-related burial needs in the context of death, dying, and loss in Kenya and Zimbabwe? The study utilized insights from a securitization theory as a theoretical framework. A desk research method and a comparative approach were used to explore the experiences of Christian churches and adherents of African indigenous communities in both Kenya and Zimbabwe. Before looking at the directives from the Ministries of Health in Kenya and Zimbabwe, the next section focuses on the theoretical framework.

Theoretical Framework

The study was guided by insights from the securitization theory. The dangers posed by COVID-19 made it a phenomenon with implications for security. Most of securitization theorists and ontological security scholars assume the securitizing actor to be the state, which evokes security to guard its survival and fend off threats against its normal institutional routine. According to Buzan et al. (1998:24), securitization includes the process through which an issue is presented as an existential threat requiring urgent measures and justifying alternative actions outside the usual prescribed procedure. According to Lauststen and Waever (2000:708) securitization "studies how security issues are produced by actors who pose something (a referent object) as existentially threatened and therefore claim a right to use an extraordinary measure to defend it." At the same time, securitization theory shows the effects of securitization as referent objects raised to a level of having a demand on survival and threatened to a point to be dealt with swiftly to avoid coming to a point of no return (Lauststen & Waever 2000:708). Therefore, securitization creates a second-order system useful in observing how main actors in the field of security studies operate.

Bramadat and Dawson (2014:7–8) consider securitization as the growing emphasis on national security, which may be understood broadly as increased international cooperation in the war on terror and narrowly as increased border controls for particular states. The Copenhagen school, common in literature, represents the body of work including that of Ole Weaver and Barry Buzan that focuses on linguistic–grammatical composition in the construction of security (Watson 2012:280–281). The theory of securitization explores the way a referent object (something) is deemed threatened and security action necessary to defend or protect it. It examines the construction of threats and the implementation of policies thereafter.

Securitization theory, therefore, includes several basic components. First, securitizing actors who announce the security situation may range from cabinet secretaries, non-governmental organizations, activists to protectors, among others. Second, it is also concerned about the threats which can be tangible like bombs, missiles, or a health issue, in this case COVID-19 pandemic. Third, the referent object comes to the fore and this is the target of the threat. Fourth, it encompasses measures taken to actively deal with the impending threat. This is where rules and regulations are announced in order to curb the spread of COVID-19 pandemic. The process of securitization has also been deemed as a speech-act in which the pronouncement itself is the act, and it is by branding or labeling an item or somebody as a security issue that it essentially takes up the place to become one (Lauststen & Waever 2000:708). Further, the very act of referring to health issues as threatened means securitizing an issue and the possibility of success in making the security move on behalf of those whose loss destroys faith and annuls being is greater than when attempting to securitize most other objects (Lauststen & Waever 2000:719). Securitization theory shows the effects of securitization as referent objects elevated to a level that makes particular demands in the name of survival and threatens that if these are not dealt with urgently and precisely, there will come a point of no return (Laustsen & Waever 2000:708). It is important to note that various organizations, such as non-governmental organizations, religious outfits, and governments are essential actors, though not the only ones, in securitization. They make announcements on whatever they consider and judge to be worth attention in terms of danger. Therefore, in Kenya and Zimbabwe, the government and the Health Ministries were arguably securitizing actors who highlighted the COVID-19 health issue as a threat to human flourishing, which makes the theory helpful for the study.

COVID-19 and Health Ministries' Directives in Kenya and Zimbabwe

The COVID-19 virus was established as the cause of pneumonia and a number of deaths in Wuhan city in China on 31 December 2019. It was reported that a combined total of 7,026,732 people had been infected with the COVID-19 virus and 403,015 deaths were recorded around the world as on 8 June 2020 (https://coronavirus.jhu.edu/). It was also projected that 83,000–190,000 people in Africa could die of COVID-19 and several millions could get infected in the first year of the pandemic if containment measures in Africa failed (WHO 2020). Notably, some warned that COVID-19 could become a death trap for many Africans unless a hands-on approach was taken by many governments. It was predicted that the number of cases that would require hospitalization would overwhelm the available medical capacity in much of Africa. It was also reported that in Africa, an estimated 3.6 million to 5.5 million COVID-19 hospitalizations would be recorded, of which 82,000–167,000 would be cases requiring oxygen, and 52,000–107,000 would be critical cases requiring breathing support and severely strain the health capacities of most countries (WHO 2020).

In recent times, COVID-19 has continued to cause sickness and mortalities due to its rapid spread to all parts of the world, including in Kenya and Zimbabwe. The WHO declared COVID-19 a global pandemic on 11 March 2020 (Cucinotta & Vanelli 2020). The Kenyan government through the Ministry of Health (MOH) press release on 13 March 2020, immediately banned all meetings, religious crusades, conferences, and events and issued advice to all Kenyans to avoid any events where many people would be gathering (Kihui 2020). In Zimbabwe, the government through Statutory Instruments, SI76/2020 and SI77/2020, empowered the Minister for the Ministry of Health and Child Care (MOHCC) to legislate measures to prevent, contain, and treat COVID-19 as a "formidable epidemic disease" (The Zimbabwean 2020). Therefore, COVID-19 had deadly impacts where Kenya and Zimbabwe were not spared.

The Kenyan Ministry of Health (MOH) together with the county officials as well as the Ministry of Health and Child Care of Zimbabwe declared and enforced interment within 72 hours of occurrence of death due to COVID-19. Mortuaries were required to clear the bodies as soon as they could whilst burials were conducted the same day the body was removed from the morgue, among other restrictions. It is clear that burials during the COVID-19 pandemic in Kenya and Zimbabwe were conducted hurriedly, especially if the deceased was known to have died from COVID-19-related complications. At the same time, COVID-19 has been securitized by the state and this had an enormous impact on burial ceremonies in Kenya and Zimbabwe.

COVID-19 pandemic had a great impact on the communities of Kenya and Zimbabwe. The measures put in place such as social distancing, curfews, and the discouraging of gatherings were rolled out as a high number of COVID-19 infections continued to be registered. Soon afterwards, there followed lockdowns, which curtailed social interactions, the social fabric, programs, and community activities, traditionally practiced in Kenya and Zimbabwe. The impact of COVID-19 led Kenyan MOH to produce a document titled, "Interim guidelines on handling of human remains infected with Covid-19" to guide all mortuaries, both public and private. This document asserts that:

> Widespread community transmission can overwhelm health systems resulting in excess deaths; therefore, guidelines are required for the safe management of bodies of the deceased persons in preparation for possible fatalities. The measures include handling of bodies at community level, hospitals, in mortuaries/funeral homes, transportation and body disposal. Complete autopsy of bodies with the disease is highly discouraged. [...] Persons diagnosed with coronavirus disease in the healthcare facilities, home or in other locations may have autopsies done in exceptional circumstances with authorization from the Chief Government Pathologist. (MOH Guidelines 2020:7–8).

The implication of this directive is that where a family desired an autopsy during the time of the pandemic and also on one who died from COVID-19-related complications, that a complete autopsy could not be done. At the same time, the guidelines were to be enforced and ministry officials deployed to the health facilities to ensure compliance. Similarly, Africa News (2020) reported that the government of Zimbabwe issued a directive on how COVID-19 victims were to be laid to rest. It was announced that the deceased was to be buried in the city where they died. This shows that strict measures were employed to prevent and contain the pandemic.

Along the same lines, the Kenyan "Interim guidelines" further added that should a death be encountered,

> The health worker must ensure that the body is handled applying strict standard precautions, including hand hygiene before and after interaction with the body and the environment, and use of appropriate personal protective equipment (PPE) at all times, place the body into leak proof and tamper proof body bags. Keep both the movement and handling of the body to a minimum. The body should be labelled and bagged/plastic wrapped immediately into a body bag. The body bag will be made of PVC, leak proof and tamper proof material. There will be double bagging of all bodies. Once the body bag been wrapped it must NOT be opened thereafter and the outermost body bag must be wiped with 0.5% sodium hypochlorite/disinfectant. (MOH guidelines 2020:10–11).

Although this directive was issued by the Kenyan MOH, its implications are instructive for understanding the Zimbabwean experience. According to Aljezeera News Agency (2021), the police in Zimbabwe alongside the MOHCC enforced the government ban of the public viewing of bodies and the tradition of having a corpse stay overnight in the family's home before burial. Therefore, in Kenya just as in Zimbabwe, once a body was disposed into a leak-proof body bag shortly after death, it was not to be opened thereafter. In practical terms, this deprived the deceased of the dignity which was normally accorded to the dead by dressing them and allowing for open viewing such that the bereaved family and friends were now unable to pay their last respects as per tradition. In addition, of particular concern was that the family and other relatives could not prove that the person in the body bag was really their kith and kin, which sharply truncated their grieving.

COVID-19 Deaths and Related Burials

Upon the arrival of COVID-19 in Kenya, the very first reported death was in March 2020, whilst in Zimbabwe, the first case of COVID-19 death was also reported in March 2020 (Muronzi 2020). According to WHO (2021), in Kenya, from 3 January 2020 to 26 November 2021, there were 254,862 confirmed cases of COVID-19 with 5,333 deaths, whilst from the same source from 3 January 2020 to 10 November 2022, there were 257,893 confirmed cases of COVID-19 with 5,606 deaths in Zimbabwe (WHO 2021). The statistics show that there was a comparative range of death and loss in Kenya and Zimbabwe. However, many deaths evoked fear and uncertainty on the disposal of human remains as people had lost the freedom to travel to attend a funeral and pay respects to their loved ones (Pentaris 2022:3). Apparently, any patient who died after developing breathing complications was deemed as having passed on from the virus effects, and was to be buried within 24 hours.

Even with these measures in place, Kenya and Zimbabwe continued to register some COVID-19-related deaths in substantial proportions. Because of fear, uncertainty, and inexperience with the pandemic, COVID-19-related burials in Kenya and Zimbabwe were conducted hurriedly. As a result, the modes of burials were no longer as detailed as per African traditions and customs and also defied some of the Christian funeral rites. This was rather distressing to the surviving family, relatives, and friends because body viewing was no longer practiced as the customary way of ascertaining the identity of the deceased and paying the last respects. In some cases, the deceased were given a "pauper's burial," which lacked dignity and respect in spite of the social status s/he once held in life. In fact, since the deceased family was equally barred from coming into contact with the deceased's body, this destabilized the families' mental and spiritual health in the context of grief and loss. It turned out that burials were no longer elaborate as per African spirituality and customs in order to curtail the further spread of the coronavirus across the country. However, in Kenya and Zimbabwe, the move was contrary to African indigenous culture and some African Christian beliefs where the dead are usually buried in the same place as their ancestors (Africa News 2021).

The health precautions imposed in both countries had their fair share of challenges. For instance, in Kenya there have been cases where due to the "body bag directive," a wrong body was claimed by a family and buried. The Star (2020) reported that on 31 July 31 2020, in Kisasi, Vihiga County, a stranger was buried instead of Rev Linus Simwa who was COVID-19 positive at the home of the latter. Both bodies were placed in similar body bags around the same time, in the same place in the Vihiga Referral Hospital morgue. The wrong body was collected by the family of the cleric. Meanwhile, several rituals had to be performed by elders before public health workers exhumed the body of an unidentified man they mistakenly buried in place of the cleric whose infected body had been left in the morgue. The apparent mix-up and labeling of bodies raise questions about the hospital's preparedness to handle bodies of those who die of the virus. However, this is not the only implication. The other one was rightly proffered by Charles Kavuludi, one of the elders from the same area, Kisasi. According to Kavuludi, such a matter is now beyond the family members because they cannot set eyes twice on someone who was already buried. He further states that some cleansing rituals were required so that the family members would not face the consequences of the spirits from the dead and ancestors (The Star 2020). In addition, according to Kavuludi, such rituals must therefore happen in the absence of all close family members so as not to look upon their dead a second time. Meanwhile, the family will be informed later that their loved ones were buried again (Lusigi 2021). This is a typical catch-22 situation where culture, law, and science seem to be on a collision path.

Clearly, there is an imbalance in the lives of the grieving family when their loved one has to be reburied in their absence. The elder brings to our attention that there are grave consequences that follow such an error of burying a total stranger in a grave that has been set aside for a family member in a particular home (The Star 2020). The spirits of the dead and ancestors do not take this lightly and there are attached consequences. A number of questions arise in this context of death and loss. For instance, whose mistake was it to bury a stranger? Was it the mortuary attendant, the MOH Kenya directive, the body bag color, or the close kin who transported the body? Because unintended spiritual and cultural consequences that befell the family are beyond the scope of this chapter, a horizontal life course study is necessary to ascertain how they appease the ancestors.

At this juncture, it can be asked: Does the value of the dead change when the cause of death is COVID-19 and how should families of the deceased cope in these times? This has implications for the policy response to death, dying, and loss. Apparently, in light of this problem, COVID-19-related burials have been securitized by the state in both Kenya and Zimbabwe. For instance, there was a marked presence of security details in both Kenya and Zimbabwe in the context of COVID-19-related deaths and burials, which brought intimidation, distress, and trauma among bereaved owing to the presence of the police in full police uniform and the Ministry of Health officials dressed in protective gear. These officials took the center-stage whilst the relatives became passive onlookers. This has an impact on the psyche of the deceased family since some of the dead were not buried by their kin but by strangers who have no emotional connection to the dead. At the same time, the deceased family members were not even allowed to come close to the casket, which definitely destabilized the deceased families' mental and spiritual health.

COVID-19 deaths and losses have come along with four aspects, which were less fraught in earlier times. First, the bereaved were affected by the grief when they lost a loved one. Second, they also had to contend with the physical separation that happened during illness and infection, prior to death. Third, the speed at which the dead must be laid to rest was also unsettling. Fourth, the context of the dead body and the new way in which it was handled rendered it largely inaccessible. Death of a loved one was associated with succeeding elevations in symptoms of various forms of psychopathology (Keyes et al. 2014). Traditionally, the burial rites and grieving period were said to allow for the living to accept the loss and further cope with the reality of the loss of a loved one (Shisanya 1996; Keyes 2014). However, when grief and grieving were not allowed to go full cycle, there are adverse psychological and mental repercussions that befall the bereaved family (Kaplow et al. 2013). Clearly, death is a rite of passage whose effect on the living leaves a huge impact in many African societies, including those in Kenya and Zimbabwe.

COVID-19 funerals in Kenya and Zimbabwe were done under tight security, with no body viewing, minimal funeral attendees, and spraying of the casket before lowering into the ground. These actions in the present times not only present an affront to African death rituals among the bereaved people in Kenya and Zimbabwe but also present mental health challenges for the bereaved. Indeed, the absence of social support and burial details associated with African tradition, African Christian life, and spirituality due to the pandemic and related stigma by reason of the above mentioned, the African spirit is being oppressed and suppressed. In the pre-COVID-19 context, the long gatherings and interactions during burials were moments for sharing and reflecting on life (Nwachuku 1992). The prohibition of such *ubuntu*-inspired spontaneous gatherings and with no decent send-off to the dead, trauma, and a host of mental health problems ensured.

According to Jacobs (1993), after an important loss, such as the death of a close friend, spouse, parent, or child, about a third of the people most directly affected will suffer harmful effects on their physical or mental health or both. It is clear that bereavements are known for causing or furthering a variety of psychosomatic and psychiatric instability. For most, about a quarter of widows and widowers may undergo clinical depression and anxiety during the very first year of bereavement (Parkes 1998). If in pre-COVID-19 times the earlier-mentioned effects of dead were experienced, one can imagine how much more are they likely to occur in the unique, challenging, and securitized acute COVID-19 circumstances in Kenya and Zimbabwe.

Securitization of COVID-19 and other Pandemics

There are dilemmas associated with the securitization of pandemics. It was also examined how security is socially constructed with the goal of prioritizing the urgency of an issue in a given context by political agents and the existential hazard it poses for the survival of the State. Some scholars have studied the securitization of health issues such as HIV and AIDS (Elbe 2006); avian flu (Youde 2008); SARS and avian flu (Wishnick 2010). The same may be applied to the deadly threats aroused by COVID-19, with the aim of preventing health dangers, justifies securitization.

The Kenya MOH Guideline states that:

> A public health official should be designated in advance to accompany the body from the hospital to the place of final disposition to ensure the safety of all those involved in the process. Follow government guidance on the conduct of funerals which includes minimizing the number of attendants to not more than fifteen and must adhere to social distancing
> (MOH Guidelines 2020:20).

Traditionally, the disposal of the dead was not a matter that was uniformly prescribed for all persons in Kenya and Zimbabwe. Rather, the normal practice was of having bodies disposed of as per people's traditions and religious prescriptions. The Kenyan MOH guideline speaks to the numbers allowed to attend the funerals and even that a stranger from the public health office should be in attendance at the burial to ensure compliance. In the case of Zimbabwe, stringent rules for burial under a task force were introduced where relatives watched from a distance. In addition, the transportation of bodies outside their places of death was forbidden. In exceptional cases, corpses could be transported to faraway places on condition that they were "hermetically sealed" and placed in "triple coffins" (Muromo 2021; Africa News 2021). Under Level 4 National Lockdown in Zimbabwe, government limited the funeral gatherings to 30 people and banned overnight vigils (Mutsaka 2021). The police, soldiers, and health officials in Zimbabwe were used in enforcing the strict COVID-19 funeral rites, which securitized death, dying, mourning, and grieving.

The announcements contained in the Kenyan MOH and the Zimbabwean Ministry of Health and Child Care touch on health-related security of the citizens and demands to be taken as critical. The existential threat presented by the Ministry of Health as securitizing actors is the imminent health threat against the Kenyan and Zimbabwe citizens alike. Indeed, the act by government officials in pronouncing the COVID-19 infection to be the targets raises the question of this security to another level. The Health Ministries alerted the public by insisting that COVID-19 is lethal and should be checked. This invokes the milieu of identity for the victims of the pandemic as Kenyans and Zimbabweans. Thus, COVID-19 is considered as a significant health threat as reported in local and international dailies. The very act of referring to the health of the nation as threatened operates as a means of securitizing it. As indicated above, the speech act labeling, which identifies something as threatening, initiates the process of securitizing it. The threat of COVID-19 against Kenyan and Zimbabwean citizens considers it as an existential threat, which could end the lives of many abruptly, limit their freedoms and health options in a way that demanded extraordinary action.

COVID-19 in Kenya and Zimbabwe: A Securitization Analysis

In the statements by the Ministries of Health in both Kenya and Zimbabwe on COVID-19, citizens were exposed to the risks of a terrible pandemic with deadly repercussions. Notably, the very act of referring to health issues as threatening means securitizing them. The threat of a collapsed health status in the two countries was portrayed as an existential risk that could bring to end the lives of many Kenyans and Zimbabweans and befits immediate action – one demanding extraordinary measures. The act by health officials to pronounce the health of citizens as targets brings their security to another level. The speech act in this statement touches upon the health of Kenyans and by the same token Zimbabweans, the existence of the state and which the Health Ministry's demands should be taken seriously. The Health Ministry sounds the alarm by insisting that those killed are Kenyans and Zimbabweans.

In the Kenyan MOH Guidelines, it is stated:

> Even though Covid-19 has been fairly well controlled in China, it has continued to cause morbidity and mortalities due to rapid spread to other

parts of the world, leading to the eventual declaration by WHO that it is a pandemic. There is hence an urgent need to have guidance on how to control the spread of the disease in Kenya. Kenya has not been spared by the disease, with multiple cases being reported in various parts of the country

(MOH Guidelines 2020:3).

The speech act from Kenyan MOH is asking for the management of the spread of the disease in the country, which will help deal with the security threats. Ideally, the audience of MOH/MOHCC includes Kenyan/Zimbabwean citizens and the state at large. In sum, the securitization scheme components, adapted from Pinto (2014:168) may be shown as below:

In Kenya, just as in Zimbabwe, the securitization of the health issue has seen the police in attendance of burials to ensure compliance. The mourners, chanting funeral dirges are to be controlled to keep social distance as ordered by police and also see to it that they are putting on face masks during the funeral. In Kenya, one example was that of a procession from a Kisumu mortuary to Chiga in Kisumu East sub-county. A convoy of police accompanied the hearse carrying a body from the mortuary. On Friday 13 June 2020 evening, thousands of mourners pelted police with stones and managed to stop the burial of the singer. A source from the police said that the officers who had been on duty were released to go and rest as some reported injuries from the encounter with angry mourners who took the casket and put it under their own custody and vigilance (https://www.standardmedia.co.ke). This shows that the people were protesting the strict regulations introduced on burials for people who succumbed to COVID-19.

Reimagination of Post-COVID-19: Critical Reflections

COVID-19 deaths came along with new aspects, which were less fraught in earlier times. First, the speed at which the dead were supposed to be laid to rest was unimaginable in an African context of burial rites. Secondly, the issue of the context of the dead body and its treatment that were inaccessible to the bereaved were a serious concern. Thirdly, it was not only the grief which people had to deal with, but, fourthly, the physical separation that happened during illness and infection, in the first place. In a post-COVID-19 era, we

Table 10.1 Securitization Scheme

Securitizing Actor	MOH/MOHCC
Existential Threat	COVID-19
Referent Object	People and their health
Speech Act	Asking for controlling the spread of the disease
Audience	Kenyan/Zimbabwean Citizens and Government

foresee that for these four aspects there are serious implications on the citizens and the state in both Kenya and Zimbabwe.

Starting with the first point, the speed at which the dead were laid to rest has financial implications for many communities who have the custom of spending too much money to feed mourners and expensive night vigils. In limiting the number of mourners we re-imagine post-COVID-19 era with fewer attendees for burials in order to curb the spread of COVID-19 pandemic from a securitization perspective. In other words, we imagine the cost of funerals being reduced in future. However, this has cultural and religious implications in a post-COVID-19 era. The fact that some close relatives may miss the hurried event to be attended by few numbers to mourn and grief with the bereaved will turn the burial ceremonies to be a less elaborate event, which used to last several days. This would minimize the goal of holding a "befitting" funeral accompanied by different rites and sacrifices, contrary to African tradition and Christian values (Omonisi 2020). The nature of the send-off may not bring complete closure to those in grief.

On the second point, the body is inaccessible to the bereaved. On this basis, our attention is drawn to orality and bodiless voices. It is imagined that the gaze on bodies will be reduced during death and burials because of securitization. When bodies are covered in body bags and viewing of the dead is banned, it follows that the dead are exempt from the gaze, so that it is voices that are emphasized and not bodies. The ideas of Smith (2005) are instructive and they are summarized here. For Smith (2005), men and women bracket and view the world in distinctive ways, in conjunction with their distinct, biographically articulated life-worlds attuned to the sensory experiences of the body. The loss of a child to its mother has a greater impact on the females than males (Smith 2005). Basing on Smith's observations, if the mourning and grieving parts of the funeral rites are not carefully handled, this would water down the interconnectedness of humanity in post-COVID-19 era. Holding closed-coffin funerals instead of open-casket events rendered death, loss, and grief as footnotes to human flourishing.

Thirdly, under the context of grief in post-COVID-19 pandemic, many parents may wrestle with the need to explain the pandemic to their children without intensifying their fear. Explaining the abrupt and securitized funerals to children may cause feelings of guilt and fear among others. Repeat burial ceremonies for the right persons could produce depressed affect and at the same time decrease family resources. Post-COVID-19 burials may come with additional losses of relationships, health, property, and status. As Pentaris (2022:3) argues, there are varied non-death-related losses including loss of freedom, loss of employment, the loss of contact with family and friends, loss of choice and access to certain services, which have been compounded by death and loss of loved ones due to COVID-19 pandemic.

Fourthly, the physical separation that happened during illness and infection can also be re-imagined in post-COVID-19-related funerals. The restrictions related to the measures of tackling the pandemic by the state and law enforcement agents brought a double tragedy in the event of the death and loss of a loved one. The inability to be near a loved one who is ill and dying has left many grievers in a helpless state of chronic and traumatic grief (Pentaris 2022). There may be increased levels of violence as a result of inadequate grieving in homes. Similarly, many children and the surviving parent would undergo stress due to limited resources, interpersonal relations, inflexible situations, and community as well as security demands. However, in post-COVID-19 it is also reimagined that burials shall be conducted without health officers and police convoys as many would have learned to conform to the practice of social distancing to promote human flourishing.

Conclusion

Burial ceremonies of COVID-19-related deaths in Kenya and Zimbabwe were securitized to ensure that the least number of people attended and further loss of lives was curbed. Additionally, in some cases no food was served to people at funeral gatherings. At the same time, securitization ensured that under the gaze of the police and other security apparatus, the Ministry of Health guidelines were adhered to and also that the dead was neither touched nor viewed by mourners. Securitization processes are embedded in power relations with a complex interplay of health ministry, the state, global health actors, economics, gender, ethnic nationalism, among other variables. The trends and long-term impact of post-COVID-19 are yet to be fully grasped, some of which have been highlighted within the chapter. Though the two countries belong to different regions of Sub-Saharan Africa, the chapter has demonstrated that they have comparable experiences on the multidimensional phenomenon of COVID-19 burial rites in Kenya and Zimbabwe.

References

Africa News. (2021). Zimbabwe Issues Directive on Covid-19 Burials. *Africa News.* https://www.africanews.com/2021/01/14/zimbabwe-issues-directive-on-covid-19-burials/, viewed on 20.10.2022.

Aljezeera News Agency. Available at: Coronavirus pandemic | Today's latest from Al Jazeera.

Bramadat, P. (2014). The Public, the Political and the Possible: Religion and Radicalization in Canada and Beyond. In *Religious Radicalization and Securitization in Canada and Beyond*. Bramadat, P. & L. Dawson (eds.). Toronto: University of Toronto Press, 3–33.

Buzan, B., O. Waever & J. De Wilde (1998). *Security: A New Framework for Analysis.* London: Routledge.

Coronavirus Resource Centre. https://coronavirus.jhu.edu/.

Cucinotta, D. & M. Vanelli. (2020). Who Declares COVID-19 a Pandemic. *Acta Biomed*, 19(1), 157–160.

Elbe, S. (2006). Should HIV/AIDS Be Securitized? The Ethical Dilemmas of Linking HIV/AIDS and Security. *International Studies Quarterly*, 50(1), 119–144.

Hampton, A.J.B. & A.R. Thiessen (2021). Introduction: Theology and Ecology in a Time of Pandemic. In *Pandemic, Ecology and Theology.* Hampton, A.J.B. (ed.). Abingdon, Oxon: Routledge, 1–3.
https://www.standardmedia.co.ke/nyanza/article/2001374894/mourners-defy-police -covid-19-rules-to-escort-body-of-ohangla-musician, viewed on 11.08.2022.
Jacobs, S. (1993). *Pathologic Grief: Maladaptation to Loss.* Washington, DC: American Psychiatric Press.
Kaplow, J.B., C.M. Layne, W.R. Saltzman, S.J. Cozza & R.S. Pynoos (2013). Using Multidimensional Grief Theory to Explore the Effects of Deployment, Reintegration, and Death on Military Youth and Families. *Clinical Child and Family Psychology Review,* 16(3), 322–340. doi: 10.1007/s10567-013-0143-1.
Keyes, K.M., C. Pratt, S. Galea, K.A. McLaughlin, K.C. Koenen & M.K. Shear (2014). The Burden of Loss: Unexpected Death of a Loved One and Psychiatric Disorders across the Life Course in a National Study. *American Journal of Psychiatry,* 171(8), 864–871.
Kihui, N. (2020, May 18). Kenya: 80% of Students Missing Virtual Learning Amid School Closures. AllAfrica.com, 18. Retrieved from https://allafrica.com/stories /202005180774.html.
Laustsen, C. & O. Waever (2000). In Defence of Religion: Sacred Referent. Objects for Securitization. *Millenium,* 29(3), 705–739.
Lusigi, B. (2021). Double Blow to Family as Man's Body Missing. *Standard Media.* https:// www.standardmedia.co.ke/rift-valley/article/2001418810/double-blow-to-family-as -mans-body-missing, viewed on 14.09.21.
Michaud, D.A. (2021). The Multidimensional Unity of Life, Theology, and COVID-19. *Pandemic, Ecology and Theology.* Hampton, A.J.B. (ed.). Abingdon, Oxon: Routledge, 66–77.
Ministry of Health. (2020). Interim Guidelines on Handling of Human Remains Infected with Covid-19. https://www.health.go.ke/wp-content/uploads/2020/06/Interim -Guidance-on-Handling-of-Human-Remains-Infected-with-COVID-19.pdf, viewed on 20.08.2022.
Muromo, L. (2021). Covid-19: Burial Rites Set to Change. *The Standard,* 17 January.
Muronzi, C. (2020). Zimbabwe Tightens Gathering Limits as COVID-19 Cases Rise. *Aljazeera News Agency.* https://www.aljazeera.com/news/2020/12/2/zimbabwe -tightens-gathering-limits-covid-19-cases-rise, viewed on 1.11.2022.
Mutsaka, F. (2021). Zimbabwe Bans Traditional Funerals to Battle Covid-19 Spike. *AP News.* https://apnews.com/article/africa-zimbabwe-coronavirus-pandemic-5f0a3ae 69bd5646d46801d4f2eea3885, viewed on 11.10.2022.
Nwachuku, D. (1992). The Christian Widow in African Culture. In *The Will to Arise: Women, Tradition and the Church in Africa.* Oduyoye, A. & M. Kanyoro (eds.). New York: Orbis Books.
Omorini, A.E. (2020). How Covid-19 Pandemic Is Changing the Africa's Elaborate Burial Rites, Mourning and Grieving. *The Pan African Medical Journal,* 3(Suppl 2), 1–4.
Parkes, C.M. (1998). Coping with Loss: Bereavement in Adult Life. *British Medical Journal,* 316(7134), 856–859. doi: 10.1136/bmj.316.7134.856.
Pentaris, P. (2022). Introduction: Capturing the Beginning of a Long Journey of Loss, Trauma and Grief. In *Death, Grief and Loss in the Context of COVID-19.* Pentaris, P. (ed.). Abingdon, Oxon: Routledge, 1–13.
Pinto, V. (2014). Exploring the Interplay between Framing and Securitization Theory: The Case of the Arab Spring Protests in Bahrain. *Revista Brasiliera de Política Internacional,* 57(1), 162–176.

Sibanda, F., T. Muyambo & E. Chitando (2022). Introduction: Religion and Public Health in the Shadow of COVID-19 Pandemic in Southern Africa. In *Religion and the COVID-19 Pandemic in Southern Africa.* Sibanda, F., T. Muyambo & E. Chitando (eds.). Abingdon, Oxon: Routledge, 1–23.

Shisanya, C. (1996). Death Rituals, the Case of the Abaluhyia of Western Kenya. In *Groaning in Faith: African Women in the Household of God.* Kanyoro, M. & N. Njoroge (eds.). Nairobi: Acton.

Smith, D. (2005). Institutional ethnography: A sociology for people. Toronto: AltaMira Press.

The Star. (2020). Body Mix-Up: Stranger Buried Instead Of COOVID-Positive Cleric. https://www.the-star.co.ke/news/2020-08-03-body-mix-up-stranger-buried-instead -of-covid-positive-cleric/, viewed on 14.09.2021.

TheZimbabwean (2020). Regulations to Curb Spread of COVID-19. https://www .thezimbabwean.co/2020/03/regulations-to-curb-spread-of-covid-19/, viewed 05.11.2022.

Watson, S. (2012). 'Framing' the Copenhagen School: Integrating the Literature on Threat Construction. *Millenium,* 40(2), 279–301.

Wishnick, E. (2010). Dilemmas of Securitization and Health Risk Management in the People's Republic of China: The Cases of SARS and Avian Influenza. *Health Policy and Planning,* 25(6), 454–466.

WHO. (2020). https://covid19.who.int/region/afro/country/cf, viewed on 23.10.2022.

WHO. (2021a). https://covid19.who.int/region/afro/country/ke, viewed on 21.10.2022.

WHO. (2021b). https://covid19.who.int/region/afro/country/zw, viewed on 21.10.2022.

Youde, J. (2008). Who's Afraid of a Chicken? Securitization and Avian Flu. *Democracy and Security,* 4(2), 148–169.

11 Karanga-Shona Funeral and Post-Funeral Rites in the COVID-19 Era

A Case Study of the VaDuma in Bikita, Zimbabwe

Beatrice Taringa¹ and Sophia Chirongoma²

Introduction

Having emerged in 2019, three years later (2021), COVID-19 is continuing to wreak havoc globally, wave after wave and with new variants sprouting. Each time a new wave emerges, it will have metamorphosed such that it continues to threaten humanity's health and well-being worldwide. The pandemic's behavior and traits necessitate a multi-pronged approach in dealing with it. From December 2019 when COVID-19 initially broke out in the city of Wuhan, Hubei Province in China, on the Asian continent (Lone and Ahmad 2020; Zhou et al. 2020), it has been spreading like wild fire across the world. For several months, the city of Wuhan was its epicenter, then it eventually spread from one continent to the other, to Europe and then to Africa. The world is now facing the fourth wave; some European countries are still experiencing heavy casualties. Surprisingly, unlike its predecessors, COVID-19's death toll is still skewing on the side of developed countries that boast of state-of-the-art healthcare facilities. This is raising questions on its causes, management, and containment. The advent of COVID-19 coincided with the fourth Industrial Revolution drive, which some sections of society have been resisting. Regrettably, the resisting communities suddenly found themselves with no choice and no time to reflect upon their religious, cultural, and traditional assets' contribution towards managing, controlling, and containing this global pandemic.

Worldwide, funeral gatherings have been identified as COVID-19 superspreaders. Hence, there has been emphasis on decongesting funeral, burial, and post-burial venues through replacing the physical space with virtual space. In response to the surging numbers of those infected with the coronavirus in Southern Africa, particularly South Africa which shares the border with Zimbabwe put in place some measures to try and contain the pandemic. Inevitably, Zimbabwe introduced stern restrictions in the movement of human communities. Since 31 March 2020, Zimbabwe has been observing various lockdown phases/levels. The implementation of these lockdown

DOI: 10.4324/9781003390732-11

measures immensely impacted on the funeral, burial, and post-burial rites for the vaDuma people who fall under Chief Ziki in Bikita. For instance, the policy that was effected at the peak of the pandemic instructing the medical practitioners, the bereaved, and the funeral parlors to treat all deaths as COVID-19 related, halted huge funeral gatherings since only 50 people were allowed to gather. These regulations struck at the core of the indigenous Shona people's understanding of death and mourning. To make matters worse, the specification that all the funeral processes and procedures must be conducted within 24 hours as well as the regulation that corpses should only be handled by specialized personnel obstructed several close family members and friends from attending funerals. It also hindered them from actively performing the funeral rituals as they would have done under normal circumstances. The restrictions on funeral attendees bring another dimension of virtual funeral attendance to the fore in the Shona people's funeral rituals. Prior to COVID-19, virtual funeral attendance and mourning used to be ridiculed. It was viewed as anti-cultural and perceived as something that is done by people who lack *Unhu/Ubuntu* (Chirongoma and Mutsvedu 2021). Additionally, some funeral insurance companies such as Nyaradzo Funeral Company are now restricting body viewing to immediate family members and in some cases, it is absolutely skipped. It is against this backdrop that this chapter zeroes into discussing post-COVID-19 funeral, burial, and post-burial rites among the Shona, using the vaDuma under Chief Ziki in Bikita district as a case study. The objective is to uncover some of the promises and opportunities emerging from the adjustments ushered in by the COVID-19 pandemic.

Background to the Study

Since Zimbabwe attained independence in 1980, the government has been striving to resuscitate cultural and traditional values. Efforts have been made to revisit and reconfigure indigenous spirituality. This includes death and burial rituals. The COVID-19 epidemic has ushered a momentous occasion for rethinking indigenous funeral rites in the post-COVID-19 era. Like other past pandemics, COVID-19 has presented a litmus test. It has necessitated the rethinking of indigenous funeral rituals and practices. Drawing insights from some recent pandemics including HIV and AIDS, cholera, typhoid, Ebola, influenza, and SAARS, the global community has since discerned the futility of procrastination whilst the epidemic is spreading exponentially. One of the major lessons learnt from the past is that exclusivity and rigidity should make way for inclusion and flexibility in the global village. This necessitates a rethinking of our cultural traditions in line with COVID-19 management, control, and prevention. It also entails applying the tenets of social reconstructionism with the end goal of securing a sustainable and healthy future. Hence, this chapter reflects on how some of the adjustments on death and burial rituals implemented by vaDuma can offer some insights on responding to COVID-19 in other communities in Zimbabwe and worldwide. It also reflects on some lessons that can be drawn from this experience as African communities gaze into the post-COVID-19 era.

As noted by Haralambos and Holborn (1995), culture is a social construct. Being a human discourse, members of the society are constantly contributing towards constructing and reconstructing culture. Ngigi and Busolo (2018) defined culture as an integrated pattern of human behavior, language, thoughts, communication actions, customs, beliefs, values, attitudes, and institutions of racial, ethnic, religious, and social groups. Culture is also a product of socialization. It shapes personalities from the cradle to the grave. It is an oasis of social and religious precincts. Thus, the vaDuma should be able to draw from their cultural wells to carve safe courses in the COVID-19 era and beyond. It is therefore pertinent for cultural lenses to properly guide its practitioners towards foolproof COVID-19 treatment initiatives, containment, management, and prevention measures. Cultural practices, norms, and values are so deeply ingrained such that culture can be perceived as a double-edged sword; i.e. it can either spur or even obstruct perceptual processes resulting in blurred rationalizations (Kanu 2007; Taringa 2014). Drawing insights from a 2018 case study conducted among the Karanga in Machivenyika village in Zaka district, Munamati and Musendekwa (2021) concluded that death and burial practices are havens for the spread of the cholera epidemic. They, therefore, recommended the rethinking of death and burial practices in relation to public health. In unison with Munamati and Musendekwa, we critique how some people tend to use the cultural guise to rigidly justify certain practices regardless of them being detrimental to people's health and well-being. As such, we reiterate the urgent need for rethinking and reconfiguring some funeral rites, which precipitate the spread of COVID-19 and other similar future pandemics. We also foreground the importance of adopting a multi-faceted approach, which facilitates deliberations on how to inculcate life-giving and life-transforming traditions in the face of COVID-19 as well as other pandemics which are yet to emerge.

In concurrence with Lawton (1980), our chapter also proffers that just as the curriculum is a selection from culture, the current COVID-19 era compels us to be proactive and accommodative especially in terms of how we perform funeral rites. As noted by Munamati and Musendekwa (2021), a common Shona practice is for mourners to gather in large numbers for some days. These massive gatherings where people "perform the ritual of *kubata maoko*, which literally means, to hold hands" [expressing solidarity through the bereavement process] (Chitakure 2017: 62), provide fertile ground for the spreading of COVID-19. Chirisa et al. (2021) expound on the unanticipated changes to such practices in the wake of COVID-19 as follows:

> In the context of the COVID-19-induced ban on social gatherings, most communal cultural practices may cease to exist in the future. The cultural and symbolic significance of death rituals, such as hand-shaking the

bereaved as a sign of sharing their sorrow, known as *kubata maoko* has been temporarily stopped by Covid-19.

(Chirisa et al. 2021: 4–5)

It was also explained that a domestic animal, normally a cow, is slaughtered for ritual purposes as well as the practical logistics of feeding the guests. Chitakure (2017: 64) explains that the ritual slaughter of the animal among the Shona is known as *nhevedzo* (accompaniment), which denotes that by slaughtering the animal and consuming its meat, the bereaved are literally pouring libations to accompany the deceased to the grave and more importantly, to the spirit world.

Furthermore, some rituals are performed after the funeral. For instance, family members and close associates gather to distribute the deceased's estate among those who are eligible to inherit. In some instances, another domestic animal will be slaughtered sometime after the funeral (three months, a year, or several years later) for the *kurova guva* (bringing back/domesticating the spirit of the dead) ceremony (Vambe 2009; Mwandayi 2011; Chitakure 2021). As elucidated by Shoko (2007), the Shona are weary that if they fail to conduct the funeral rites properly, this may raise the ire of the spirit of the deceased, which will inflict misfortunes among the living relatives. It is against this backdrop that our chapter propounds for continual adaptation of the Shona people's burial rituals in line with COVID- 19 regulations and other future epidemics whilst remaining within the critical threshold to ensure that the dead will not mete out punishment among the living. Striking a balance between curbing the COVID-19 pandemic and other future communicable diseases is crucial because public health awareness, protection, and care-giving are mandatory in our times and more importantly for posterity. Hence, this chapter examines some facets of the funeral practices performed by vaDuma. This examination will assist us to assess whether these practices expose or protect members of the vaDuma community from the adverse effects of COVID-19. Tapping into the experiences of the vaDuma people, the chapter also examines whether the existing intervention programs may have underestimated the impact of culture in the management, control, and prevention of the spread of COVID-19 among the Shona people in Zimbabwe. It is our contention that any hesitancy in implementing the much-needed drastic cultural modifications might result in the wiping out of human communities not only among the vaDuma community in Bikita, but other indigenous communities which share common beliefs and practices with vaDuma.

Theoretical Framework

The theoretical framework illuminates the study's methodological design (Mpofu et al., 2013). The discussion is undergirded by the social reconstruction theory in sync with the *Unhu/Ubuntu* philosophy. As explicated by Letsiou (2014), the process of social reconstruction entails making culture relevant to the daily lived realities. It elicits a progressive approach towards life. This enhances the agency of societal members to take charge of their lives. The main focus is to mobilize the Shona in particular, the vaDuma to become agents of cultural change in relation to COVID-19 management, control, and prevention. It propounds a reconfiguration of the Shona religio-cultural aspects to do with funeral, burial, and post-burial practices in the COVID-19 era and beyond using vaDuma of Chief Ziki in Bikita district as a case study. In concurrence with Munamati and Musendekwa (2021), we argue that the funeral, burial, and post-burial practices of the vaDuma people cannot remain unchanged if these practices are meant to serve its members during the COVID-19 era and beyond. We, therefore, propose that the funeral and post-burial rituals must be reconfigured in a COVID-19-sensitive style that is life-saving. We envisage that this would instill indigenous responsive measures in the wake of COVID-19 and other pandemics that might emerge in the future.

The social reconstruction theory is characteristic of postmodernism. It is a cultural and ethnic framework competing with existing norms and powers that have the propensity of sacrificing Africans and their social rights on the altar of elevating the Western modes of knowing to a higher pedestal. In line with Letsiou's (2014) approach, it is our conviction that social reconstructionism is the appropriate theory for the purposes of this study. Social reconstructionism critiques the Eurocentric view of intervention programs that are entirely bio-medical whilst neglecting the religio-cultural factors in epidemic containment. The same sentiments were raised by Munamati and Musendekwa (2021), who after examining the ripple effects of Shona burial practices in Zaka district concluded that funeral practices serve as a harbinger for spreading the cholera pandemic. Following in the same footsteps, this chapter propounds for the reconfiguration of the vaDuma burial practices as a crucial survival strategy in the COVID-19 era and beyond. Kanu (2007) defines tradition as a set of beliefs, practices, values, and modes of thinking that are inherited from the past and that may organize and regulate ways of living and of making sense of the world. Kanu further argues that tradition exists only in constant altera-tion and as such it can be rethought, transmuted, and recreated in novel ways in response to the meanings and demands of emergent situations. In the same vein, we highlight the urgent need for vaDuma community to reframe and rethink their inherited funeral rituals in light of the COVID-19 pandemic containment framework. The reconfigured religio-cultural framework should become an empowering tool for preserving societal health and well-being in the COVID-19 era and beyond.

Through reconstructing their religio-cultural values, vaDuma community will be better equipped to effectively manage not only pandemics but also vari-ous other situations threatening their health and well-being. This approach also obliges them to be flexible and adaptive to enable them to embrace continu-ous changes in their socioeconomic and political arenas. Thus, the ideology of social reconstruction can be linked to the collective production of meaning and knowledge through interaction. In line with the social reconstruction theory,

Kanu (2007) tenders that tradition is neither monolithic nor merely preserved and handed down to subsequent generations. In Kanu's view, tradition has been handed down consecutively over time. Hence, traditions undergo changes since the circumstances for the receiving generation are never exactly the same as those of the transmitting one. Granted, vaDuma ancestors that handed down the current funeral rituals had no inkling of the COVID-19 pandemic. Henceforth, the current vaDuma community needs to unpack and repackage the funeral ritual framework congruent with the COVID-19 situation as well as taking contingent measures for other future airborne pandemics.

Research Methodology

The chapter adopts the inductive theory as well as the interpretivist epistemology. As noted by Bryman (2012: 6), the inductive theory "implies that a set of theoretical ideas drive the collection and analysis of data." In sync with Morgan and Sklar (2012: 73), we are cognizant of the fact that "reality is a social construction phenomenon and there are multiple realities." Similarly, Creswell (2009: 8) restates that, "there are varied and multiple truths, leading the researcher to look for complexity of views rather than narrowing the few categories or ideas." Hence, this chapter looks at reality from the vantage point of vaDuma people, focusing particularly on their capacity to adopt COVID-19-sensitive funeral and post-burial practices. The key findings presented here are drawn from interviews conducted with a homogenous and representative sample of 20 study participants. This includes five village heads, one advisor for each village head, as well as two male and two female adults from each village head's area of jurisdiction in Chief Ziki's chiefdom. Selecting the study participants was made in line with Punch's (2009: 162) affirmation that "we cannot research on everyone, everywhere, doing everything." They were asked questions pertaining to the resilience of vaDuma community when it comes to renegotiating funeral and post-burial rituals in light of the COVID-19 pandemic. The decision to focus on funeral and post-burial rituals was also informed by the understanding that religious and cultural beliefs serve as a frame of reference in people's behavior and mental operations. This was also confirmed by the previous researches reviewed in this study, which noted that religious and cultural beliefs have also contributed to the spread of epidemics in the past (Munamati and Musendekwa 2021).

For the collection and presentation of data, we triangulated textual analysis of COVID-19 sensitization communications and interview excerpts. As noted by Punch (2009: 133), "data collection and analysis are done in cycles and stops after two repetitions and even continue until theoretical saturation is achieved." For data analysis, we made use of the conventional content analysis of the interview excerpts with a specific focus on how vaDuma have adopted COVID-19-sensitive funeral and post-burial rites. Besides the critical analysis, the data were also triangulated with discourse analysis to help in describing, interpreting, and explaining such relationships as well as trying to account for the resilience of vaDuma funeral and post-burial practices. The key themes that emerged from this field research have been presented thematically.

Significance of the Chapter

There has been considerable amount of literature focusing on death, burial, and post-burial practices in Zimbabwe (Bourdillon 1987; Shoko 2007; Vambe 2009; Mwandayi 2011; Saidi 2017; Chitakure 2017, 2021). Other scholars have also restated the vitality of reconfiguring funeral rituals during the era of pandemics (Munamati and Musendekwa 2021; Chirisa et al. 2021). Writing about the essential need for transforming some cultural practices within the context of the HIV and AIDS pandemic in Africa, Chitando (2008) reiterates that cultural traditions are not cast in stone, hence, they cannot remain static especially in times of crisis. Discussing the Shona people's understanding of death and how they conduct funerals in contemporary Zimbabwe, Saidi (2017) proffers that there's a need for reconfiguring identities as societies participate in funeral rituals. In the same light, Chirisa et al. (2021) also mention how COVID-19 has drastically altered countless deeply cherished Zimbabwean indigenous practices, including how communities conduct funerals. However, there seems to be a scholarly gap in terms of literature addressing how specific indigenous communities are transforming their funeral practices during the COVID-19 era and beyond. There also seems to be a scholarly lacuna on literature propounding for how to practically reconfigure indigenous African funeral practices in compliance with the COVID-19 safety regulations without rendering asunder some core traditional funeral practices. These are dimensions that this chapter seeks to address. Focusing on the vaDuma in Bikita district, this chapter emphasizes the need for African indigenous communities to be the ones who determine what is sensible and life-preserving when transforming cultural traditions, particularly when it comes to conducting funeral and post-burial rites during the COVID-19 era and beyond. It also proposes possible ways in which indigenous communities can possibly strike a balance in terms of culturally transforming some of their funeral rites in a COVID-19-compliant manner whilst preserving some practices which do not expose cultural practitioners to COVID-19.

Brief Review of Related Literature

A review of related literature assists researchers to locate the study alongside similar scholarly works. This study is located within the context of indigenous African funeral and post-burial rituals. It also fits within literature which addresses the interface of dominant religio–cultural traditions and the spread of pandemics in Africa. Our study finds resonance with Munamati and Musendekwa (2021) who make the following remarks:

> African burial practices are a threat to public health in Zimbabwe. They expose people since their practice need the living to get in contact with the

corpse ... African burial practices [are] another underlying factor responsible for the spread of cholera in Zimbabwe... neglecting the impact of
African burial practices limits our horizon in combating determinants of
the spread of cholera in Zimbabwe.

(Munamati and Musendekwa 2021: 6–7)

Drawing insights from the conclusions and the recommendations raised by
Munamati and Musendekwa (2021), this study focuses on exploring how
funeral and post-funeral rituals among the Shona can be reconfigured in a
manner which insulates the community from exposure to COVID-19 as well
as curb the spread of similar pandemics in the future. Whilst acknowledging
the pertinent need for reconfiguring the Shona funeral rites, this study also
cautions against hasty changes that are insensitive to the enshrined cultural
traditions which define and humanize the Shona. This is also iterated by Saidi
(2017) who confers that:

> Death and funerals offer a context that draws very interesting semiotic
> signals that define death, the dead and management of death itself ... there
> exists an attempt to demarcate the dead from the living without necessar-
> ily questioning cultural belief systems as well as connections to the world
> of the dead who are culturally assumed to have assumed power of the
> spiritual.

(Saidi 2017: 353)

Hence, this study calls for a balanced, flexible, and accommodative reconfiguring of Shona funeral and post-funeral rituals to ensure that they effectively
respond to the crisis posed by COVID-19 as well as enhance their resilience
to similar future pandemics. However, we are also alert to the danger of completely disrupting the ingrained traditions such that it threatens to destroy the
community's understanding of death and the attendant rituals. The active
involvement of the community's gatekeepers is therefore crucial whenever
embarking on such an undertaking. Chitakure (2021: 104) explains this point
as follows:

> ancestors are unpredictable, and sometimes vindictive. Although all the
> death rituals should be performed meticulously, the living family mem-
> bers have to prepare for any eventuality that may arise because of any-
> thing that may aggrieve the spirit of the deceased during his [her] last
> days.

The above excerpt lays bare the fact that funeral rituals have a primary significance for the Shona people. Funeral rituals serve a dual purpose, to express
the bereaved family's respect and honor for the dearly departed as well as safeguarding against aggravating the anger of the deceased's spirit. Chirisa et al.
(2021) also bemoan the manner in which some of the COVID-19 safety

measures have negatively impacted the indigenous Zimbabwean populace's religio-cultural practices. They highlight that:

> Getting closure and saying "goodbye" to departed loved ones is critical for all human beings, and doing this communally is of prime importance in most African cultures. However, the dawning of the COVID-19 epidemic has changed everything in terms of social intercourse, traditions and relations ... In the context of the COVID-19 epidemic, not only has death and the living-dead [ancestors] lost their spiritual significance and status, these communally respected cultures may disappear altogether and lose respect as deaths become more medicalised and policed due to the epidemic.
>
> (Chirisa et al. 2021: 4)

The above sentiments necessitate undertaking a study anchored upon establishing a middle path to ensure that the re-concenceptualizing of funeral rituals will not annihilate those practices which are worthwhile preserving. Maintaining the same thrust, Vambe (2009) reaffirms the central importance of the Shona post-funeral ritual called *kurova guva* (domesticating/bringing back the spirit of the dead). This is an integral part of processing grief, particularly for the bereaved family. Hence, close friends, associates, and members of the extended family will gather to perform this ritual. He puts it across as follows:

> While the Shona are not perceived as a group with homogeneous cultural values, there is general agreement that *Kurova Guva* is a distinct Shona cultural rite of passage ... The *Kurova Guva* ritual-myth ceremony reasserts the continued spiritual existence of the dead person by seeking to bring that person back into the community of ancestral spirits that are recognised by the dead person's surviving family members ... the physical death of the flesh is not the ultimate terminus of "human" life.
>
> (Vambe 2009: 112)

Similarly, Chitakure (2017) foregrounds the centrality of *kurova guva/kugadzira mufi* ritual among the Karanga-Shona. He elucidates this point in the following words: the word *kugadzira*, that is mostly used by the Karanga of Masvingo for this process means to make or produce. In this case, it refers to the making of an ancestor (Chitakure 2017: 64). Cognizant of the central importance that the Shona people place on *kurova guva* ceremony, we are therefore proposing that when reconfiguring this ritual, there must be concerted efforts to preserve its essence whilst endeavoring to be compliant with COVID-19 safety regulations. For instance, the ritual can be performed by a smaller number of people who will be observing all safety protocols so as to minimize the spread of any communicable viruses or bacteria. Furthermore, we concur with Chirisa et al. (2021), who caution against the danger of embracing changes which might end up being detrimental to the society's social fiber. They state their point as follows:

> The COVID-19 epidemic appears to be adding to the already in motion reconfiguration, re-conceptualisation and even re-evaluation of the functions of certain social and religious institutions in the society. Communally, celebrated events, such as births, deaths and marriages may become less popular and visible but may become privatised or individualised. So, the subsequent question is will Zimbabweans live and adapt, or die with these changes in their culture and society?
>
> (Chirisa et al. 2021: 4–5)

Responding to the issues raised by the scholars cited above, this study draws insights from the vaDuma in Bikita to illustrate that it is possible to reconfigure and re-conceptualize the funeral and post-funeral rituals in line with COVID-19 protocols without completely decimating the core religio-cultural values. Furthermore, using vaDuma as a case study, we propose some practical steps that can be adopted in embracing the changes to ensure that indigenous communities are well equipped to deal with the current global pandemic as well as similar future pandemics.

Below, we present the key issues emerging from the field research. The discussion is anchored on how vaDuma are aligning funeral and post-burial rituals in light of the COVID- 19 pandemic as well as how this has implications for the future. These are presented in thematic form below.

Presenting the Study Findings

Introduction

As has been noted above, the study participants also affirmed the fact that just like other preceding pandemic, COVID-19 has necessitated the reconfiguring and reconceptualization of how African communities are socially organized. As such, funeral and post-burial rituals have been equally impacted. The key issues emerging from the interviews have been divided into two segments: first, we discuss some recurring issues raised by the study participants pertaining to the changes embraced on funeral rituals during the COVID-19 era; second, we present some keys issues that were raised regarding the adjustments made to the post-funeral rituals. We conclude this section by highlighting some lessons and opportunities for the future in Africa as we continue to grapple with the aftermaths of the COVID-19 era.

Reconfiguring Funeral Rituals during the COVID-19 Era

VaDuma in Bikita shared various adjustments that have been implemented on the funeral and post-burial rituals. Study participant 1 shared the following:

Since the ushering in of this *dzibwamupengo* (COVID-19), whenever death occurs in the village, only the closest family members will gather at the deceased's homestead before and after burial. The rest only go there briefly during the day *kundobata mavoko* (to express condolences to the bereaved). More people will arrive on the day when the body will spend the night at the homestead. After burial, again, only the closest relatives will remain behind, whilst the rest will be dispersing.

Clearly, the "new normal" has introduced a totally new way of mourning as well as a new way of showing solidarity with the bereaved. Study participant 2 added that:

> In the past, all the newly arrived mourners would express condolences by moving around the homestead, shaking the hands of everybody gathered, whilst saying *nematambudziko/nedzinoparadza* (condolences/sorry about your loss). In some cases, the close family members and friends would embrace each other and console each other as they cried together. However, now the handshakes and embracing is forbidden due to the COVID-19 safety measures. Instead, mourners can either use the elbow greeting or just wave at each other whilst vocalizing the words *nematambudziko/nedzinoparadza*.

The other changes that have been introduced were outlined by study participant 3 who said:

> The buses from the funeral parlours which used to ferry mourners have either stopped or they sometimes reduce the number of passengers. The hearse used to ferry at least one or several close relatives of the deceased but now it only ferries the deceased. This has considerably reduced the number of mourners. Also, the washing and dressing of the corpse which used to be performed by the closest family members is now being conducted by the funeral service companies before transporting the body to its final resting place.

The ritual washing of the body has been a long-held tradition among the Shona. Unfortunately, the risk of spreading COVID-19 has led to the temporary halting of this ritual. Whilst this is a noble initiative, it takes away the bereaved family's opportunity to actively participate in this final parting ritual. Instead of bathing the corpse, now, it is the bereaved who have to constantly sanitize their hands as well as wear masks throughout the time they are surrounded by mourners. This was expressed by study participant 4 as follows:

> Upon arrival at a homestead where there's a funeral, there will be ushers standing at all the entry points, who will ensure that they have administered a hand sanitizer whilst offering clean water for hand washing. At

some funerals, mourners will also be provided with disposal masks to ensure that all safety measures have been observed.

Whereas in the past, body viewing was a public affair, now it's usually a preserve for the immediate family members. In the event when one dies due to COVID-19-related illness, then there will be no body viewing. Study participant 5 shared the following:

> There have been some funerals in this community where body viewing was skipped because the person had died due to COVID-19. The bereaved were inconsolable because for most people, body viewing accords them an opportunity to see their loved one for the last time. This helps them to bid farewell to the deceased. What is even more painful is that for COVID-19 cases, the coffin will be carried by health personnel and even the burial will be conducted by health professionals. As a result, the bereaved, together with fellow church members [who usually lead the burial procedures], will be reduced to mere spectators.

The risk of contamination has led to the adoption of all these measures. Failure to observe the safety measures will continue to make funeral gatherings hot spots for spreading the pandemic. In an endeavor to reduce the length of time when people will be gathered for the funeral, most families have resorted to conducting the burial within the shortest period possible. This means that some close family members who are either out of the country or residing somewhere far from where the burial will be conducted will end up missing the funeral. This has increased the use of technology to facilitate the virtual funeral attendance for those who would have failed to physically attend the funeral. The gradual adoption of virtual funeral guests was mentioned by study participant 6; she said:

> It used to be unthinkable for a close relation to fail to attend the funeral of their kin. Sometimes, the burial date would be pushed further ahead in order to allow time for mourners to travel from all corners of the world so as to converge at the funeral. Nowadays, the travel restrictions have made it difficult for people to travel from one province to the other and it becomes even more complex if someone has to cross borders. Instead, people are resorting to using technology to allow mourners to participate via cyberspace.

Hence, whereas virtual funeral guests used to be frowned upon and they were considered as people who want to show off their technological prowess, nowadays, blended funerals have become the order of the day.

Aligning Post-Burial Rituals with COVID-19 Safety Procedures

The COVID-19 pandemic has also prompted the reconfiguration of post-burial rituals. Study participant 7 expounded this as follows:

The ritual of *kugova nhumbi dzemufi* (distributing the deceased's estate) which used to be presided over by a huge number of relatives and friends is now being conducted by a much smaller number of people who would have remained after the burial. However, if the person died of COVID-19, his/her clothes will not be distributed because of the fear of spreading the virus.

Having to dispose of a deceased relative's clothing items is a really heartbreaking process because among the Shona, inheriting a loved one's personal effects gives them a sense of affinity and continuity. Thus, discarding the items is tantamount to cutting off ties with the deceased. Difficult as it is, this has been necessitated by the crisis in our midst. Another new development is the introduction of disinfecting a homestead after the mourners have dispersed. Study participant 8 explained it thus:

> Soon after the bulk of the mourners have left after the burial, some bereaved families have embraced the tradition of disinfecting the homestead in line with COVID-19 safety measures. Although some community members initially critiqued this due to the belief that it appeared as if they were disrespecting the dead and the mourners, generally, people have come to appreciate this as an important safety measure to safeguard against the spread of COVID-19.

Before the outbreak of COVID-19, this would have been regarded as anathema but now vaDuma and other African communities have come to realize the efficacy of such precautionary measures.

Another common post-burial ritual among the Karanga-Shona is *masukafoshoro*, literally meaning "cleaning off the dirty from the shovels." This ritual is usually conducted after a month or a few months after the burial. It is intended to serve as an opportunity for the bereaved to express their token of gratitude to their surrounding community members who assisted them with material resources, manual labor, and their physical presence during the funeral. Study participant 9 described the adjustments made to this ritual as follows:

> Pre-COVID-19, local people would start gathering for the *masukafoshoro* ceremony at least the evening before the ceremony. They would be socializing, singing, dancing, and drinking traditional beer and maheu (locally brewed non-alcoholic beverage). However, due to restrictions on big gatherings, nowadays, only the few close relatives traveling from afar will arrive the day before. Otherwise, all the local people will arrive in the morning on the day of the ceremony and they will depart on the same day at the end of ceremony. In some cases, those who can afford will simply transact money via eco-cash (mobile money transfer facility) into the accounts of individual community members who will then individually buy their food and beer which was supposed to be consumed at the event. This is

intended to reduce incidences of gathering people together as this exposes the community members to the susceptibility of COVID-19 infection.

The innovations mentioned above are pragmatic measures that can be adopted in other African communities to mitigate the spread of COVID-19 and other similar epidemics which might emerge in the future.

As has been noted earlier, for the Karanga-Shona people, the ritual for *magadziro/kugadzira mufi/ kurova guva* (domesticating/bringing back home the spirit of the dead/transforming the deceased's spirit into an ancestor) is a very important rite of passage. COVID-19 has also occasioned some modifications to this ritual. Study participant 10 articulated these as follows:

> Normally, *magadziro* will be conducted between 6 months to two or three years after burial. This is a huge gathering where the deceased's family will slaughter a cow, prepare a lot of food and traditional beverage to be consumed on the day of the ceremony. The ceremony begins at night where the participants will be drinking traditional beer whilst singing and dancing throughout the night. It will be concluded the following morning when people will visit the gravesite to pour some libations to welcome the deceased's spirit into the ancestral realm. Since the outbreak of COVID-19, some families have deferred conducting such ceremonies until after COVID-19 is officially under control. Hence, the period between burial and the conducting of the ceremony has been considerably increased. Others are conducting the ceremony but they have significantly reduced the number of participants.

Clearly the communal spirit, which is characteristic of the *magadziro* ritual, has been negatively impacted. However, it is heartening to note that the vaDuma people in Bikita have managed to adjust some of the aspects whilst preserving the integral part of the ritual. Being proactive in that manner helps to prepare African indigenous communities to deal with the current crisis as well as any future pandemics of this nature.

Due to the profound influence of Christianity in Zimbabwe, just like other African communities, in some families, the *manyaradzo* (Christian memorial service to console the bereaved) often takes the place of *magadziro*. This is whereby members of the church where the bereaved used to fellowship will gather to conduct a church service commemorating the life of the deceased whilst preaching to the bereaved to counsel them and encourage them to live an upright Christian life in preparation for their own death. Just like *magadziro*, study participant 11 explained that the scheduling of this ceremony, the processes followed, and the number of participants have all been reconfigured. All these changes are significant indicators of the community's ability to re-conceptualize their traditions for their own benefit as well as for the benefit of future generations. Below, we discuss some important lessons learnt from the insights shared by the study participants.

Lessons Learnt from COVID-19 and Opportunities for the Future

Reflecting on the related literature, which has been reviewed, as well as the insights emerging from the study participants presented above, it is apparent that COVID-19 has wrought changes and a renegotiating of religio-cultural traditions, including funeral and post-burial rituals. Whilst this chapter is based on a case study of the vaDuma in Bikita, their innovative modifications of funeral and post-funeral rituals in the wake of COVID-19 can be embraced as important signposts for how other African indigenous communities can deal with future pandemics.

For instance, making use of virtual platforms to facilitate electronic funeral attendance is a progressive move in the current times since we are living in a global village where information, communication, and technology (ICT) has taken charge in almost all circles of life. This is a befitting reconstruction of religio-cultural practices particularly for millions of Zimbabweans who are scattered across the globe in pursuance of educational and employment opportunities. Granted, vaDuma have revolutionized their funeral rituals in line with global technological trends. There is a high likelihood that electronic funeral attendance, which was initially perceived as a deviance, will soon become the norm not only in Zimbabwe but globally. Besides the convenience afforded to the bereaved who will be separated from their family and friends by time and space, it also greatly contributes towards decongesting funeral venues. Thus, virtual mourning has ceased to be viewed neither as a show off nor a sign of lacking *Ubuntu/Unhu*. As Chirongoma and Mutsvedu (2021: 160) aptly put it across, "Zimbabwe is a classic case whereby ICT helps to reinforce community bonds as prescribed by *Ubuntu/Unhu*." This also affirms Kanu's (2007) view that tradition only exists in constant alteration, it can be rethought, transmuted, and recreated in novel ways in response to the meanings and demands of an emergent situation. Undoubtedly, some of these changes that have been embraced during the COVID-19 era reveal that it is impossible to revert to traditional ways and reverse all the gains that have been made this far. There is no more turning back as diasporians will ever be there and the virtual operating space is gaining ground as it is more appealing in the social, religious, and economic environment we are living in.

By adopting the tradition of disinfecting and fumigating the homestead after the funeral as well as transforming some funeral and post-burial practices as described by the study participants cited above, confirms that vaDuma rituals are products of human discourse which can be deconstructed and reconstructed to address specific needs. This fits in well with the African Union's Agenda 2063, which calls for cultural dynamism, mutation, and reconfiguration within the context of globalization. VaDuma community's flexibility and ability to align cultural intangible resources ensures their survival amidst the tidal wave of COVID-19 as well as similar pandemics they might encounter in the future. The transformative stance in funeral rituals adds credence to

Kershaw's (2018) view, who whilst writing within the context of the HIV and AIDS epidemic noted the efficacy of the decision made by the Kargbo in Sierra Leone – to bury all deceased people in a hygienic way regardless of the cause of death in 2016. He noted that this move significantly reduced stigmatization. The same approach can be adopted when conducting burials and post-funeral rituals in the context of COVID-19. If all African nation states were to adopt such a stance even beyond the COVID-19 era, this would make a world of difference when it comes to containing any emergent airborne pandemics.

Another important lesson learnt from this case study is the fact that when reconfiguring religio-cultural traditions, the top-down approach is not the best way forward. Rather, intervention strategies whereby the health personnel conduct sensitization workshops and brainstorming sessions with the community gatekeepers who will cascade the information into the community is a better approach. The discussions with the study participants also revealed that the process of reconfiguring the funeral and post-burial rituals was a success mainly because of the bottom-up approach, which enhanced community ownership of the processes. Peering into the future, these are issues that also need to be taken into consideration whenever dealing with a crisis similar to the COVID-19 pandemic.

Based on our findings, we also suggest the pertinent need for acknowledging that for some people, it is not easy to discard traditional and cultural resources as these have been rubbed into them to such an extent that they erroneously appear natural and biological. This seemingly makes people prioritize their cultural traditions without making enough room to accommodate other pressing scientific facts, which necessitate urgent adjustments. Such a rigid stance has the propensity of putting communities at risk in the context of COVID-19 as well as other similar emergent pandemics in the future. In this light, there is therefore need for sensitivity and being accommodative when introducing major shifts in religio-cultural practices. This should entail adopting a middle path whereby all precautionary measures are fitted into the affected people's culture, resultantly coming up with a hybridized version. In line with the social reconstruction theory, the COVID-19 response measures among vaDuma in Bikita have foregrounded the futility of cultural rigidity. It has also reaffirmed the positive benefits of cultural fluidity and flexibility. Thus, moving ahead into the post-COVID-19 era, the African traditional religio-cultural framework should be construed in such a way that its adherents are well equipped to cleverly maneuver and take a safe route whilst navigating any unanticipated social, economic, and political challenges. In essence, whether it is funeral rituals or any other African religio-cultural traditions, they must be life-sustaining and they must capacitate the practitioners to continue floating regardless of the intensity of the turbulence in which they are sailing.

Conclusion

COVID-19 has literally taken the world by storm. Based on our case study, it is evident that vaDuma funeral rituals are facing drastic transformative processes.

Willingly or unwillingly, vaDuma find themselves engaging in a religio-cultural reconfiguration in line with COVID- 19 safety measures. This is in sync with the social reconstruction theory, which is the theoretical framework adopted in this chapter. The active participation of the vaDuma community from the grassroots in reshaping their intangible cultural heritage is central to ensuring compliance and it minimizes the likelihood of tissue rejection. Normally, when the transition is so fast and abrupt and does not accord religio-cultural systems time to acclimatize, systems are subjected to cultural shock. Hence, our discussion has restated that a middle-path approach is needed. The fact remains, after COVID-19, that the vaDuma traditional, religio-cultural funeral, burial, and post-burial practices will never be the same. COVID-19 has also ushered in new developments like professionals conducting funeral rituals and practices. Similarly, new business innovations like hiring professional mourners, funeral events managers, and video recording funeral proceedings have become more popularized. These changes will continue to be part and parcel of African funeral practices even beyond the COVID-19 era. The ushering in of COVID-19 response measures has also demystified the funeral rituals and practices like body viewing, putting sand into the grave, bathing the corpse, the furor about having the body lying in state for the whole night, hand shaking and accompanying the deceased's body in a hearse. Undoubtedly, a case study of the vaDuma has brought to the fore some significant lessons that can equip other African communities on how to deal with epidemics in the future. In conclusion, it is our conviction that if similar studies were to be conducted on other African indigenous communities, this would provide more empirical evidence to guide Africans in mapping the way forward beyond the COVID-19 era.

Notes

1 Belvedere Technical Teachers College, Research Methods & Statistics.
2 (a) Midlands State University, Department of Religious Studies and Ethics; (b) Research Fellow in the Resarch Institute in Theology and Religious Studies at the University of South Africa.

References

Bourdillon, M. F. C. (1987). *The Shona Peoples: An Ethnography of the Contemporary Shona, with Special Reference to Their Religion*. Gweru: Mambo Press.
Bryman, A. (2012). *Social Research Methods* (4th ed.). Oxford: Oxford University Press.
Chirisa, I., et al. (2021). The Impact and Implications of COVID-19: Reflections on the Zimbabwean Society. *Social Sciences & Humanities Open*, 4(1), 1–10. https://doi.org/10.1016/j.ssaho.2021.100183.
Chirongoma, S. and Mutsvedu, L. (2021). The Ambivalent Role of Technology on Human Relationships: An Afrocentric Exploration In B. D. Okyere-Manu (ed.), *African Values, Ethics and Technology: Questions, Issues and Approaches*. London: Springer, Palgrave and MacMillan Publishers, pp. 155–172.

Chitakure, J. (2017). *African Traditional Religion Encounters Christianity: The Resilience of a Demonized Religion*. Oregon: Pickwick Publications.

Chitakure, J. (2021). *Death Rituals among the Karanga of Zimbabwe: Praxis, Significance, and Changes*. Oregon: Wipf and Stock Publishers.

Chitando, E. (2008). Religious Ethics, HIV and AIDS and Masculinities in Southern Africa. In R. Nicolson (ed.), *Persons in Community: African Ethics in a Global Culture* (pp. 1- 18). Durban: University of KwaZulu-Natal Press.

Creswell, J. W. (2009). *Research Design: Qualitative, Quantitative and Mixed Methods Approach* (3rd ed.). London: Sage Publications.

Haralambos, M. and Holborn, M. (1995). *Sociology: Themes and Perspectives*. Glasgow: Collins Educational

Kanu, Y. (2007). Tradition and Educational Reconstruction in Africa Post-Colonial and Global Times: The Case of Sierra Leone. *African Studies Quarterly*, 10(3), 65–84.

Kershaw, H. (2018). Remembering the Don't Die of Ignorance' Campaign Online London Hygiene and Tropical Medicine. Available at http://placing thepublic.Ishtm.ac.uk/rem embering-the-don't-die-of-ignorance-campaign. Accessed 05/12/2019.

Lawton, D. (1980). Curriculum Planning and Technological Change. *Education + Training*, 22(4), 124–124. https://doi.org/10.1108/eb016710.

Letsiou, M. (2014). *ART Intervention and Social Reconstruction in Education: Secondary Education, ART Education Researched*. Greece: Athens School of Fine Art.

Lone, S. A. and Ahmad, A. (2020). COVID-19 Pandemic – An African Perspective. *Emerging Microbes and Infections*, 9(1), 1300–1308. https://doi.org/10.1080/22221751 .2020.1775132.

Morgan, B. and Sklar, R. H. (2012). Sampling and Research Paradigms. In J. G. Maree (Ed.), *Complete Your Thesis or Dissertation successfully: Practical Guidelines*. Cape Town: Juta.

Mpofu, V., Otulaja, F. S., and Mushayikwa, E. (2013). Towards Culturally Relevant Classroom Science: A Theoretical Framework Focusing on Traditional Plant Healing. *Cultural Studies of Science Education*, 9, 221–242.

Munamati, S. and Musendekwa, M. (2021). African Burial Practices as Havens That Promote the Spread of Cholera in Zimbabwe. *International Journal of Applied Research on Public Health Management*, 7(1), 1–10.

Mwandayi, C. (2011). *Death and After-Life Rituals in the Eyes of the Shona: Dialogue with Shona Customs in the Quest for Authentic Inculturation*. Bamberg: University of Bamberg Press.

Ngigi, S. and Busolo, D. (2018). Behaviour Change Communication in Health Promotion: Approaches, Practices and Promising Application. *International Journal of Innovative Research and Development*, 7(19), 84–95.

Punch, K. F. (2009). *Introduction to Research Methods in Education*. Thousand Oaks: Sage.

Saidi, U. (2017). *Agonya Neiko Mfanha Uyu?* Of Death and Funerals – A Semiotic Exploration of the Shona Funeral Ritual in Zimbabwe. *African Identities*, 15(4), 353–366. https://doi .org/10.1080/14725843.2017.1319758.

Shoko, T. (2007). *Karanga Indigenous Religion in Zimbabwe: Health and Well-Being*. Ashgate Publishing Limited.

Vambe, M. T. (2009). The Function of Songs in the Shona Ritual-Myth of *Kurova Guva*. *Muziki*, 6(1), 112–119. https://doi.org/10.1080/18125980903037393.

Taringa, B. (2014). Implications of Portrayal of Women in Shona Proverbs. *Zimbabwe Journal of Educational Research (ZJER)*, 26(3), 395–409.

Zhou, P., et al. (2020). A Pneumonia Outbreak Associated with a New Coronavirus of Probable Bat Origin. *Nature*, 579(7798), 270–273.

12 The COVID-19 Restrictions and Clashes with Shona Cultural Practices and Values

Post-COVID Era Lessons for Zimbabwe

Liveson Tatira, Shamiso Tatira, and
Gaynor Paradza

Introduction

This chapter focuses on the case of Zimbabwe's Shona people's conduct of funerals and weddings in response to the global COVID-19 restrictions in order to highlight the importance of local culture and values in the domestication of global provisions. The Zimbabwe government has launched several campaigns and widely disseminated information about COVID-19 in print and electronic media. Zimbabwe has high literacy and wide access to cellphone, radio, and television reception. As a result, there is high awareness of the pandemic and its consequences in the country. Although the regulations and restrictions imposed by government are to mitigate the spread of COVID-19, the restrictions on civil freedoms have had an adverse impact on how Shona people observe and celebrate life cycle events of funerals and weddings. This work highlights the experience of Shona people's funerals and weddings in the framework of COVID-19-induced restrictions on gatherings.

The chapter illustrates how the organization of Shona funerals and weddings has evolved in response to the World Health Organization (WHO) regulations aimed at curbing the spread of COVID-19. After the chapter deliberates on the aforementioned issues and that of social distance, sanitization, and quarantine, it proposes some lessons to be learnt by Zimbabwe. Before it delves on the issue of funerals, the argument puts afore the methodology used, World Health Organization (WHO) regulations on COVID-19 (a case of Zimbabwe), Shona culture and values, the singing and dancing, weddings, sanitization and social distance, quarantine, post-COVID era lessons for Zimbabwe, and conclusion.

Methodology

The primary data were drawn through participant observation by the authors who attended funerals before and during the COVID-19 pandemic. Since COVID-19 pandemic is about two years old in Zimbabwe, there is a dearth of scientific evidence on the phenomena under enquiry. As a result, the authors

DOI: 10.4324/9781003390732-12

relied heavily on observation; specifically participant observation. Participant observation according to Best and Kahn (2006) is an attempt to observe events as they naturally occur from within. The participant observer methodology generates rich data and insights but is biased towards the observers who in this case would be close relatives of the deceased. This undermines the neutrality of the observation. In line with Cohen, Manion, and Morrison (2010), the authors triangulated their observations with engagements with people who also attended other Shona funerals in Zimbabwe. On this basis, the authors are confident that the findings provide useful insights on how the Shona people in Zimbabwe localize the COVID-19 restrictions on gatherings during funerals and weddings.

World Health Organization (WHO) Regulations on COVID-19 (the Case of Zimbabwe)

Zimbabwe is a country in Southern Africa with a population of about 15 million people. The country's first COVID-19 case was detected on 21 March 2020 (The Zimbabwe Herald, 21 March, 2020). However, this virus had been in China for over two and half months before it was recorded in Zimbabwe. Bruns, Kraguljac, and Bruns (2020) note that the novel coronavirus 2019 (COVID-19) was first recognized and reported in Hubei Province of China on 31 December, 2019.

At the time of writing, figures from the Ministry of Health indicate that there have been 123,000 infections and 4,293 deaths because of the pandemic. In an effort to manage the pandemic, the Government of Zimbabwe adopted a variety of measures. These included the World Health Organization (WHO) regulations on prevention, containment, control, and treatment of COVID-19. The Zimbabwe government declared a national lockdown in 27 March 2020, through the Government Statutory Instrument 83 of 2020 Public Health (COVID-19) Prevention, Containment and Treatment (National Lockdown), Order, 2020 (zimlii.org/zw/legislation/si/2020/83 Accessed 5 August 2021). In addition, the government imposed social distancing, self-quarantine for 14 days, quarantine in centers, wearing of face masks, frequent washing of hands, and limiting gatherings to 50 people at funerals. The issue of numbers has since been reviewed upwards from 50 to 100, down to 30. The number of days one is required to be in quarantine centers have been revised from time to time. At the time of writing, the country was under level-four lockdown whose complimentary restrictions included a limit on the number people who could attend a funeral, ban on funeral wakes, and total ban on weddings and other social gatherings through the Public Health (COVID-19 Prevention, Containment and Treatment) (National Lockdown) (No.2) (Amendment) Order, 2021(No.9), (gazettes. africa/archives/zw/2021/zw-government-gazzette- dated – 2021-01-02-no-3pdf Accessed 2 February 2022).

Shona Culture and Values

Shona people are an ethnic grouping that is found in Southern Africa with most of them located in Zimbabwe. The Shona comprise 85% of the people in Zimbabwe (Tatira, 2004). Although there are variations, there are general values and traditions that they observe throughout the life cycle. There are cultural practices around birth of a child, marriage, and death (Meekers, 1993). The cultural practices around a marriage and death and burial of an individual involve the mobilization of the extended family, friends, and representatives of social networks like church and workmates. The Shona people have a high regard for solidarity and togetherness (Gelfand, 1973; Bourdillion, 1975; Gombe, 1986; Tatira, 2010). It does not matter whether the occasion is a sorrowful or joyous one. Such values drive many of them to attend funerals and weddings in large numbers.

The next section highlights the cultural dynamics around funerals as the Shona people respond to the COVID-19 restrictions.

What Does a Funeral Mean to a Shona Person?

Generally, Shona funerals are organized on the basis of extended family mobilization and consultations. These begin from the announcement of the death and can continue for a few days after burial. In urban settings, normally a delegation of close relatives moves in different offices processing papers to facilitate the burial of the deceased. The Shona people are communalist in their dispositions especially on issues of bereavement. They feel compelled to attend funerals (Tatira, 2010; Gombe, 1986; Bourdillon 1975 Gelfand, 1973). Singing and dancing are part and parcel of Shona gatherings; be they rituals, funerals, weddings, and parties. Every such gathering attracts a sizeable number of people. There is a common belief, among the Shona, that the more people in attendance the better. For this reason, and many more, limited numbers as stipulated by the COVID-19 regulations that might be 30, 50, or 100, at any form of gatherings including funerals are difficult to maintain.

The question of what does a funeral mean to a Shona person, if properly answered would help to understand why it is difficult or impossible for most Shona people to adhere to the stipulations of limited numbers at funerals, to self-quarantine, and social distancing.

To a Shona person, by this we mean a well-groomed Shona person, he/she is expected to do certain things and at the same time avoid doing certain things in order for one to be acceptable or feel acceptable in society. As such, certain behavior is difficult to stop especially if the measures threaten or are perceived to threaten how individuals handle their activities.

A funeral in a locality, especially in rural areas, means that the whole locality has been thrown into mourning. Life is temporarily suspended and people are expected to join the bereaved family until conclusion of the burial. This also means that a day or more soon after burial, people are not expected to work in their fields through the declaration of *mahakurimwi* (day(s) of mourning)

(Gombe, 1986). During the declared days of mourning, a villager who might be tempted to work in the fields is fined by the village head. Most of the Shona people who stay in the urban centers have rural backgrounds (Tatira, 2004) and to a large extent observe the same practices as their rural counterparts. It is not surprising that even in towns close neighbors generally suspend their activities in order to attend funerals.

Among the Shona, funerals are public events where neighbors, relatives, and close friends are obliged to attend. Failure to attend a funeral without a valid excuse is not taken lightly among the Shona people. As a result, friends, close relatives, and neighbors sometimes have to go out of their way in order to attend a funeral, hence the Shona say, *Rufu ndimakokorodze/maunganidze* (Death gathers many people together). This is regardless of the gender or age of the deceased. Failure to commiserate may undermine the existing reciprocal relationships and associated benefits.

The Singing and Dancing

Singing and dancing play a central role at Shona gatherings. It is not an exaggeration to say that when it comes to singing, it occupies a large space in Shona life. You find the Shona people singing when they are happy (weddings and parties), sorrowful (funerals), working (threshing corn, stumping grain, weeding), caring for the baby (lullabies), and many more. Finnegan (1970) also notes the same phenomenon among people of Africa, while Pongweni (1982) observed the importance of songs in the Liberation of Zimbabwe and Kaemmer (1989) explains the issue of social power and music among the Shona. Singing has a powerful effect of bringing people together as it is a vehicle through which collective emotions are harnessed. It has the incredible power of bringing back memories of the past and connecting people with the future. Singing can lift people from the real world to an imaginary one depending on the song. Therefore, it cannot be contested that singing finds itself a special place in the lives of the Shona people. When it comes to funeral, singing is mostly accompanied by dance. In singing and dancing at funeral, people would be relieving themselves of the pain and grief associated with the losing of a beloved one. The singing and dancing provides a space for people to move away from concentrating about the loss and divert or more appropriately let out their bottled emotions to singing and dancing. Singing and dancing temporarily sedate people in such moments of emotional pressure. One would find that most of the singing during the night before burial takes place where the corpse lie in state. Such singing also provides for a necessary time-passing activity since it would be unbearable for mourners to cry throughout the night. This activity requires a sizeable number of people who will be close to each other so that their voices are harmonized as they sing. This automatically means that the issue of social distance is ignored. More so that of putting on masks is mostly done away with. Mourners cannot possibly sing and dance throughout the night while wearing masks. It would not be an exaggeration that during the first and second wave, all the funerals attended by the authors of this chapter, the observations on the issue of singing and dancing while not wearing masks was a common feature at funerals held by most Shona people in Zimbabwe in spite of the COVID-19 restrictions. The issue of singing and not wearing of masks at funerals is not only peculiar to Zimbabwe but is also reported in South Africa. Jaja, Anyanwu, and Jaja (2020) report of funerals in South Africa where a lot of singing takes place at funerals with people not wearing masks.

As we have earlier on pointed out, the restrictions on numbers is not respected and to some extent the issue of social distancing and wearing mask. This means that there is a danger of spreading of the virus at funerals. The threat is sometimes ignored because of cultural solidarity and a general conformity to the cultural dictates about Shona funerals.

It is only during the third wave where a noticeable change has been noted where if opportunity avails, many people sing with masks. Night vigils in the case of COVID-19 deaths are no longer much practiced. But generally, scores of close people gather at the deceased's home. This is so possibly for two reasons that the corpse is not allowed to lie in state at the homestead and that such funerals are generally supervised by health personnel.

From the observations made, let it be emphasized that where the person has died of COVID-19, people might not have all night dancing and singing but when the body is taken for burial from parlor, there is still some singing though in masks. The issues of numbers still go beyond the stipulated numbers. Close relatives, friends, neighbors, work mates, and fellow congregates, if the deceased was a church member, still find themselves obligated to mourn with the bereaved family. This does not imply that all members of the mentioned groups attend but those who do attend make a crowd, which would be above the stipulated number. The Shona seem not to have problems with sanitization, masking (except in some cases when singing), and to some extent social distancing; what they have problem with is not to attend a funeral because the numbers that are required have been met. This is because most Shona people find closure by attending the funeral and also doing so is a means of maintaining healthy social relations not to also mentioning that attending a funeral is regarded as a social duty.

The other gathering among the Shona people, which generally fails to conform to the restriction of numbers, is the wedding. In the next subsection we would like to investigate how weddings give challenges in terms of required limited numbers.

Weddings

Among the Shona people, weddings are highly celebrated events as they are regarded as special events in a person's adulthood. They are taken as occasions to celebrate the beginning of a new life as people move from singlehood to marriage and for those already in marriage as a beginning of another phase of life in a marriage after wedding. As a result, weddings among the Shona tend to attract a large number of guests. The wedding, among the Shona, in some cases has substituted, the *mapemberero* (a Shona traditional feast meant to welcome a bride). Many people, who included relatives, friends, and neighbors were invited to join the celebrating family (Janhi, 1970; Bourdillon, 1975; Chigwedere, 1982; Gombe, 1986; Tatira, 2010). The tradition of inviting many people seems not to have died with the introduction of weddings.

Therefore, the issue of restricted numbers at weddings becomes problematic but not to the same extent as at funerals. Weddings become less challenging in that when one is not invited one is not under pressure to attend. However, the problem of numbers would still arise when the host figures out who to invite among many prospective guests. The host would have a headache over which people not to invite since relatives, close friends, and neighbors all matter a lot. There would always be pressure on the part of the host not leave some of the close relatives, friends, and neighbors. This is because if such people would be left out, they would most likely not take it lightly and relationships could be negatively affected.

The uninvited relatives would feel that they are only appreciated during bereavement as they would generally attend funerals that befall the host family. We can better appreciate the challenges of adhering to the stipulated numbers, if we do not lose sight of the fact that a wedding involves two families – that of the bride and the bridegroom. Those who might be familiar with the Shona culture might be aware that people, who matter in such families, would be well over 50 years. Culturally, these people who matter are not invitees but are a part to the wedding; without them, culturally, there would be no meaningful or fulfilling wedding. Such people would include, but not limited to, parents and their siblings from both sides, aunts, uncles, grannies, cousins, and nephews. Some of the relatives are supposed to carry out some cultural duties before and soon after the wedding. It is a common practice that on the eve of the wedding, representatives from the bridegroom's family go to the in-laws to seek permission to have the groom leave her parents to join her soon-to-be husband. The delegation would bring the bride's clothes and her other belongings to the bridegroom's place while she would join her new family soon after the wedding.

A delegation of relatives from the groom would, normally, soon after wedding, bring the groom to her in-laws. This cultural event is marked by celebration which is usually accompanied by singing, dancing, and eating. This generally concludes the wedding process though this might vary from family to family.

Among the listed relatives who attend the wedding, there would be other people who are the following, the bridesmaids, groomsmen, and a few representatives from the church, minister of religion, and the mediator, most often they come with their spouses. The mediator is the person who would have played an important role of bringing the two families together and facilitated the process of payment of bride wealth *(roora)* (Gombe, 1986. Tatira, 2010). All such groups of people might not be relatives but nevertheless they are expected not only to attend but also to participate at the wedding in their different capacities. As a result, the stipulated numbers are hard to adhere to and many weddings continue to flout the stipulations.

As for dancing and singing, people do it though most of them would be in masks. There would be church songs as well as popular choruses and at other weddings traditional songs. Therefore, singing is not dispensed with. The bridal team obviously dances oblivious of the social distance as some dances require physical contact. However, the rest of the guests generally would be cautious of social distance especially with people they are not familiar with. All what we are saying are not speculations but real incidences that we observed at different weddings.

Sanitization and Social Distance

In all the gatherings, we have observed that sanitization is not a problem. This is because the Shona are generally hygienic people; even in their indigenous knowledge they have taboos which touch on hygiene (Tatira, 2000). They have taboos on washing of hands after people have participated in burial, before eating and after eating. There are also taboos on avoiding of washing hands with dirty water. People are discouraged from not washing hands after burial as it is said that they would experience bad dreams. This does not mean that when children grow up to become adults they would still believe in such taboos, but because they would have been socialized to be hygienic so they would continue to wash their hands.

Therefore, in regard to sanitization, generally Shona cultural practice and values do not clash with COVID-19 protocols and as such there is no problem of violating the regulation as a way of resistance. However, we are not insinuating that all people wash hands or sanitize at all times, but failure to do so as mentioned would not be out of a clash with expectations.

The idea of social distance is not a straightforward issue when we come to the Shona people. Generally Shona people are warm and feel comfortable when they are close to each other, for instance, when they converse, walk, and gather. This is true when they are with people familiar to them. Being apart from others would be taken as either that one is proud, or is in an unpleasant mood or some of the negatives which go with self-isolation. All such comments about individuals are passed if the situation is normal and, therefore, inviting people to wonder about the exhibition of abnormal behavior. The requirement of social distancing for a cause like that of COVID-19 is therefore understandable to the Shona people.

Quarantine

Among the Shona cultural practices, quarantine of people with certain illness was practiced ever since. People who were very ill or with "strange" diseases were isolated from the rest of the people. The elderly people would take such an individual out of the homestead and nurse him/her away from the other members. It is only a few close relatives who were allowed to visit the sick. These would brief him/her and the people nursing him/her about the situation back home. This helped the person not to feel the full burden of isolation as he/she somehow remained connected with what was taking place back home. The ill person would only be brought back when fully recovered. Therefore, the idea of quarantine is not quite resisted and even that of self-isolation. The problem with self-isolation is that of the general lack of space to self-isolate, especially in urban crowded households. There are situations where many people stay in one room and use the same toilet and bathroom. In such a situation, self-isolation becomes a structural problem rather than a cultural one.

Post-COVID-19 Era Lessons for Zimbabwe

As much as we believe that diseases require medical solutions to combat them, we still contend that they also equally need social remedies to fully combat them. In the case of COVID-19, the sociocultural aspect also plays a very important role in fighting the pandemic. What people value and believe to be the essence of their humanity cannot be simply wished away because there is a pandemic. What is important and should be learnt is that in a situation of COVID-19, health authorities should find a win–win situation. This is a scenario where the strong cultural aspects are taken aboard with the regulations, especially when it comes to funerals and to a less extent, weddings.

Taking into consideration that there is nowhere in Shona culture where one would possibly prevent people from mourning with the bereaved family, issues of numbers should not be as minimal as they currently stand at 30, 50, and 100. We have explained the problem of numbers at the beginning of this chapter. People would rather flout the regulations rather than not attend the funeral of their beloved ones. The issue of numbers should be practical; take for example in a village, how many people are expected to dig and prepare a grave? A conservative number would be 25, which means the funeral gathering would only be short of five to reach the Government of Zimbabwe's expected number. This number does not even include the directly bereaved members. The directly bereaved members, culturally, are generally excluded from digging the grave as they would be mourning their departed relative.

To make matters worse, the numbers of 30, 50, and 100 are the same in urban, peri-urban, and rural areas. The cultural expectations and demands are not uniform across the geographical divide. The numbers should be reviewed upwards depending on the geographical location of the funeral. Because of required limited numbers which apply to all areas, you would find that people continue to gather in their numbers at funerals be it urban or rural areas. The most important lesson to be learnt is that numbers should not be limited to unrealistic levels. What is most important is to have people maintain social distance, sanitization and masking up. It might sound a not-quite-well-thought-out statement but with the existing few numbers in place, people have continued to disregard those numbers. We would not like to promote the feeling that people are willfully disregarding regulations but to know that culturally they are feted to behave in a way they do. If they fail to do so they lose their humanity especially as Shona people.

The same lessons should be learnt on weddings; the numbers should be realistic and people should be encouraged to have their weddings in open spaces or venues that allow for social distancing. This would assist in a long way to accommodate immediate relatives, neighbors, friends, and a sample of other groups that matter. Without taking the above into consideration, the weddings would remain flouting the numbers in crammed venues thus posing more harm as they become potential super-spreaders of COVID-19. Still, the geographical divide might be considered rather than a flat number across the divide.

On quarantine as we have noted there is not much conflict. To improve the quarantine system, close relatives must be allowed to visit the center to see and talk with the quarantined person whilst maintaining a stipulated distance. This might be even talking to each other over a phone from a distance of sight. This might reduce instances of running away from the quarantine centers as experienced in Zimbabwe.

Conclusion

Zimbabwe was not spared by the COVID-19 pandemic like all other countries across the globe. The country instituted COVID-19 restrictions to curtail the spread of the disease. Some of the restrictions have, however, posed a big challenge to the Shona cultural practices and values. The issue of limited numbers at funerals and weddings has resulted in people flouting the limit. This is because such gatherings attract a lot of people and attendance in the case of funeral is almost obligatory to close relatives, friends, and neighbors who happen to be many in Shona society.

On weddings, the bare minimum of people who are expected to attend among the Shona would be beyond the required limit. Both situations of funerals and weddings cause headaches to Shona people as they would be unable to limit people to the required numbers. This is because of the strong kinship ties and high expectations of society on attendance of such gatherings. It is almost an offense for one not to attend a funeral or wedding when culturally one would be expected to attend.

On the issue of social distancing, sanitization, and quarantine, the Shona people do not have much problems as pointed out in the course of the discussion. As has been argued, the Shona people are hygienic and in their indigenous knowledge have taboos which encourage them to be hygienic. It is only the issue of social distance and quarantine which can give them a bit of a problem but can be managed by allowing people to congregate in spacious places and also allow the quarantined a visit or visits by limited close relatives.

Limiting of numbers without taking into consideration the social and cultural matrix of people does not in any way solve the problem. What is supposed to be done is to have realistic numbers in place and then insure that the protocols of social distancing, masking, sanitization, and others are followed. The issue of numbers as we have argued should not be the same across the geographical divide. It should be understood that cultural pressure on certain gatherings is intense in rural areas compared to urban areas when we consider the strong spirit of neighborliness that prevails in rural areas. But it should be stressed that both the urbanites and the rural are nevertheless, in their way, culturally bound to attend gatherings where they are considered to be close relatives, friends, and neighbors.

Reference

Best, J.W. and Kahn, J.V. (2006). *Research in Education*. Boston: Pearson Education Inc.

Bourdillon, M.F.C. (1975). *The Shona People*. Gweru: Mambo Press.

Bruns, D.P., Kraguljac, N.V. and Bruns, T.R. (2020). COVID-19 Facts, Cultural Considerations and Risks of Stigmatisation. *Journal of Transcultural Nursing*, 31(4), 326–332.

Chigwedere, A. (1982). *Lobolo-the Pros and Cons*. Harare: Books for Africa.

Cohen, L., Manion, L. and Morrison, K. (2010). *Research in Education*. Milton Park: Routledge.

Finnegan, R. (1970). *Oral Literature in Africa*. Cambridge: Cambridge University Press.

Gelfand, M. (1973). *The Genuine Shona People: Survival Values of an African Culture*. Gwelo: Mambo Press.

Gombe, J.M. (1986). *Tsika dzaVaShona*. Harare: College Press.

Janhi, L. (1970). Roora and Marriage. In Keleff, C. and Kileff, P. (eds.), *Shona Customs*. Gwelo: Mambo Press, pp. 33–41.

Jaja, I.F., Anyanwu, M.U. and Jaja, C.J.I. (2020). Social Distancing: How Religion, Culture and Burial Ceremony Undermine the Effort to Curb COVID-19 in South Africa. *Emerging Microbes and Infections*, 9(1), 1077–1079. https://doi.org/10.1080/22221751 .2020.1769501.

Kaemmer, J.E. (1989). Social Power and Music Change Among the Shona. *Ethnomusicology*, 33(1), 31–45.

Mekeers, D. (1993). The Noble Custom of Roora: The Marriage Practices of the Shona of Zimbabwe. *Ethnology*, 32(1), 35–54.

Pongweni, A.J.C. (1982). *Songs That Won the Liberation War*. Harare: College Press.

Tatira, L. (2000). *Zviera ZvaVaShona*. Gweru: Mambo Press.

Tatira, L. (2004). Beyond the Dog's Name: A Silent Dialogue among the Shona People. *Journal of Folklore Research*, 41(1), 85–98.

Tatira, L. (2010). *Shona Culture*. Germany: LAP.

13 Beyond COVID-19

Reimagining Religious and Political Futures in Zimbabwe: A Decolonial Paradigm

Tobias Marevesa

Introduction

The outbreak of the COVID-19 pandemic at the end of 2019 has brought the world at large to a standstill as it came in different waves globally. This coronavirus disease has affected human life in a number of ways in the field of education, economy, politics, and religion, among other facets of life. The upsurge of coronavirus has had a global impact financially, mentally, psychologically, religiously, politically, economically, and educationally (closure of schools and universities). It has restricted movement, affected health facilities, and forced people to be quarantined (Marevesa & Mavengano, 2021). Zimbabwe was not spared by the effects of the coronavirus in different facets of life. Everyone was vulnerable to this pandemic, regardless of being rich or poor. The disease does not differentiate between power and race, and has no boundaries. The chapter seeks to explore and reimagine the religious and political environment in Zimbabwe and beyond in the context of post-COVID-19 era. The pandemic has brought other challenges such as labor shortages, inequality, and interdependence. This should encourage Zimbabweans to find a pathway to the new future, that is, the post-COVID-19 era. There is a very significant number of people who sacrificed their lives for others by accepting to become frontline and foot soldiers in the fight against the pandemic. These include petrol attendants, nurses, doctors, pharmacists, electricians, cleaners, and engineers who continued working while everyone was under lockdown. In this chapter, as we rethink and reimagine the post-COVID-19 future, it is important to reflect on millions of human lives that are globally being lost due to this pandemic. A crisis of this magnitude requires an opportunity to pave the way for a new future of Zimbabwe and Africa at large. Yet, it could be problematic to reimagine and rethink a new and different post-COVID-19 Zimbabwe without the external interference of the West, economically, politically, and religiously, among other spheres. This chapter argues that all problems or realities that hinder [Africa] from forming its own futures rest in religion and politics in Zimbabwe. It can be argued that the present realities in Zimbabwe determine how the future will become. This chapter will make an attempt to grapple briefly with the interrelatedness and the entanglement of "coloniality

DOI: 10.4324/9781003390732-13

of power, Knowledge and being as constitutive elements of global coloniality as a power structure which makes it difficult for [Zimbabweans] ... to create their own futures" (Ndlovu-Gatsheni, 2020:182). This study will be guided by the following questions: What are the challenges encountered by Africa during the pandemic which should be addressed in the post–COVID-19 era? What is the role of religion, economics, and politics, among others, in preparing Zimbabwe for possible future pandemics? How can the lessons drawn from the pandemic inform Zimbabweans to re-imagine the future trajectories of the country in the various domains?

Theoretical Framework: A Decolonial Paradigm

Decoloniality is a concept of the postcolonial, which seeks to give a colonial testimony of the third world countries with their narratives of minorities (Bhabha, 2003). This theory focuses on colonial "amnesia and creating a tabula rasa with a view to rewrite and rethinking of all aspects of the colonial process addressing the question of history, culture, identity, ethnicity, gender, language, and education" (Ndlovu, 2021). Rethinking and reimagining the post–COVID-19 Zimbabwe in the context of religion and politics is located within the postcolonial theory. Ndlovu-Gatsheni (2015) is apt in arguing that decoloniality cannot just be perceived only as an epistemological and political movement aiming at the liberation of those who were colonized by the global coloniality, but should also be understood as a way of one's thinking, doing, and knowing. To reimagine and rethink of the situation after COVID-19, focusing on the political and religious realities in Zimbabwe, is a way of thinking and knowing because it is difficult to "uncolonise" and "decolonize" the mind of Zimbabweans. Is it possible for the post–COVID-19 era to have a decolonized religious and political landscape in Zimbabwe?

There is an idea of decolonial turn, which argues that there are various forms of colonialisms in the American context, which produced a matrix of power (Mignolo, 2011; Restrepo & Rojas, 2012; Quijano, 2010). This concept of decolonial turn has been premised on the configuration that promotes a command of coloniality. It can be noted that coloniality cannot be only perceived politically, but can also refer to military regime. It goes further "creating a subjectivity based on the differentiation according to sex, race and class" (Buttelli & Bruyns, 2019). Decolonial turn pays much attention to the matrix of power created and based on the three suppressed issues on sex, race, and class with their epistemological and philosophical significances.

The concepts of coloniality and decoloniality are both corporal and intellectual realities that originated from the physical developments of colonization and decolonization. According to Maldonado-Torres (2007), coloniality and decoloniality are not similar from the procedures of colonization and decolonization, but colonization is a historical reality that can be situated in a particular historical periodization. Yet, Ndlovu notes that "in contrast, coloniality and decoloniality refer to the logic, metaphysics, ontology, and matrix of power created by the massive processes of colonization and decolonisation" (Ndlovu, 2021:5). The terms coloniality and decoloniality are interconnected and inter-twined to hegemonic narratives and Western modernity. It is significant at this moment to consider Maldonado-Torres (2007), who offers three taxonomies of coloniality and decoloniality which are based on power, knowledge, and being. He goes on to argue that coloniality of power entails integrating cul-ture and structure, coloniality of being combines space and time and, lastly, coloniality of knowledge incorporates method and objects. It is important to the colonial logics and structures embedded in coloniality in the present times. This chapter has engaged in dialogues about rethinking and reimagining the decolonized post-COVID-19 Zimbabwe in the context of religion and poli-tics. Coloniality has formed inedible ways of being and seeing genuineness, how Africans also have grasped the grammar of coloniality stored in what Ndlovu-Gatsheni (2020) terms "cognitive empires." It is important to have a decolonized post-COVID-19 Zimbabwe, but is it possible to have a future reli-gious and political environment without a decolonized mind of Zimbabweans? This decolonization of the mind is significant in that, people would be able to appreciate their Indigenous Knowledge Systems (IKS) (traditional herbs) and the African indigenous independent churches. Thus, the decolonial paradigm is a pertinent approach in attempting to envisage the futures of Zimbabwe after the COVID-19 pandemic.

The Crisis of COVID-19: An Overview

The COVID-19 pandemic which erupted in China, Wuhan, end of December 2019, brought the world to a standstill. Its impact beyond the borders of China was felt in international health delivery systems. It had sociopolitical and eco-nomic ramifications worldwide. In the Zimbabwean context, a fragile public health system was hard hit as well as the educational sector, political landscape, religious practices, among other effects (Shumba et al., 2020). Zimbabwe with its ailing economy and a severely incapacitated and flimsy public healthcare sys-tem could not respond satisfactorily to the threat of this novel pandemic. The WHO proclaimed COVID-19 pandemic a global disaster and pronounced mitigation in a myriad of ways: vigorous education on the pandemic, strict national lockdowns, COVID-19 tests, social distancing, personal hygiene, quarantining, among others. The public health mitigating measures to curb the spread of COVID-19 pandemic has exacerbated the Zimbabwean economic crisis, which severely affected the livelihoods of several people. A number of Zimbabweans are informally employed and they survive from hand to mouth (Chirisa, 2018). It was catastrophic to have an abrupt closure of both formal and informal sectors, for example, demolition of wares (Kubatana.net, 2020), which resulted in the unexpected loss of incomes where food security was threatened in different households. A number of people succumbed to the virus. The religious and political activities were affected greatly because of social distancing, which did not allow people to congregate. Church and religious activities which were affected include celebration of the Holy Communion, baptism, crusades, all night prayers, handshakes, live church services, among others. Politically, by-elections and rallies were put on halt, affecting those who anticipated to become legislators. Ideally, the religious and political activities were banned and were done online. This brief historical overview of the menacing COVID-19 pandemic led to the re-imagining and re-thinking of the post-COVID-19 era in the context of religious and political environments in Zimbabwe.

The Future is Present

The future of Zimbabwe after the COVID-19 pandemic in the areas of religion and politics is not a question of chance. It will come as a result of the present day where there are struggles against the coloniality of power, being, and knowledge as they constitute essentials of global coloniality. According to the African Union (AU) (2013), the agenda 2063 foresees the future of Africa in the unity of Africa, wealth, harmony, and integration. The AU's vision should be driven by Africans with the dynamic powers functioning within the worldwide environment. Zimbabwe falls within the framework of pan-Africanism, which emphasizes unity, integration, solidarity, and self-reliance (African Union, 2013). There should be a careful consideration of Zimbabwe's capacity of creating her own destiny, that is, being in charge of her future and being able to plan her own independent trajectories of development. Ndlovu-Gatsheni (2020), in agreement with this claim, argues that this mentality may remind us of the arguments of Karl Marx when he talked about people constructing their own history in an environment which they have chosen. Will the Zimbabwean situation allow her to chart a new pathway for a new religious and political future? However, can Zimbabwe and Africa be able to have different post-COVID-19 futures? This can only be achieved by defeating the global coloniality, that is, when Zimbabwe and Africa at large will be able to create their own futures (Ndlovu-Gatsheni, 2020).

What can change Zimbabwe and Africa to have a "decolonized" and "uni-colonial" mindset? These concepts are just idealistic because, who will decolonize and uncolonize Zimbabwe? It is difficult to imagine who will determine the parameters and mechanisms of decolonization. It is likely that the present scenario will inform the post-COVID-19 era even if Zimbabwe has vision 2030. The political and religious realities that are manifesting in this present context in Zimbabwe may not change in the future because there are no indications on the ground which point to that. However, the religious practices may change because of the effects of the COVID-19 pandemic. There are various changes and suspensions that were made by different churches during worship services. In the African indigenous religions, the COVID-19 pandemic has also forced adherence to alteration of their veneration processes. The same applies to the Islamic religious practices which also changed because of the effects of coronavirus. These issues will be discussed in the next section.

The Christian-African Indigenous Religion Praxes in Zimbabwe: The Post-COVID-19 Era

This section seeks to rethink and reimagine the religious environment that could be in the post-COVID-19 in Zimbabwe and beyond. It is difficult to reimagine a situation which is yet to come when focusing on the religious environment. If we go by Ndlovu-Gatsheni (2020), there will be very little changes in the futures of COVID-19 in Zimbabwe and beyond when he talked about people constructing their own history in an environment which they have chosen. In this regard, it is the Zimbabweans who should reconfigure their own religious history, which will manifest itself in the future of Zimbabwe. Ndlovu-Gatsheni (2020) also contends that the future of Zimbabwe's religious situation can only change if there is a defeat of global coloniality. This is when the Zimbabweans will be able to create their own religious futures. According to Mutalemwa (2021), religious leaders are not representing the faithful but they are answerable to God, while the laity are answerable to the leadership. This situation may be found in the post-COVID-19 environment because the present informs the future. There are lessons that can be observed today and can be relevant to the future of Zimbabwe, that is, the post-COVID-19 period (Mutalemwa, 2021). For instance, there are lessons that are drawn from the current COVID-19 crisis in the areas of communication, science, education, and business, where professionalism is needed to guide leadership to deal with people's responses.

In the Christian religion, there are beliefs and practices which were foregone during this COVID-19 pandemic period because they were against the mitigatory measures which were put in place. Such practices are like the Eucharist (Lord's Super or Holy Communion), which is a central rite in Christianity where bread and wine are sanctified by the ordained pastor and taken by the pastor and his members in a particular congregation, in line with Jesus' command at his Last Supper, which says, "Do this in remembrance of me" (1 Corinthians 12:24). This is practiced by different churches such as the Roman Catholic, Anglican, Pentecostals, and other Protestant churches. This practice is called a sacrament and signifies Christ's union with his followers who are faithful (Price, 2008). Before the outbreak of COVID-19 in Zimbabwe, most churches were administering the Eucharist, which used one cup to drink wine which symbolized the blood of Jesus. They also used the bread as part of the Eucharist, which symbolized the body of Jesus. It can be understood that in the post-COVID-19 era, very little will change in the administration of the Holy Communion by ordained ministers and in other proceedings of church services. During the COVID-19 pandemic, different churches had to suspend the celebrations of the Eucharist, whereas other churches made some adjustments by giving members different cups each for the purpose of partaking the wine (Chukwuma, 2021). It is likely that in the post-COVID-19 era, the administration of the Eucharist will have some adjustments when it is served by ministers of religion. There is a high probability that the Holy Communion may end being administered online while members are in their homes (Chukwuma, 2021). However, to receive the Eucharist while members are at their homes will weaken the sacredness and essence of the institution. Certain practices by different churches today may be suspended in the post-COVID-19 era in Zimbabwe. In the post-COVID-19 era, there is a likelihood that most of the churches may end up performing most of their activities online, such as preaching, Bible studies, Holy Communion, and conferences. This is probably so because it has become the norm during the lockdowns and even after there is a probability that people may want to continue with tele-evangelism.

In the context of African indigenous religions in Africa and Zimbabwe in particular, the post-COVID-19 era will be rejuvenated in the sense that the Africans have tested the efficacy of the traditional medicine during the coronavirus era. The use of traditional herbs will be highly regarded as what is evident in Tanzania and Madagascar, where the state presidents confirmed the effectiveness of the use of herbs to cure coronavirus (Marevesa, Mavengano & Nkamta, 2021). African leaders are beginning to appreciate the value of traditional herbs in curbing the coronavirus. This is evident in that recently, Ramaphosa the president of South Africa, in an interview with SABC News, indicated that his country is turning to traditional medicine and home remedies to cure COVID-19 (SABC News, 10 January 2021). Ramaphosa went on to attack the West for going political on the COVID-19 pandemic, especially on the use of traditional medicine. He joined the other African leaders such as the Presidents of Tanzania and Madagascar in condemning the West for not appreciating the African efforts in inventing traditional medicines, which have demonstrated their effectiveness in curbing the virus. Other African leaders are complaining that Omicron is being treated politically by the West, rather than on medical lines. The whole world, as it is known historically, is divided into the Global North and South where Africa belongs to the South. In the southern hemisphere we are less developed and because of coloniality, the people in the southern part are referred to as subalterns by those in the Global North (Marevesa, Mavengano & Nkamta, 2021). Yet the Global South is not as less developed as those in the North might want to perceive. Those in the Global South have their IKS, which are competitive and can support the type of livelihoods that Africans may depend on. The African medical solutions are always in tandem with the context, so the African context will find African indigenous religion and IKS coming to the center of the operation of the people during the coronavirus. There has been a breakthrough or discoveries during the coronavirus, where the West was found wanting, with their own people also suffering due to the limitations of their so-called scientific discoveries and vaccinations. It is high time IKSs were put to test or retried so that people can learn from them because their remedies are found to be in tandem with organic system that are always pro-health rather than toxic, because most of the Western conventional medicines are toxic and have side effects that could be harmful to humanity (Matiashe, 2021). So the future of African indigenous medicine is promising and should be tapped from and this makes

African indigenous religion remain resilient together with its knowledge system (Ndlovu-Gatsheni, 2020). It is high time people ran away from Western-invented knowledge. The toxic elements in their medical discoveries should be taken with caution and so too their vaccines, which should not be forced. African indigenous religions and IKSs have the chance to come to the center in the post-COVID-19 era as a viable option for medicines for different ailments.

It is problematic that the international superpowers are skeptical about the knowledge that is coming from Africa, but that could be valuable in the cure of coronavirus infection. This skepticism brings to the fore the epistemic and ontological problems and questions about the knowledge that is generated in Africa. Of significance is, how is the African question of epistemology created from the Western ontology? In light of this, Ndlovu-Gatsheni (2020:373) is apt when he asked a mind-blowing philosophical question, which goes: "[h]ow can Africa confront the Cartesian constructs that project the Global North as the master of reason and the Global South as the subaltern other?" Any traditional medicine that comes from Africa is considered useless and subaltern. Yet the traditional medicines have proved to be useful in the cure of coronavirus infection from its advent up to date. Basing on what has been discussed in this section, it is highly probable that African indigenous religion and the IKS will be very popular in the post-COVID-19 era because Zimbabweans would have tested the efficacy of the traditional medicine. That means every other belief and practice of this religion will be taken on board. In the post-COVID-19 era, it is possible that African traditional herbs may be preferred by Zimbabweans to the conventional Western medicines, which have proved to be toxic.

Reimagining the Political Futures in Zimbabwe in the Post-COVID-19 Era

This section will focus on the political terrain that is envisaged in the post-COVID-19 era in Zimbabwe. The political landscape that will be considered in this chapter will include aspects such as economics, health, and education, which relate to political discourse in Zimbabwe. The outbreak of coronavirus disease (COVID-19) in China, Wuhan, at the end of December 2019 brought the world to a standstill in all facets of life (Marcus, 2020). Its global spread had its distressing effects, witnessed in public health danger and a challenge in development, and it had socioeconomic and political consequences in many countries, including Zimbabwe (Harapan et al., 2020) Zimbabwe, being in an environment where there were economic challenges to develop herself, coupled with a very fragile health delivery system, had to impose national lockdowns and dynamic health campaigns in responding to the threat of the pandemic (Shumba et al., 2020:270).

Africa was the last continent to confirm its first COVID-19 case, a continent that is characterized by poverty, poor health delivery systems, and conflicts (WHO, 2020). Irrefutably, the continent had ample time to prepare for the imminent catastrophic pandemic. Yet it is troubling and distressing to note that there was nothing that could be done to prepare for the pandemic because of the poor economies and health delivery systems in Africa. According to the WHO (2020), it was on March 11, 2020, when the WHO proclaimed that the virus was a global pandemic. According to Shumba et al. (2020), countries in Africa, such as Zimbabwe, had confirmed cases of coronavirus. The cases which were confirmed in Zimbabwe and beyond involved people from other countries and Zimbabweans who had traveled abroad, specifically the West and China (Rodriguez-Morales et al., 2020). Shumba et al. (2020) argued that "[a] top-ranking government official and ruling ZANU (PF) National Chairperson, Defence Minister, Oppah Muchinguri sparked controversy after claiming that COVID-19 was God's punishment on Western countries that include the United States of America for imposing sanctions on Zimbabwe." It is probable that the minister in question had seen a trend that the Western counties were hit hard as compared to Africa and Zimbabwe in particular. It is a reality that more people in the Western countries died because of the COVID-19 pandemic, but it was a reckless statement from such a high profile and a senior government official. The minister uttered these statements when she was "addressing a political rally in Chinhoyi, a city located 116 kilometers northwest of Harare, at a time when Zimbabwe had not officially registered any COVID-19 case" (Ndebele, 2019). It is regrettable that such an irresponsible statement from respected members of authority may possibly derail the efforts by health personnel to curb the pandemic. However, President Mnangagwa the following morning issued a statement emphasizing that government "empathizes with the affected people around the globe" (Mutsaka, 2020), but he did not mention Muchinguri's name. The statement by the President was a diplomatic way of correcting Muchinguri's irresponsible utterances. It is apparent that Muchinguri may have been affected by colonialism. Then, is it possible for the post-COVID-19 era to have a Zimbabwe which is free from such clashes between Africa and the West? Ndlovu-Gatsheni (2020) is right in saying that there is need for Africans and Zimbabweans, in particular, to have a decoloniality of the mind, where Zimbabweans can create their own history without the West. Yet, it is difficult to decolonize people's minds and put in place measures to make sure that people are decolonized. It is, therefore, likely that politically, there will be no real change in the post-COVID-19 environment in Zimbabwe.

Zimbabwe and Africa are very far from a post-COVID-19 situation, but should wait for the vaccination efforts which governments are advocating, for getting assistance from China and beyond. Yet, there are indications that the world is heading towards a post-COVID-19. There is development of informal markets, the localization of economic activity, the growth of businesses based in rural areas, and the increase in expansion of small towns and growth points. These are signs that there is an upward growth of the economy and perhaps we are going towards the post-COVID-19 era.

The mitigatory measures which were implemented by the governments and being enforced by WHO to curb the spread of coronavirus in Zimbabwe and beyond resulted in the economic crisis, which affected the lives of many people (Chirisa, 2018). The majority of Zimbabweans are employed informally and their survival is from hand to mouth. There were sudden closures of business activities (informal and formal) and in some cases wares were destroyed (Kubatana.net, 2020), resulting in loss of all the acquired resources. Before the outbreak of COVID-19, "the World Food Programme (WFP) had predicted that more that 7.7 million people, half of Zimbabwe's population, would face food insecurity at the peak of the lean season" (WFP, 2019). According to Zamchiya et al. (2020), although the lockdowns were significant, they were not accompanied by mitigatory measures to help those who were in need. The mitigation measures against the deadly virus were good for the people, but imposing lockdowns on people who were threatened by hunger without giving the vulnerable people some basic needs was a disaster. The government and Non-Governmental Organizations could have helped reduce the impact of the lockdowns in households with lower income, probably by allocating transfers of money or through food assistance programs that could have eased the problem of food shortages for both urban and rural people.

There were lessons which were learnt during this COVID-19 pandemic in Zimbabwe and beyond. The COVID-19 pandemic has affected economies, health delivery systems, politics, religious practices, education, industry, and many other areas. It is the past and the present experiences of coronavirus that inform the future of Zimbabwe and Africa in the post-COVID-19 era. The outbreak of the COVID-19 pandemic triggered the re-manifestation of exclusionary and de/colonial logics, which should be castigated in order to re-imagine the Zimbabwean future in the post-COVID-19 era (Ndlovu-Gatsheni, 2020). The coronavirus disease has exacerbated binary conceptualization of humanity in general and Africa is further pushed into oblivion. This chapter has provided a research study that seeks to re-think global public health matters from a decolonial school of thought (Ndlovu-Gatsheni, 2020). How can Zimbabweans re-imagine and re-position Zimbabwe in the post-COVID-19? This chapter challenges the role of African governments, particularly the Zimbabwe government, in promoting the recovery process in the various facets affected by the coronavirus pandemic. Can Zimbabwe evaluate the power and economic dialectics of COVID-19, navigate the tumultuous challenges generated thereof, both at continental levels, institute and come up with appropriate systems for future pandemics?

Conclusion

This chapter has established that the outbreak of the novel COVID-19 pandemic has immensely affected all facets of humanity globally. Zimbabwe was not spared the far-reaching ravages of the coronavirus disease, as is evident in the socioeconomic, education, politics, religion, infrastructural development, health delivery system, among others. As the world is grappling with the contagious global pandemic of the coronavirus, also popularly known as COVID-19, it is necessary to provide scholarly introspections into the lessons drawn from the pandemic, in an effort to re-imagine the future possibilities of Africa. The study also observed that the coronavirus disease in Zimbabwe triggered research innovations in both conventional and traditional medicines. It is a fact that Africa is a fundamental part of the world, hence there is need to consider the role of the continent in medical breakthroughs that will save humanity at the global level. As part of debates about the future of Africa, the continent should not lag behind in global medicinal developments. Therefore, African researchers should engage in a polemic dialogue about Africa's place in medicinal inventions in the global arena. Due to the problems which were brought about by the virus, there is need to find a pathway into the new future. The insights of decoloniality were usefully utilized in this research to interrogate the reimagined post-COVID-19 pandemic in religious and political situation in Zimbabwe. The chapter has asked questions such as: Can Zimbabweans create a Zimbabwean future which is free from coloniality? Will Zimbabwe in the post-COVID-19 era be able to "uncolonize" and "decolonize" the knowledge formed by coloniality in the context of both religion and politics? It was observed that very insignificant things can be changed in the future of Zimbabwe in both religion and politics. The process of uncolonizing the mind of the African, particularly the Zimbabwean, is a daunting and mammoth task.

References

Bhabha, H. K. (2003). Postmodernism/postcolonialism. In R. S. Nelson & R. Shiff (Eds.), *Critical terms for art history* (pp. 435–451). Chicago: University of Chicago Press.

Buttelli, F. G. K., & Le Bruyns, C. (2019). Liberation theology and decolonization? Contemporary perspectives for systematic theology. *Alternation Special Edition, 24*, 198–221.

Chirisa, I. (2018). Peri-Urban informal trading Zimbabwe: A case study of women in the sector (WIIS) in Ruwa. *Asian Journal of Development Studies, 7*(1), 21–37.

Chukwuma, O. G. (2021). The impact of the COVID-19 outbreak on religious practices of churches in Nigeria. *HTS Teologiese Studies/Theological Studies, 77*(4), a6377. https://doi.org/10.4102/hts.v77i4.6377.

Harapan, H. et al. (2020). Coronavirus disease 2019 (COVID-19): A literature review. *Journal of Infection and Public Health, 13*(5), 667–673.

Kubatana.net. (2020). Burning of confiscated vegetables in Mutare must be investigated source: Vendors initiative for social and economic transformation (VISET), 3 April 2020 economy health, human rights. Retrieved from http://kubatana.net/2021/9/03/burning-of-confiscated-vegetables-in-mutare-must-be-investigate/.

Maldonado-Torres, N. (2007). On the coloniality of being: Contribution to the development of a concept. *Cultural Studies, 21*(2–3, March/May), 240–270.

Marcus, T. (2020). Coronavirus: US-China battle behind the scenes [blog post]. Retrieved July 2021, from https://www.bbc.com/news/world-52008453.

Marevesa, T., Mavengano, E., & Nkamta, P. N. (2021). Home remedies as a medical development in the context of the Covid-19 pandemic in Zimbabwe: A cultural memory paradigm. *Gender and Behaviour, 19*(1), 17371–17384.

Matiashe, F. S. (2021). Covid-19 vaccines face a trust gap against some traditional African remedies. *Quartz AFRICA qz.com.*

Mignolo, W. D. (2011). *The dark side of western modernity: Global futures, decolonial options.* Durham, NC and London: Duke University Press.

Mutalemwa, G. (2021). In search for peace amidst COVID-19: Reimagining politics, religion, and culture in Africa. *Journal of Sociology and Development, 4*(1), 98–104.

Mutsaka, F. (2020). Zimbabwe official says coronavirus punishes U.S. for Sanctions, *PBSO News Hour*, Associate Press, www.pbs.org.

Ndebele, N. (2019). Zimbabwean healthcare system: 'A silent genocide'. *Daily Maverick.* Retrieved July 2021, from https://www.dailymaverick.co.za/article/2019-10-22 -zimbabwean-healthcare-system-a-silent-genocide/.

Ndlovu, S. (2021). Decolonisation of the Zimbabwean linguistic landscape through renaming: A quantitative and linguistic landscaping analysis. *African Identities*, 1–18. https://doi.org/10.1080/14725843.2021.1910013.

Ndlovu-Gatsheni, S. J. (2015). Decoloniality as the future of Africa. *History Compass, 10*(13), 485–496. https://doi.org/10.1111/hic3.12264.

Ndlovu-Gatsheni, S. J. (2020). Global coloniality and the challenges of creating African futures. *Strategic Review for Southern Africa, 36*(2), 181–202.

Price, C. P. (2008). *Eucharist.* Redmond, WA: Microsoft Encarta, Microsoft Corporation.

Quijano, A. (2010). Colonialidade do poder e classificacao social. In B. S. Santos & M. P. Meneses (Eds.), *Epistemologias do Sul.* Portugal: Ed. Cortez, 84–130.

Restrepo, E., & Rojas, A. (2012). *Inflexion Decolonial: Fuentes, Conceptos y Cuestionamientos.* Colombia: Universidad del Cauca.

SABC News. (2021). Traditional and home remedies remain a strong belief among South Africans, January 10, 2021. Retrieved June 2021, from https://www.youtube.com.s

Shumba, K. et al. (2020). Politicising the COVID-19 pandemic in Zimbabwe: Implications for public health and governance. *African Journal of Governance and Development, 9*(1), 270–286.

World Food Programme. (2019). Zimbabwe in the grip of hunger. Retrieved July 2021, from https://insight.wfp.org/zimbabwe-in-the-grip-of-hunger-4a689447acbc.

World Health Organisation. (2020). WHO director general's opening remarks at the media briefing on COVID-19, March 11. Retrieved August 2021, from https://www.who.int /dg/speeches/detail/who-director-general-s-opening-remarks-at-the-media-briefing -oncovid-19-march-2020.

Zamchiya, P. et al. (2020). Zimbabwe's Covid-19 lockdown: Ensuring the right to food for the poor. Retrieved from https://www.future-agricultures.org/blog/zimbabwes-covid -19-lockdown-ensuring-the-right-to-food-for-the-poor/.

14 The Socioeconomic Ramification of COVID-19 to the Economically Disadvantaged Members of the Community in Harare during 2020 Lockdowns

A Practical-theological Approach to the Post-COVID-19 Era

Gusha Isheanesu Sextus

Introduction

Pandemics have been part and parcel of the history of humanity since the prehistoric periods. Over 20 deadly global pandemics have been documented till today and some of them are Plague of Athens (430 BC); The Black Death (1346–1553); Flu Pandemic (1889–1890); and Ebola Epidemic (2014–2016). Millions of people have succumbed to various pandemics since the period in antiquity. COVID-19 is one such deadly pandemic that has destabilized the world. I concur with Abdullah A. Balkhair's sentiment that "throughout history, infectious diseases have caused havoc among societies" (Balkhair 2020). The acronym COVID-19 simply stands for Corona (CO), Virus (VI), Disease (D), and 19 (the year 2019 when the first case was discovered in China). When the first case of the virus was discovered in Wuhan, China, in December 2019, many people did not take the news seriously because the common thinking was that it was one of the deadly pandemics like SARS that had hit China in the past two decades (Chamburuka and Gusha 2020: 4). The devastating effects of the pandemic were underestimated by the people, especially those who were geographically far from China. The virulent nature of the pandemic immediately put the world into panic as people began to die in the other parts of the world. The World Health Organization was left with no option but to declare it, "a health emergency of international concern on 30 January 2020 before it was further declared a pandemic on 11 March 2020" (World Health Organization, 30/01/2020). It was from this time forward that serious precautionary measures such as travel bans, banning of social gatherings, closure of public institutions, and the final lockdowns of the economy were adapted by several governments. It is within the context of this background that this chapter discusses the socioeconomic ramifications of COVID-19 to

DOI: 10.4324/9781003390732-14

the economically disadvantaged members of the community in Harare during the 2020 lockdowns. The chapter is limited to six significant lockdown orders in 2020 because these economic lockdown measures were too many to exhaust in one chapter and they are still ongoing to the time of writing this chapter. The research will employ the practical-theological approach as the theoretical framework of the research.

The Practical Theological Approach

The practical-theological approach is derived from the discipline of practical theology. It is therefore important to define practical theology and then later discuss the methodology itself. Firstly, practical theology is conceived as a subdiscipline of systematic theology and this is why it took centuries to develop a clear methodology for theology. H. David Schuringa argues that, "it is not real theology but simply application of theology" (Schuringa 2000:4). The arguments on whether it is real theology or not is not the subject of this chapter and hence needs no further exploration. The father of practical theology in terms of the coinage of the term is a Dutch theologian from the University of Utrecht by the name G. Voetius. Although he coined the name he never developed a systematic methodology of the theology because his point of departure was that every theology should be practical. It was after 150 years that practical theology was officially unveiled as a distinct discipline by the German theologian, Fredrich Schleiermarcher. Douglas Wilson concurs that, "in modern theology it was Friedrich Schleiermarcher who first developed the area of practical theology" (Wilson 2020:24). Wilson further argues that, "the central discussion of practical theology is the issue of the relationship between theory and praxis" (Wilson 2020, p. 14). Praxis has to do with issues on how theory or skill is embodied in real-life situations or contexts. Systematic theology seems to be dealing with abstract concepts such as the concept of God, salvation, and atonement. These concepts appear to be more theoretical; hence practical theology is centered on how such concepts can be embodied in real-life situations. This is why it is often taken as applied theology. According to Wilson, "theory without good practice is invalid theory" (Wilson 2020, p. 14). Wilson's sentiments tally very well with the book of James where the author argues that faith without works is dead. Theology therefore accommodates other disciplines such as those from social sciences in order to analyze how the church as the custodian of theology functions in the community. Practical theology therefore becomes the host of pastoral care and all other related church ministry activities. Schuringa concludes that practical theology acts as a bridge between seminary life and the real world of ministry (Schuringa 2000, p. 4). I would further argue that the bridge extends from the pulpit or altar to the community. Theology therefore encompasses issues such as, "business ethics and family life, political commitments and lifestyle choices" (Wand 2017, p. 20). Joyce Ann Mercer further argues that, "practical theology is concerned not simply to describe reality and to make sense of it, but to seek transformation toward the love and justice of God for all people" (Mercer 2021, p. 436). Economic issues, poverty, and justice are also issues of interest for practical theology.

Why has a practical theological approach been adopted for this chapter? It was Richard Osmer in 2008 who laid out an impressive methodology of theology for contemporary readers. He argues that practical theology has four primary tasks, which are:

1. Descriptive: What is going on? That is, gathering information to better understand particular episodes, situations, or contexts.
2. Interpretive: Why is this going on? Entering into dialogue with the social sciences to interpret and explain why certain actions and patterns are taking place.
3. Normative: What ought to be going on? Raising normative questions from the perspectives of theology, ethics, and other fields.
4. Pragmatic: How might we respond? Forming action plan and undertaking specific responses that seek to shape the episode, situations, or contexts in desirable directions. (Osmer 2011, p. 2)

Therefore, the above four tasks will constitute the theoretical framework of the practical theological approach for this chapter. What is going on? That is, COVID-19 and lockdowns in Harare. A detailed narration on the situation on the ground is needed. Why is this going on? A detailed analysis of why lockdowns were issued in Harare is needed and its impact on the economically disadvantaged people. What ought to be going on? A detailed discussion on what the government ought to do to these economically disadvantaged people during the lockdowns for them to have descent lives is needed. Was there a better way of doing things while saving people's lives? How might we respond? Here, recommendations are made for home-grown solutions that are sustainable and life preserving. This is the layout of how the practical theological approach will interact and investigate available data.

The Lockdowns as a Mitigating Measure against the Spread of COVID-19

In this section, the researcher narrates the situation on the ground or context. The subject area is lockdowns in Harare during the outbreak of the COVID-19 pandemic. The sources for this narration will be the six *State of the Nation Address* by the president of Zimbabwe, CDE Emmerson Mnangagwa. These were the legal promulgations of the lockdowns. First, before narrating the story of national lockdowns in Zimbabwe, there is need for a brief background as to how the pandemic arrived in Zimbabwe. The threat of the pandemic was becoming real as cases of positive infections of the virus were reported in the neighboring countries like South Africa and Botswana. The government reacted to the threat of the incoming virus by declaring coronavirus to be a national disaster. The declaration was made by His Excellency, Emmerson Dambudzo Mnangagwa, the president of Zimbabwe on his 17 March 2020, State of the Nation Address. In the address the following measures were introduced: first, the Zimbabwe International Trade Fair scheduled for April was cancelled; second, the country's annual Independence celebrations scheduled for 18 April were also cancelled; third, all sporting activities were cancelled as well; four, all gatherings of more than 100 people were also banned for the next 100 days; five, all government premises were to be equipped with COVID-19 screening facilities and private business were encouraged to do the same; six, schools were to remain open for the last two weeks of the term but the opening dates were to be announced later by the government depending on the situation on the ground; seven, a national communication task force was set to communicate all matters regarding the pandemic; eight, all resources earmarked for the cancelled events were to be channeled towards drought mitigation work as well as help people who were to be affected by the virus. The president, however, warned the people that if the situation worsened the government was going to introduce more drastic measures. The address left people in a state of panic and confusion.

What happened later after the State of the Nation address? Three days after the address to the nation by the president the first COVID-19 positive case was reported in the resort town, Victoria Falls, on the 20 March 2020. The patient had a traveling history of having traveled to the United Kingdom and then returned back through South Africa. The announcement of the first case by the Minister of Health sent many people and the business fraternity into panic. A day later on the 21 March two more cases were confirmed, and on the 23 March the first death of the journalist Zororo Makamba was reported. Danger was looming at a fast pace and the government needed to take decisions to combat the spread of the virus before many people die. This was the genesis of national lockdowns that are the subject of this chapter.

The First National Lockdown Order

It was on 23 March that the president issued a directive for the first national lockdown and prescribed measures were to take place with immediate effect. Security forces and health personnel were to be deployed to enforce the national lockdown. Summarized below are the measures that were to take effect:

National borders were to remain open for essential travels and goods. Human trafficking was banned except for returning residents. Returning resident was to undergo stringent Covid-19 screening process as well as mandatory one-day quarantine. Domestic traveling was banned except for essential services. All entertainment and social gatherings were banned. Hospital and clinic visits were restricted to one per day and for one relative per patient. Public gatherings were reduced to 50 people and including churches. Visits to informal markets were reduced and people were discouraged to make such visits. All transport operators were to comply with health safety measures. Companies were encouraged to innovate and reduce human concentration at work. Where possible, people were encouraged to work from home.

(President's State of the Nation Address
23/03/2020)

In the next section, after narrating the history of the economic lockdowns during COVID-19, we shall analyze the impact of lockdowns on economically disadvantaged people. However, before engaging in such a discussion, certain facts need to be outlined from the outset. Zimbabwe is a country with 80–90% of people earning a living through the informal sector. This involves traveling to other countries especially neighboring countries in the SADC region such as Malawi, Mozambique, South Africa, Namibia, Zambia, Lesotho, Swaziland, and Botswana to procure goods for re-selling back home. Some go to far-away countries such as China, United Arab Emirates, and India to buy goods for reselling back home. Many people in the country run informal business such as manufacturing furniture, selling groceries, and clothes. Some survive by horticultural projects especially in the rural areas and peri-urban areas and their market is in the cities' informal markets. Informal transporters are also part of a thriving informal sector. Now that the visits to informal markets have been discouraged and reduced, what would be the impact of such presidential pronouncement?

The Second National Lockdown Order

The numbers of positive cases continued to escalate regardless of the introduced lockdown measures and four days later on the 27 March a severe lockdown measure was declared by the president. This was a total lockdown as compared to the first one with severe and stringent measures. The lockdown was to commence the midnight of 30 March and was to last for 21 days. This means that the second lockdown would end on 20 April 2020. Here is a summary of the imposed restrictions:

> People were to stay at home and movement was restricted to essential services like buying food and medicine. Only workers in essential services were exempted from the directive. Funeral gatherings were limited to only 50 people. Visits to hospitals and clinics were to remain one visitor per patient per day. Those refueling their cars were to remain seated in their cars. Only food markets were to remain open while other nonfood markets were to be closed. All public transporters were to be suspended except Zimbabwe United Passenger's Company and public commission buses. Informal markets were to be closed.
>
> (State of the Nation Address 27/03/2020)

This was more devastating than the first lockdown especially in a country with more than 80% of the people engaged in informal economic sector. The president however admitted that this was a hard decision to be taken by his government. It was not meant to be a punishment but could not be avoided since it was an opportunity to save millions of lives. This was a justified cause by a responsible government in protecting citizens but the question remains: What would be the plight of economically marginalized people in such a situation? Did the government have the capacity to cater to the welfare of people in need in such a context? These and other things are the subject of our discussion later on in the chapter.

The Third National Lockdown Order

The second lockdown did not completely arrest the scourge of COVID-19 and the number of positive cases continued to increase. The 21 days' lockdown which was supposed to lapse on the midnight of 19 April had to be extended. This means to some it is the second lockdown that was being extended while for others it was the third lockdown. On 19 April 2020, the president held another State of the Nation Address to the nation regarding the position of the government on the spreading of the virus. The lockdown was extended for another 14 days and this means that people were to remain under lockdown from 30 March to 3 May. People were to stay at home for five weeks without income especially those in the informal sector. The argument for the extension of the lockdown was lack of sufficient resources to sustainably fight the virus (State of the Nation Address: 19/04/2020). In his address the president admitted that the lockdown was not a cure to the pandemic but a way of slowing down the transmission while other sustainable measures were being sought. Therefore, three objectives of the lockdown were to:

> "Flatten and then arrest the infection curve.
> Raise the line of tests through expanded testing and,
> See more Covid-19 recoveries so our health institutions are not overburdened."
>
> *(http://www.veritaszim.net, 2020)*

The same measures that were passed in the second lockdown announcement remained in place. People were to stay at home and movements restricted to essential services. The informal sector was to remain closed and public gatherings banned. This means that the economically disadvantaged were to endure another two weeks' spell of not having revenue. While the objectives of saving lives were being achieved other survival challenges were looming for those without formal jobs and consistent revenue.

The Fourth National Lockdown Order

The third lockdown measures did not completely stop the spreading of the virus and things were getting worse while people were expecting the ending of the lockdown restrictions on 3 May 2020. However, on Friday1 May 2020, new measures were announced by the president in his State of the Nation Address. The third lockdown which was supposed to end on 3 May was further extended by another 14 days meaning that people were to remain locked at their homes. These were seven weeks of unbroken lockdown period and the pressure was now piling on the government's economy. This means that certain conditions were supposed to be eased for people's survival as well as the survival of the country's economy. The pronouncements saw the relaxing of conditions for the manufacturing and mining industries. These are the sectors that are key drivers of the country's economy as well as the business ventures of top business people in the country. Now the economic heat caused by COVID-19 was being felt even by those with strong economic muscles as well as those with strong political muscle. Therefore, by opening the mining and manufacturing industry they were not rescuing the country's economy but they were also refilling their pockets that were drained by the lockdown measures. The economically disadvantaged, especially those not involved in small-scale mining, remained in abject poverty as they were to remain at their homes. All other restrictions were to remain in place. It was at this period that the general public began to express their sentiments about how the economic lockdown were impacting on their lives. The objectives of slowing down the rapid spread of the virus were, however, achieved regardless of the challenges that were being faced by the people.

The Fifth National Lockdown Order

On the 16 May, new announcements were made by the president concerning lockdown restrictions. In the opening remarks of his speech he made a positive and promising statement:

> Zimbabwe must once again be open. The freedoms we promised at the outset of the new dispensation must once again be felt across the whole of our society. Freedom of assembly, freedoms of speech and religion, freedom to vote in free and open elections, and freedom to flourish.
>
> (*http://www.veritaszim.net*, 2020)

Where were these positive comments leading to? Where they leading to the easing up of lockdown restrictions? What is evident from the opening remarks is that the president was responding to the public discourse on the effects of national lockdowns of the plight of the people. The following adjustments were made as the country was to be placed under level two of the economic lockdown:

> First, people from the informal sector were supposed to be registered with immediate effect. This was the only way they could resume their operations. Second, church services were restricted to 50 people and ensuring

that they follow safety measures. Third, unnecessary traveling remained banned. Fourth, the legislation of suspension of rentals was lifted. The owners of the property and tenets were to agree on terms of payment.

(*http://www.veritaszim.net*, 2020)

Things were now easing up as the informal sector that sustains the majority of the people was now given the green light to open but on conditions of formalizing the registering of the companies and adhering to COVID-19 protocols. This was the opportunity for the economically disadvantaged people to regain the income that was lost over a period of nearly eight weeks. The review of these lockdown measures was now indefinite and what mattered now was the situation of the group as advised to the president by the national taskforce.

The Sixth National Lockdown Order

The significant address on the lockdown updates by the president was done on 21 July 2020. What was the COVID-19 situation, both globally and domestically? Over 8.1 million people globally were tested positive for COVID-19 and over 600,000 lives were lost. Africa recorded over 721,000 positive cases and more than 15,100 deaths. Zimbabwe recorded 1,713 positive cases and 26 deaths. Such statistics posed a health crisis to the nation, hence there was need for one more stringent measure to protect life. The following measures were put in place to preserve lives:

> First, people not working under essential services were to stay at home. Second, the wearing of masks remained mandatory. Third, the use of sanitizers and other hygienic measures to remain in place. Fourth, all public spaces were to compulsorily screen people. Fifth, social distancing at all times remained mandatory. Sixth, business hours were reduced that is between 0800HRS until 1500HRS. Seventh, curfew between 18:00 and 06:00 to be enforced by security forces. Eighth, all companies were to adhere to World Health Organization standards. Ninth, informal companies that were registered were the only ones allowed to work. Tenth, food-selling businesses were to remain opened. Eleventh, intercity transport businesses remained closed. Twelfth, approved transporters were to adhere to WHO regulations. Thirteenth, public assembling for any purposes remained banned. Fourteenth, escaping from quarantine centers was a criminal offense. Fifteenth, anyone found intentionally spreading the virus was to be severely punished.
>
> (*http://www.veritaszim.net*, 2020)

Things went from bad to worse as more stringent measures were announced thereby throwing the plight of the economically disadvantaged people into more crises. This means people had to endure more tough conditions for an indefinite period. Was there any hope for the poor in such a context? What economic recovery methods were put in place by the government for the ordinary people who were now in danger of a new pandemic called hunger? These are some of the questions that will be explored later in this chapter. So far, the researcher was on the descriptive part of the practical theological approach. This part responds to the question, 'What is going on?'

The Impact of Lockdowns on the Economically Disadvantaged Members of the Community

This section moves to the second task of the practical theological approach, which is the interpretive one. Here the research responds to the question, "Why is this going on?" This is where the researcher interrogates the impact of lockdowns on the economically disadvantaged people. The sources of gathering information in this section are mainly interviews and desktop researches. Firstly, there is need to unpack this category of the economically disadvantaged people in Zimbabwe before exploring how they were affected in by the lockdowns.

Exploring the Categories of Economic Classes in Zimbabwe

The subject of economic classes within a defined country is a debatable one because economists and politicians are sometimes not in agreement on which instruments to use. There are times when they are globally agreed measurements of defining economic classes but disagreements arise in the interpretation and application of the instruments. How many economic classes are supposed to be in a country with an economy that is running smoothly? What determines economic classes and result in the social stratification of a nation? In general terms, the economic value of a person is measured by the person's income in relation to the prices of the important goods. Karl Max believed that a typical society has three economic classes: bourgeoisie, land owners, and proletariat. Are these classes still in existence in the contemporary world? Many communities have the following three classes: upper, middle, and lower class. What determines the categorization of these classes in the 21st century economy? Many countries use an instrument that looks at the Poverty Datum Line (PGL). What is this line all about? According to Leonard Sengere, "it is the minimum amount needed to attain a minimum level of health and decency in life" (Sengere 29/09/2021). This is the minimum amount of money needed by an individual or family per month to cover basic costs (Sengere 29/09/2021). This is where we find a contention between politicians and economists because the later normally tend to be conservative in order to defend their political will. What are the things that are used to measure the PDL? The first thing is food. This is the minimum amount needed by an individual in a given period, for example in a month. This food is not determined by specific foods as is the case in the Zimbabwean's context where the National Consumer Council talks of the breadbasket with specific items. It is measured in terms of the calories. The next items are the non-food essentials.

Things included in this category are rentals and household essentials needed by an individual so as not to be considered poor. Leonard Sengere argues that

> there is always confusion between the Total Consumption Poverty Line (TPCL) and the Poverty Datum Line. This measure is the one we often think about when we hear 'poverty datum line'. The TPCL is the sum of the Food Poverty Line and the non-food essentials. So it represents the least amount of money an individual or family needs to cover their food, rentals, clothing and other essentials (Sengere 29/09/2021).

This means that what we should use in measuring poverty and classifying people into economic classes is the TPCL and not PDL.

Why is this information important for our argument here? It helps to determine the classes of people in Zimbabwe who constitute a bracket of economically disadvantaged people. Official information concerning the usage of these instruments or measurements in Zimbabwe is produced by the Zimstat. However, their information is disputed by many economists as it is taken to be more conservative and not in tandem with the reality on the ground. For example, in a combined report by the Zimstat and World Bank it was acknowledged that:

> Poverty measurement methodologies require periodic updating in response to improved data and analytical techniques, changing conditions and consumption habits, and new consensus on which expenditures should be included in the welfare aggregate. Therefore, it was necessary to update the approach used to measure poverty in Zimbabwe.
>
> (Zimstat and World Bank 2020)

The same sentiments were acknowledged by Zimstat in their report: "they produce the official Poverty Datum Lines which are not comparable to cost of living indicators produced by other players on the market" (Zimstat: 31/12/2020). What is the latest official TPCL for one person in Zimbabwe? As of July 2021, the TPCL was placed at ZWD$6,126.00. This means that a family of six people needs ZWD$36.756.00 per month to live a decent life and not to be considered economically disadvantaged people. This is the official measure according to the government, but it is widely disputed by the other economic players on the ground that it is not in line with daily economic performances on the ground.

What are the economic classes in Zimbabwe? Ryan Gosha gives us some interesting economic classes of Zimbabwe. He concurs with Roger Southall who argues that "the middle class has since disappeared" (Southall 2020:542). Gosha proposed nine economic and political classes in Zimbabwe and below is a discussion of these classes:

1. The Deep State

According to Gosho, "this is a combo of government leaders and top finance leaders" (Gosho 30/08/2020). This is the group of people in the pinnacle of both economic and political power. The group includes the Presidium, Ministers, Military Chiefs, Police Commissioners, Chief Justice, Central Intelligence Boss, Airforce Commander, Brigadiers, Reserve Bank Governor, Commercial Bank of Zimbabwe Chief Executive Officer, Zimbabwe Revenue Authority Commissioner General, National Social Security Authority Chief Executive Officer, Zimbabwe National Road Association Chief Executive Officer, and lastly Air Zimbabwe Chief Executive Officer.

2. Oligarchs

Gosho argues that, "these are a very small class of wealthy people, mostly businesspeople" (Gosho 30/08/2020). These people have the capacity to interact with the above 'Deep State' and sometimes they can capture them because of the abundant wealth (Gosho 30/08/2020). This is where we talk of state capture by such people. In Zimbabwe we normally refer to these people as 'queen bee'. They include business moguls such as Strive Masiiwa of Econet, Kudakwashe Tagwirei of Sakunda Holdings, Billy Rautenbach of Green Fuel Investments, and John Bredenkemp founder of Casalee Group.

3. New Nobility

According to Gosho, "these ones are royalty. They do not attempt to manage the political process. They manage their business and can influence policy through normal channels and lobbying" (Gosho 30/08/2020). They deal with politicians behind the scene and this group is diverse as it includes people such as Zed Koudounaris, who is the chairperson of ACIA Aero Leasing Group Board; the Late Mohammed Musa (wholesaler); the founder of Croco Motors, Moses Chingwena; the Late Sam Levy, who owned the country's most beautiful shopping mall, Sam Levy; Exodus Makumbe, who is the founder and owner of Exodus and Company Private Limited and is also in the platinum business; Busisa Moyo, who is the chief executive officer of United Refineries; Late Genius Kadungure, who was in the gas industry; Shingi Munyeza cleric and entrepreneur; Emmanuel Makandiwa, cleric and entrepreneur; Ezekiel Guti, cleric and entrepreneur; Passion Java, cleric and entrepreneur; Walter Magaya, cleric and entrepreneur; Phillip Chiyangwa, politician, sport administrator, and businessman; Super Mandiwanzira, journalist and businessman; and Frank Buyanga, United Kingdom-born businessman. This is the group where the Shona term 'mbinga' is applied. The term means a wealthy person.

4. Upper Caste

This is a class that has employees who are mainly in the managerial level. According to Gosho, "they do not own the means of production but they are technocrats and professionals managing the affairs of the classes above them" (Gosho 30/08/2020). They are the think tanks for the Deep State, Oligarch, and Nobility. This is where we see the executive managers, finance directors, and some chief executive officers. One such person in that category is Tawanda Nyambirai.

5. State Nomenklatura

These are civil servants involved in the administration of government affairs. Gosho argues that "they are high-level government employees appointed to key positions" (Gosho 30/08/2020). These people lead boards of important government parastatals such as Vehicle Inspection Department, NETONE, Grain Marketing in Board, Zimpost, and embassies.

6. False Middle Class

Gosho called them the false middle class because his argument is that, "the middle class is non-existent in Zimbabwe" (Gosho 30/08/2020). Either one is in the upper classes or in the lower classes. There is no middle class in the Zimbabwean economy. These are the people who work for banks, big multinational companies such as Delta, OK stores, Zimplats, Mimosa, and Econet. They are middle-level managers.

7. The Hustling Creatives

These are people who work for themselves without being formally employed by a company or an organization. According to Gosho, "these are mostly hustlers who are making it in the largely informal economy" Gosho (30/08/2020). The above seven classes are not among the economically disadvantaged people. Therefore, these are the people who could not have felt the impact of the lockdowns since the majority of them would be under the category of essential workers. They continue to earn their benefits and packages. However, the difference could be with hustling creatives who depend on the level of their hustling and the products of their businesses.

8. The Working Poor

According to Gosho, "these are the real taxpayers. They are shouldering the burden. The working poor exist in both public sector and the private sector"

(Gosho 30/08/2020). These include teachers, nurses, junior doctors, bulk of civil servants, tiny retailers, farmers, vendors, and small-scale hustlers. These are the people who supplement their income through extra jobs like doing extra lessons for students and running small poultry projects.

9. The Unemployed

This is the most pathetic group to exist in a country. Gosho postulates that, "this class is made up of people who are not meaningfully working" (Gosho 30/08/2020). They survive on illegal deals and part-time jobs. Most of them resort to criminal activities. This group is made up of mainly young people who have recently graduated and cannot secure employment. These last two groups, including the children, are the economically disadvantaged people who are the subject of this chapter. Surprisingly, these are only three groups out of ten but they constitute the bulk of the population. This is the group of 6 million people who are living in extreme poverty (The UN Common Country Analysis 2021). Below is a table by Gosho, which summarizes these classes in figures:

Deep State	1,000
Oligarchs	100
The New Nobility	5,000
Upper Caste	100,000
State Nomenklatura	200,000
False Middle Class	300,000
The Hustling Creatives	400,000
The Working Poor	3,500,000
The Unemployed	4,500 000
Under 18	5,000,000
Total	14,006,100

Gosho 30/08/2020

Therefore, when talking of the impact of national lockdowns on the economically disadvantaged people, the researcher is dealing with a subject that affected the majority of the people in the country. These are the people who constitute more than 90% of the country's population.

A Detailed Analysis of the Ramification of 2020 National Lockdown on the Economically Disadvantaged People

National lockdowns in 2020 achieved the goal of reducing the spreading of the virus and lives were saved but the economic impact on people was heavily felt. Several groups of people within the bracket of the working poor, unemployed, children, and destitute were affected severely in one way or another. This section discusses how the following groups of people were affected: teachers, vendors, and rural horticulturists. I have decided to choose these three groups only for the sake of space and time.

1. Teachers

Teachers are some of the professionals who are underpaid in Zimbabwe. Their salaries are so meager to the extent that they have to be creative hustlers to survive. According to a story in the online press called *Kubatana.net*;

> Teacher's salaries have been eroded to less than 50% of the Total Consumption Poverty Line (TCPL) due to inflation and the rise in cost of living and some of the demands by teachers are basic welfare issues like housing which has proven to be a great challenge especially for those stationed in rural areas who stay in subhuman conditions and are often exposed to risk due to the conditions they will be staying under.

This is a group of people who are informally employed but with meager salaries. During lockdown they still receive their monthly salaries in full but the challenge was that there was no room for them to hustle in order to augment their salaries. In Zimbabwe, the tradition of extra lessons after the normal school times has become common and a major source of income for teachers. Tendai Sithole (pseudonym) in an interview admitted that her income was mainly sustained by the extra private lessons she conducts in a car garage in the evenings. This means with COVID-19 such extra income activities were banned. Fortunately she owned her house and hence did not have to pay rent but she had to pay for electricity and council rates. Government decreed that school lessons were to be offered online by the authorized organs especially through the radio. However, "internet access is considered a luxury and costs are prohibitive for poorer families" (*The Guardian*: 18/02/2021). This is equally true even for university professors; they could not afford the costs of internet and many employees rely on company internet facilities. Kundai Dungeni (pseudonym) also acknowledged that life had become difficult during the lockdown as he struggled to feed his family of five children. The government had directed that food shops will remain open for the purpose of people securing food but the major problem was getting the required money to buy food. The end result was that many teachers defied the presidential decree on lockdown measures by opening private backdoor classes at their homes. Sheila Tembo (pseudonym) testified that they had to bribe the police, council, and health officers to continue with the classes. This also put their health at risk as they had to risk contracting the virus because COVID-19 protocols were not properly observed in the backyard schools. It was now a quest for survival. Some teachers have big classes with an average of 50 students and they get paid between USD$6 and USD$10 per month. Therefore, a teacher with 50 students would earn between USD$300 and USD$500. The major challenge was with those teachers without their own homes. This means they had nowhere to hold their classes. Tildah Guramba (pseudonym) admitted that her landlord refused her the permission to hold classes at the premises of the house she was renting and had to teach students on WhatsApp. Though teachers struggled, their profession is better in that they could still get clients during the lockdown especially those in the high-density suburbs.

2. Vendors

These were the people who survived by selling some food items such as vegetables, cigarettes, freezits, beverages, and airtime. These are the people who are not formally employed and their income depends on their daily sales. Their small businesses are not formally registered and they do not have business premises for them to operate from. Some of them operate from the gates of their houses and some from the roadside. Mebbo Masawi (pseudonym) who sells freezits for school at the school gate during the school term lamented that her survival was at stake with the lockdown as schools were closed indefinitely. Though the government had directed that landlords should not evict their tenants from the houses for failure to pay rent, some defied the order. Mebbo was one such person who was threatened with eviction and the Anglican Cathedral of St Mary's and All Saints in Harare had to intervene by paying her one month's rent through the Dean's discretionary fund. Sheila Chipunza who sells vegetables and small food items at small tuckshop at her house admitted that things were not easy for as well during the lockdown. The major challenge was for her to go to the wholesale to order some food items to replenish her tuckshop. She did not have the required travel documents to travel to the wholesale because her business was informal. People who run such small informal business do not have much profit to save for future use. They survive form hand to mouth and during the lockdown they did not have savings to rely on. As vendors were lamenting the pain of COVID-19 lockdown on their daily welfare, more pain was infused on them by the government. Simbarashe Gukurume and Marjoke Oosterom argue that "the government made use of the opportunity to push through reforms of informal markets, making no attempt to warn or consult vendors whose stalls were bulldozed" (Gukurume and Oosterom 2020). The timing of the government to demolish people's informal markets at this time was heavily questioned by human rights experts. Instead of channeling all available resources on fighting the pandemic, the government had to prioritize the demolishing of informal markets. The sudden announcement of the lockdown measures did not give vendors enough time to stock up food for the family. Vendors thrive in crowded spaces like the city center, market places, and bus terminus. All these places were closed and empty during the lockdown and this impacted heavily on their sales.

3. Rural Horticulturists

In Zimbabwe, agriculture is one of the pillars of the economy. Horticultural farming is one of the lucrative agricultural activities in peri-urban rural areas such as Domboshawa, Murehwa, Lowe Gweru, Chiundura, Mvuma, and Seke. These are small-scale gardeners who specialize in vegetables that are then transported to the nearby city markets. This is a business that needs a lot of planning, discipline, and hardworking. Many horticulturists registered losses during the lockdown period. Firstly, when the lockdown was announced many of them had crops especially tomatoes that were about to ripe. This means there was need for transporting the crop to the urban market. Secondly, transporting products to the market became very difficult because of banned intercity travels. Cleopas Nhira (pseudonym) lamented that during the lockdown he lost two acres of ripe tomatoes as securing transport to the market was difficult. His friend was turned back home on his way to the market and the transporter had to offload the whole load along the road for the monkeys and baboons to feed. This was a huge loss as the transporter was paid his money in full. Thirdly, the market in the city was not vibrant as before because many people were staying at home. Therefore, it means efforts to go to the city markets were a waste of time as these markets were not performing as usual. Fourthly, many urbanites resorted to gardening as well because of lack of activity. This means they produced enough vegetables for their consumption. Martin Mhaka Chirume concurs that he had enough vegetables at his church house in Melfort Park. He had to donate some of the vegetables to the nearby orphanage. Therefore, the income of the horticulturists dwindled and this was a threat for their survival. They had to dry some of their vegetables for their own future consumption. This was a loss for the people who had invested in the project in the form of inputs, pesticides, and labor.

The Way Forward for the Post-COVID-19 Era: Application of the Practical Theological Approach to the Research Findings

It has emerged from the research that the lockdowns were necessary in order to save lives. In terms of the third task of the practical theological approach that is raising a normative question: "What ought to be going?" There was no other better ethical solution than closing down the economy in order to save lives. A lost economy can be recovered in the future but the same cannot happen to a lost life. Therefore, from a practical theological perspective, saving life becomes a major priority. The government did well by protecting millions of lives from dying from the virus. It is common that in every solution there is bound to be new challenges that arise. It has emerged from the research that though the lockdown measures played a vital role in saving lives, the economically disadvantaged people suffered a lot. The majority could not raise enough income to meet the family's basic needs. Millions of people were to languish in poverty and some social challenges in the form of domestic violence increased. These findings take us to the fourth task of the practical theological approach of asking a pragmatic question: "How might we respond?" This is where solutions to the new challenges caused by the lockdown are proffered. Here we are answering the question: "Was there a better way of doing it by the government?"

The pandemic has taught us and our leadership that disasters are bound to happen at any time both at the global and local levels. Humanity has also learnt that pandemics sweep away the entire humanity and close down even powerful economies. However, what measures need to be put in place in the future to lessen the suffering of people during the pandemics?

First, our national budget should reserve adequate funds to fight disasters in the future especially subsidizing people's resources in times of crisis. This has happened in other western countries where people's salaries have been subsidized under COVID-19 hardship grants. During pandemics or other disasters people's incomes are affected because some companies close down or operate below capacity. This means that the government also needs to have policies of assisting struggling companies during such periods. Second, the health sector needs a lot of investment to be capacitated to fight such pandemics. During the period under review, testing and treatment of COVID-19 as well as remunerating frontline workers were key for the fighting of the pandemic

Second, the government needed to subsidize people's food pantry by channeling certain resources towards feeding people. The government needed to identify starving people and prepare food hampers for them through parastatals such as Grain Marketing in Board and CMED. The country's food banks, especially the GMB, responsible for the storage and distribution of grains should keep enough reserves to be given at subsidized rates to the starving communities. This is where the maize reserves in the Grain Marketing in Board silos were supposed to be availed to the people at very subsidized rates and free for the unemployed. Many people were exposed to starving and the church and other non-profit organizations played a vital role in assisting such vulnerable people. Lots of promises were made during the State of the Nation addresses on meeting the needs of the people during the lockdown periods. There were no officially known social welfare reports on the distribution of food to the starving areas in high-density suburbs.

Third, the government was supposed to use other stakeholders such as the church in meeting some of the needs of the people starving. The government in the future should invite other stakeholders and set aside political interests when confronted with disasters like COVID-19. In the previous lockdowns, churches and their personnel were treated as non-essential services hence they played a vital role informally in addressing peoples needs. The church was left out in the humanitarian efforts as it was placed under non-essential services and this means exclusion in the fight against the pandemic. The Dean of the Anglican Cathedral of Harare and his clergy during that time had to supply several starving families in Chitungwiza, Highfield, Mbare, Glen Norah, Mufakose, and Glen View with weekly food hampers. Though the church was closed it had the capacity to meet some of the essential needs of those starving during lockdowns. The Anglican Diocese of Harare through her overseas link, The Diocese of Rochester in England, donated over 500 food hampers and seed packs to the rural communities in the Mashonaland provinces. It is the duty of the government to feed, protect, and care for the citizens. This is what was happening with other governments who gave COVID-19 allowances to the citizens. Though the government of

Zimbabwe did not have such resources it was important to involve other key stakeholders for help.

Four, transparency on the COVID-19 grants was needed. The government received millions of grants from the World Health Organization but there is no clarity as to how the resources were distributed. On 24 March 2021, African Field Epidemiology Network (AFENET) issued a statement that they have received the case of mismanagement of COVID-19 grants by the Government of Zimbabwe. Below is an extract of the statement:

> AFENET (the fund manager) and Africa CDC (on whose behalf AFENET manages the fund) are neither involved in any way nor sanctioned the alleged corrupt use of the funds. We take these allegations very seriously and are happy that the issues are being investigated. Furthermore, we are glad that the case is in court for determination. We look forward to the findings of the investigation and the court's pronouncement on the case to guide our next line of action. We take this opportunity to assure our many partners of our commitment to the highest levels of compliance, probity, transparency and accountability in the management of resources we receive.
>
> (AFENET Letter 24/03/2021)

It is sad that while the world is fighting to raise funds for dealing with the pandemic, some were busy looting them and this appeared to be the case in Zimbabwe. The issue of corruption has been a cancer that has eaten the moral fiber of the nation. In the future, systems should be put in place especially an independent body to administer disaster grants.

Five, the government was supposed to postpone the plans of demolishing illegal informal business structures to reduce mental health pressure on the people who were already being traumatized by the virus. This was a misplaced priority that demonstrated a gesture of an uncaring leadership. A caring government goes beyond the crime committed by setting up of illegal structures and ask the question, "Why are people in this predicament?" "Why would the government invest time in demolishing structures in crises periods instead of investing in developing a vaccine like what other countries were doing?" In the future, political agenda and other non-essential projects should be postponed while people direct their energy towards fighting the pandemic.

Six, our institution of higher learning should develop models and home-grown initiatives of mitigating crisis. It appears as if the government cut and paste policies of fighting disasters from other countries and some of them were not applicable to our context. The fiscal policy should channel resources towards research and development of home-grown solutions to disasters. Policies should be informed by strong research not assumptions. Many people noticed that our measures and restrictions were mainly informed by South African policies and this was a major concern for many people because the two countries are not at the same level in terms of resources.

Conclusion

Though the government took the best decision in locking down the economy to preserve lives, what lacked was a holistic approach to saving lives. The holistic approach involves being inclusive and proffer better solutions to the people's problems as has been established by the practical theological approach. The research after engaging the practical theological approach concludes that in addition to national economic lockdown, the government needed to consider seriously the welfare of the economically disadvantaged people. This was through meeting the basic needs of the poor and in partnership with other vital stakeholders such as the church, nongovernmental and civic organizations. Having learnt from the past, the post-COVID-19 era should be a period of adopting new ways of doing things and strengthening the preparedness of our institutions in fighting future health and natural disasters. Disasters will remain part and parcel of our lives and hence the need to be proactive by developing home-grown policies to mitigate disasters based on well-informed research. Investment in disaster preparedness is no longer a luxury but a necessity.

References

AFENET Letter 24/03/2021.

Balkhair, A. A. (2020). COVID-19 Pandemic: A New Chapter in the History of Infectious Diseases. *Oman Medical Journal, 35*(2), e123. https://doi.org/10.5001/omj.2020.41. (Accessed 14/12/2021).

Chamburuka, P. M. and Gusha, I. S. (2020). An Exegesis of the Parable of the Good Samaritan (Lk 10:25–35) and Its Relevance to the Challenges Caused by COVID-19. *HTS Teologiese Studies/Theological Studies, 76*(1), a6096. https://doi.org/10.4102/hts .v76i1.6096. (Accessed 20/01/2021).

Gosho, R. (2020). Zimbabwe's Power-Wealth Hierarchical Classes. https://ryangosha .medium.com/zimbabwes-power-wealth-hierarchical-classes-e53b61bad6d8. (Accessed 15/12/2021).

Mercer, J. A. (2021). Economics, Class, and Classicism. In B. J. Miller-Mclemare (Ed.), *The Wiley-Blackwell Companion to Practical Theology* (pp. 432–442). Oxford: Blackwell Publishing Limited.

Osmer, R. (2011). Practical Theology: A Current International Perspective. *HTS Teologiese Studies/Theological Studies, 67*(2), Art.1058. http://dx.doi.org/6.4102/hts.v67i1.1058. (Accessed 14/12/2021).

Schuringa, D. H. (2000). What Is Practical Theology. *Calvin Theological Journal, 34*, 1–13.

Sengere, L. (2021). Breaking Down the Poverty Info Released by Zimstat, Zim Situation Dire. *Techzim.* Available at: Breaking down the poverty info released by ZIMSTAT, Zim situation dire - Techzim

Simbarashe, G. and Marjoke, O. (2020). The Impact of the Covid 19 Lockdown on Zimbabwe's Informal Economy. Institute of Development Studies. https://www.ids .ac.uk/opinions/the-impact-of-the-covid-19-lockdown-on-zimbabwes-informal -economy/. (Accessed 14/08/2021).

Southall, R. (2020). Flight and Fortitude: The Decline of the Middle Class in Zimbabwe. *Africa, 90*(3), 529–557.

The Guardian. (2021). https://www.theguardian.com/global-development/2021/feb/18/ educating-zimbabwe-home-schools-defy-lockdown-in-townships. (Accessed 20/04/2021).

The United Nations Common Country Analysis Zimbabwe. (2021). Harare: UN Resident Coordinator's Office.

Ward, P. (2017). *Introducing Practical Theology: Mission, Ministry, and the Life of the Church.* Grand Rapids: Baker Academic.

Wilson, D. 2020. *Ploductivity: A Practical Theology of Work and Wealth.* Moscow: Canon Press Zimstat. (Accessed 31/12/2020).

Zimstat and World Bank. 2020. Zimbabwe Poverty Update. 2017–19. Joint Report. Harare.

World Health Organization. (2020). Statement on the Second Meeting of the International Health Regulations (2005) Emergency Committee Regarding the Outbreak of Novel Coronavirus (2019-Ncov). Geneva. 30/01/2020. https://www.who.int/news/item /30-01-2020-statement-on-the-second-meeting-of-the-international-health-regulations-(2005)-emergency-committee-regarding-the-outbreak-of-novel-coronavirus-(2019-ncov). (Accessed 11/12/2021).

Interviews

Tendai Sithole, Harare. (Accessed 15/12/2021).
Kundai Dungeni, Harare. (Accessed 15/12/2021).
Tildah Guramba, Harare. (Accessed 15/12/2021).
Mebbo Masawi, Harare. (Accessed 15/12/2021).
Sheila Chipunza, Murehwa. (Accessed 16/12/2021).
Cleopas Nhira, Murehwa. (Accessed 16/12/2021).

15 Conclusion

The Post-COVID-19 – The Future of Public Health in Zimbabwe

Ernest Jakaza

The Future of Public Health in Zimbabwe

The unprecedented moment that the history of humankind and the entire planet (WHO, 2020) encountered has been projected to return in various forms and this requires preparedness and planning for their mitigation. Social media platforms have been singled out as perpetrators of COVID-19 infordemic (WHO, 2020). Much of the research has been carried out on social media misinformation in disseminating news on the origins, spread, deaths, and even COVID-19 vaccinations (Mhute, Mangeya and Jakaza, 2021, Brennen et al., 2020, Howard, 2021). In as much as some sections of the society might be able to discern that these are jokes about the pandemic, some ended up believing the misinformation and the unsuspecting social media news consumers suffered.

Gwaravanda (Chapter 2, this volume), through the use of the Socratic sieve, presented lessons that can be drawn from misinformation about COVID-19 origins, transmission, treatment, and vaccination in order to project the future of public health in Zimbabwe and the world in general. He argues that as it is now known that social media promotes and disseminates untrustworthy information, and to try and minimize the problem, better ways can be suggested that include health authorities rebutting or refuting misinformation by posting accurate information on social media platforms, public broadcasters, and the print media can also be used to correct misinformation on COVID-19, increasing the health literacy of social media users so that individuals can decide on information before passing it to the next person, educating social media users on how to determine what information is reliable and to encourage them to assume personal responsibility for not circulating false information.

The future of public health and journalistic education is also another critical area of concern. In projecting the future, Hove and Alufandika (Chapter 3, this volume) observed that there is a need for in-service training of journalists as well as outsourcing of well-equipped professionals in order to improve journalistic practices in the country. They argue that there is also a need to train citizen journalists so that we can bridge that gap between professional and unprofessional news gathers. Thus, this recommendation, in line with the

DOI: 10.4324/9781003390732-15

future of journalistic practices in post-COVID-19 in Zimbabwe, para-professional journalists should be trained so that they can partly identify and exhibit journalistic ethos.

The advent of COVID-19 imposed new communication, socio-cultural, and public health practices. Governments and the World Health Organization came up with mitigatory measures for the prevention of COVID-19 that were cascaded down to the rural communities. These measures impacted the way of life and a number of African cultural practices realized in *nhimbe* and funerals (Gwindingwe and Zinomwe, Chapter 4, this volume; Maseno and Sibanda, Chapter 10, this volume; Ndlovu, Chapter 9, this volume; Taringa and Chirongoma, Chapter 11, this volume).

The effects of the pandemic on people's socio-cultural practices affected their communal form of life. Rural livelihoods' cultural occasions like funerals and *nhimbes* were shredded as they were interfered with when large gatherings were criminalized and made taboo. This effect "portends a possibility of the emergence of new cultural order and the new forms of communication that negate existing socio-cultural order and impacted on community development" (Gwindinge and Zinomwe, Chapter 4, this volume). The future of public health lies in preserving these deliberative communicative platforms like *Nhimbe* as they are a socio-cultural therapy that rids society of social vices in a euphemistic way. If people are denied such platforms, the (rural) communities, their social fabric will be negatively impacted. In the same understanding, Ndlovu (Chapter 9, this volume) also argues that "some African IKS are not in any way retrogressive but could be applied globally to save humanity from the scourge of pandemics." The COVID-19 projected a reconfigured landscape in funeral rites and other African practices.

Language is a resource, a people's identity, and also a tool that defines the future. The place of local languages in communicating the pandemic and insidious ways to compart it is an area of contention in Africa and Zimbabwe. Researches in this volume (Mavengano, Chapter 5, this volume; Mhute, Chapter 6, this volume; Nyoni and Nyoni, Chapter 7, this volume) are of the opinion that the future of public health rests with continental intellectuals who are supposed to have a deep retrospection and introspection on their language-policy-inspired dependency syndrome and reclaim their responsibilities, and rise up to the demands of the situation. In as much as borrowing and other morphologization processes are part of a language's growth and expansion, the place of indigenous languages in communicating the pandemic might open up avenues for home-grown solutions and survival strategies.

References

Brennen, J. S., Simon, F., Howard, P. N. and Nielsen, R. K. (2020). Types, sources, and claims of COVID-19 misinformation. Retrieved October 25, 2021, from https://reutersinstitute.politics.ox.ac.uk/types-sources-and-claims-covid-19-misinformation.

Howard, P. (2021). Misinformation and the coronavirus resistance. Retrieved October 15, 2021, from https://www.oii.ox.ac.uk/blog/misinformation-and-the-coronavirus-resistance/.

Mhute, I., Mangeya, H. and Jakaza, E. (2021). Endangering the endangered: Impact of fake corona virus social media communications, Covid 19 ramifications in Zimbabwe, Africa and beyond-An interdisciplinary perspective. *Pharos Journal of Theology*, *102*, 1–11.

Mhute, I., Mangeya, H. and Jakaza, E. (2022). *Endangering the endangered: A case of fake COVID-19 social media news in Zimbabwe*. Generis Publishing.

WHO. (2020). Retrieved April 27, 2020, from https://www.sokodirectory.com.

Index

2019 novel coronavirus (2019-nCov) 76

ABX matrix model of communication 39
acronyms 81
actual consequence view 21
Adebileje, A. 78
Adeleke, A. 78
affixation 80
African burial practices 141–142
African Field Epidemiology Network (AFENET) 191
African language policies: cultural dependency theory 67; direction of scientists and researchers' focus 69–70; lessons for post-COVID-19 era 72–73; opportunities ignored by scientists and researchers 70–72; as promoters of cultural dependency 67–68
African religion 108, 111; fundamental aspects of 9
African Union (AU) 166
African Vaccine Regulatory Forum (ALVAREF) 69
Afrika, L. O. 108
Agamben, Giorgio 5
Agrawal, A. 111
Ahmed, A. 78
Aikenhead, G. S. 110
Aktaş, F. 110
Albarracin, D. 65, 66
Alfandika, L. 40
Aljezeera News Agency 124
alternative public sphere theory 40, 41
amanzi cleansing ceremony 116
analytic statements 20
Anyanwu, M. U. 157
Aronson, J. 112
Ary, D. 81
Asian Development Bank 65

Bächtiger, A. 43
backformation 81
Balkhair, Abdullah A. 174
Bamgbose, A. 55, 58
Banda, D. 26–27
Barnhardt, R. 110, 111
Battiste, M. 111
Benkler, Y. 45, 46
Best, J. W. 154
Bhabha, Homi 57
biopolitical power 5
Blanche, M. S. 112
blending 81
Blumler, J. G. 93
Bodini, C. 109
body bag directive 126
borrowing language 81; *jebwa* 85; *korona* (corona) 84–85; *kovhidhi* (COVID) 84; *masiki* (mask) 84
boundary jumping 69
Bramadat, P. 122
Briggs, J. 111
Bronstein, J. 92, 103
Bruns, D. P. 154
Bruns, T. R. 154
Bryman, A. 140
burial ceremonies, Kenya and Zimbabwe: COVID-19 and Health Ministries' Directives 123–125; deaths and 125–128; post-COVID-19, reimagination of 130–132; securitization analysis 129–130
Busolo, D. 137
Buzan, B. 122

Cachia, A. 70
Cajete, G. A. 110
Canagarajah, S. 50, 52, 55
carnivalesque festivals 44
Cartesian perspectivism 1

Cartesian thinking 11
Castells, M. 28
center–periphery model of humanity 57
Centre for Disease Control (CDC)
    Foundation 106
Chateuka, D. N. 40
Chikasha, J. 57
chikovhidhi 87
Chirisa, I. 137, 141–143
Chirongoma, S. 149
chisekete 85–86
Chitakure, J. 138, 142, 143
Chitando, E. 141
Cilliers, L. 95
clipping 81
cognitive empires 52, 56, 165
Cohen, L. 154
communication 39
compounding 81; *dzihwamupengo/
    dzibwamupengo* 83–84
content analysis 81
conversion 81
Copenhagen school 122
corona vocabulary 78
COVID-19 pandemic, Zimbabwe 75;
    biopolitics of 4–5; burial rites *see* burial
    ceremonies, Kenya and Zimbabwe;
    crisis of 165–166; funeral gatherings and
    nhimbes 43–44; funeral rituals 144–146;
    journalism education in 33–34; language
    change *see* language change, COVID-
    19 pandemic; lessons drawn from
    misinformation 20–22; lessons learnt
    149–150; linguistic binarisms 57–59;
    and lockdowns in Harare 176–177; *see
    also* lockdowns, Harare; Online Health
    Communities (OHCs) *see* virtual/
    online communities; post-burial rituals
    146–148; reflections on 2–4; and social
    media 15–16; *see also individual entries*
COVID-Organics 70
Creswell, J. W. 81, 140
Critical Discourse Analysis (CDA) 10
Cui, J. 109
cultural communication 37, 38; pattern 42;
    regulative signs 39, 40
cultural dependency theory 67, 69
culture, defined 137
curfews 42

Danzey, E. 85
daranganwa (spaced grain) 86
Dare/Dariro 40, 41
Darni, D 78

Dawson, L. 122
De Ceukelaire, W. 109
decolonial conversations 51
decoloniality 164
decolonial turn 164
Dei, G. J. 111
deliberative democracy 38, 40, 41, 43, 47
Dennis, M. J. 65
digital media technology 24, 28; use of 33
digital revolution 25
dismemberment 52
do-it-yourself journalism 27
Drugs for Neglected Diseases initiative
    (DNDi) 69–71
Durrheim, K. 112
dzihwamupengo/dzibwamupengo 83

economically disadvantaged people,
    lockdown impact on: economic and
    political classes 183–186; economic
    classes, categories of 182–183;
    ramification of national lockdown on
    186–189; rural horticulturists 188–190;
    teachers 187–188; vendors 188
economic and political classes of people:
    Deep State 184; false middle class 185;
    hustling creatives 185; New Nobility
    184; Oligarchs 184; State Nomenklatura
    185; unemployed 186; upper caste 185;
    working poor 185–186
Edeling, J. H. 68
education 5.0 32
Eliastam, J. 39
Elibol, E. 106, 109
emotional support 92, 100
English 53, 58; discursive contours,
    language ideologies 51–53; as lingua
    franca 53–57; linguistic binarisms,
    COVID-19 pandemic 57–59; post-
    COVID-19 moral order 59–60
entrée 94
ethical egoism 21
ethics in practice 95
Eurocentric monolingual reductionism 51
European exceptionalism 55
everything shop approach 32
expected utility 21

Fanon, F. 5
Finnegan, R. 156
Flores, D. S. 68
foreseeable consequence 21
Foucault, M. 5
Fourie, Pieter J. 27

Fraser, Nancy 37, 38, 40, 41
funeral gatherings 39, 45,
    135, 178
funeral vigils 45

Ghebreyesus, Tedros Adhanom 4
globalization discourse 59
Gombe, J. M. 38, 43, 47
goodness 17, 18, 21; ethical
    principle of 20
Gosha, Ryan 183–186
Grain Marketing in Board 190
Green, B. M. 93, 102
Grosfoguel, R. 52
Güner, H. R. 106, 110
Gwindingwe, G. 40

Habermas, Jurgen 40, 41; public sphere
    theory 38, 40
Halliday, Michael Alexander Kirkwood 79
Han, J. 109
handwashing 97, 115
Haralambos, M. 137
Hasanoğlu, İ. 110
He, S. 109
Health Centre Committee 40
health education 16
Heller, M. 58
Hens, L. 111
Hochheimer, J. L. 26–27
Hock, H. H. 84
Holborn, M. 137
Holloway, I. 111
Holy Communion 166, 167
homo significans 80
Horrell, L. N. 102
horticultural farming 188
Hove, M. L. 51, 53

Idang, G. E. 107, 108, 111
Ifeoma, O. 67
indigenous knowledge systems (IKS) 68,
    69, 71, 110–111, 165
indigenous languages 54, 60–61
inductive theory 140
infodemic 14, 15
information, communication, and
    technology (ICT) 149
information dissemination system 7
International Committee on Taxonomy of
    Viruses (ICTV) 76
internet-linked platforms 46
Islam, M. 78
Israeli Ministry of Health 68

Jacobs, L. C. 81
Jacobs, S. 128
Jaja, C. J. I. 157
Jaja, I. F. 157
jebha 85
Jia, P. 109
Joseph, B. D. 84
journalism education 26, 28; in COVID-
    19 era 33–34; debates in 27; digital
    media technologies 27–28; media and
    communication studies 27; pedagogical
    theory to meaning-based practice 25–27;
    qualitative research method 29–30;
    teaching digital skills and techniques in
    30–33
junga 86

Kachru, B. B. 52, 54, 55
Kaemmer, J. E. 156
Kahn, J. V. 154
Kanu, Y. 139, 140, 149
Katz, E. 93
Kavuludi, Charles 126
Kawagley, O. A. 110, 111
Keith, R. 78
Kenyan Interim guidelines 125
Kenyan Ministry of Health 124
Kershaw, H. 150
Khanpour, H. 103
Khotimah, K. 78
korona 84–85
Kraguljac, N. V. 154
Kubatana. net 187
kugadzira 143
kugova nhumbi dzemufi ritual 147
Kupolati, O. 78
kurova guva ceremony 138, 143

Laksono, K. 78
language change, COVID-19 pandemic
    79; anticipated contribution, society
    and scholarship 76; data gathering
    81–82; linguistic items 83–87; systemic
    functional approach 79–80; word
    formation ways 80–81
language ideology 51; discursive contours
    of 51–53
language of theory 20
language-policy-inspired dependency
    syndrome 72
language politics 49, 55, 60
language use/discourse 51, 53, 75
Laustsen, C. 122
Lawton, D. 137

Letsiou, M. 138, 139
Li, F. 109
linguicism 51
Linguistic Human Rights Theory 50
lockdowns, Harare 176; fifth national
   lockdown order 180–181; first national
   lockdown order 177–178; fourth
   national lockdown order 179–180; second national lockdown order 178–179;
   sixth national lockdown order 181–182;
   third national lockdown order 179
logical analysis 20

Macionis, J. J. 75
madaranganwa (Social and Physical
   Distancing) 86–87
magadziro ritual 148
Magwaza,T. S. C. 113
Makoni, S. 57
Maldonado-Torres, N. 164, 165
Mandaza, I. 6
Manion, L. 154
Mapara, J. 68, 69, 71
Maposa, R. S. 111
Maroyi, A. 71
Martin-Jones, M. 58
masukafoshoro 147
Matsuda, P. K. 52
Mavengano, E. 51, 53
Mavhinga, D. 5
Max, Karl 182
Mbiti, J. S. 39, 108
media system 28
Melber, H. 3, 5
Mercer, Joyce Ann 175
Mestrovic, T. 68
mhlonhlo herb 115
Michigan State University 78
Middle East Respiratory Syndrome
   Coronavirus (MERS-CoV) 109
Mignolo, Walter 51, 52
Minimum Body of Knowledge (MBK)
   30, 32
Ministry of Health and Child Care
   (MOHCC) 96, 124
misinformation, COVID-19 14;
   categorization 15; lessons drawn 19–22;
   social media impact 16
Morgan, B. 140
Morrison, K. 154
Moyo, C. 108
multidimensional architecture of language
   79
multilingual crisis communication 49

Mumpande, I. 54, 55, 57
Munamati, S. 137, 139, 141, 142
Musendekwa, M. 137, 139, 141, 142
Mutalemwa, G. 167
Mutsvedu, L. 149
Muyambo, T. 111
Mweri, G. J. 78

narrowing 87
National Consumer Council 182
National Qualification Framework (NQF)
   30
Naveh, S. 92
Ncube, L. 40, 41, 46, 47
Ndebele cosmology 107, 108, 113
Ndebele funeral rites 106; COVID-19
   virus 109; Indigenous Knowledge
   Systems (IKS) 110–111; Ndebele
   religion 107–109; public health 109–
   110; quarantine 114–115;
   research methodology 111–112;
   sanitizing 115–116; social distancing
   112–114; warmth and testing
   116–117
Ndebele religion 107–109
Ndebele spirituality 114, 115
Ndlovu, C. D. 114
Ndlovu, S. 108
Ndlovu-Gatsheni, S. J. 1, 52, 56, 57, 60,
   164, 166, 167, 169, 170
netnography 93; data analysis 95; data
   collection in 94–95; entrée 94; ethical
   considerations 95–96; strategy of enquiry
   93–94
networked public sphere 45
Newcomb's model of communication
   39; *see also* ABX matrix model of
   communication
new cultural order 37
new normal 25, 42, 75, 145
Ngigi, S. 137
Nhari, L. G. 109
Nhemachena, A. 70
nhevedzo (accompaniment) 138
nhimbe/humwe 37, 38, 41, 43
Nkuna, H. P. 55, 56, 60
Norwegian Agency for Rural
   Development (NORAD) 25
Notari, A. 116
Nouvellet, P. 110
Nyathi, P. 108
Nye, J. S. Jr. 57
Nyoni, M. 79, 82
Nzveura 43

Occupation Health and Safety 2
Ogawa, M. 110
Okunna, S. 67
Online Health Communities (OHCs)
91–93, 102, 103; COVID-19-related
thematic issues 96–99; *see also* virtual/
online communities
online health groups 93
Osmer, Richard 176
overnight gatherings 44
ox-drawn scotch carts 37

Page, C. 5
Pairin, U. 78
pauper's burial 126
Pennycook, A. 54
Pentaris, P. 121, 131
personal protective equipment (PPE) 124
Phillipson, Robert 50, 52, 54
physical distancing 86
plain text posts 96
Pongweni, A. J.C. 156
post-COVID-19 era, Zimbabwe:
Christian-African indigenous religion
praxes 167–169; practical-theological
approach 175–176, 189–191;
reimagining political futures in 169–171;
in religion and politics 166; *see also*
individual entries
Poverty Datum Line (PGL) 182, 183
poverty measurement methodologies 183
practical theology 175; primary tasks 176
procedural ethics 95
Public Health Act 40
public healthcare system 57
public health communication 49, 56, 61
public health education 7
public health sector 2
public service delivery 6–7
public sphere theory 37, 40, 41
Punch, K. F. 140

Rajoelina, Andry 70
Ranger, T. 115
Razavieh, A. 81
reductive process 68
Reeler, T. 6
Rizwan, A. 57
Rodney-Gumede, Y. 28

Saidi, U. 141, 142
Santos, B. de S. 11
Schleiermarcher, Fredrich 175
Schuringa, H. David 175

scientific theory 19
securitization theory 122, 123; basic
components of 122; of COVID-19 and
other pandemics 128–129
semantically broadened items: *chisekete*
85–86; *junga* 86; *madaranganwa* (Social
and Physical Distancing) 86–87
semiotic/transactional school 39
Sengere, Leonard 182, 183
severe acute respiratory syndrome
coronavirus 2 (SARS-CoV-2) 14, 65, 76
Shi, Z. L. 109
Shoko, T. 138
Shona cultural practices and values 155;
funerals 155–156; participant observation
153–154; post-COVID-19 era
lessons 160–161; quarantine 159–160;
sanitization and social distance 159;
singing and dancing 156–157; weddings
157–159; WHO regulations on
COVID-19 154
Shona language 75, 79
Shona linguistic expressions 82
Shumba, K. 7
Shuttleworth, J. 78
sieve of truth 17
sieve of usefulness 17, 18
silk (*rebvu*) 86
Silverstein, M. 51
Singh, P. R. 71
Sinopharm COVID-19 vaccine 16
Sklar, R. H. 140
Skutnabb-Kangas, T. 50, 51
Smith, D. 131
social distancing 45, 86, 112–114, 161
social equilibrium 39
social media 14, 20, 22, 82, 93; COVID-
19 and 15–16, 29; defined 15;
misinformation on 15–16, 20; usage 91
social reconstruction theory 138, 139, 150,
151
social vices 47, 195
Socratic sieve 8, 15, 17; lessons in 19–22;
limitations 18; three sieves test 17–18
Sorensen, C. 81
Sridhar, A. 106
state–citizens conflict 5
state of exception 5
state power, theorization of 5
Su, S. 109
Suharton, S. 78
symbolic communication platforms 43
synthetic statements 20
systematic theology 175

Systemic Functional Approach 81
Systemic Functional Grammar (SFG) 79,
    80; theoretical claims of 80
Systemic Functional Linguistics 79

Tabatabaeizadeh, S. A. 109
taboo system 108
Tacco, F. M. de S. 102
Tollefson, J. W. 54
Tomaselli, K. G. 40, 41, 46, 47
Total Consumption Poverty Line (TPCL)
    183, 187
totalitarianism 5
tradition, defined 139
Trask, R. L. 77
triple-test filter 18
Tshili, N. 45

Ubuntu 39; and communication 39–40;
    funeral gatherings in 44–45
Ubuntu/Unhu 149
ukuphalala, ritual of 117
ukuphosa ilitshe, rite of 114
ukuyabonisa 116
ukuzila 114
Umeogu, B. 67
umnyama (misfortune) 113
umsuzwane (*Lippia javanica*) 115
UNESCO Courier 52, 56
Unhu/Ubuntu philosophy 138
United Nations Department of Economic
    and Social Affairs (UN DESA) 77
United Nations Development Program
    (UNDP) 65, 72
University of Zimbabwe 25
Uses and Gratifications Theory (U&GT)
    93
uzumbani tea 115

vaccination cards 16
vaccination misinformation 16
vaDuma, COVID-19 136–141; funeral
    rituals 144–146; lessons learnt 149–150;
    post-burial rituals, safety procedures
    146–148
Vambe, M. T. 143
Van Djik, T.A. 80
Viljoen, K. 95
virtual/online communities, COVID-
    19 91, 92; goals and motivations,
    Zimbabweans joining group 99–101;
    and gratification 101–102; role in public
    health 92–93; thematic issues 96–99
Voetius, G. 175

Waever, O. 122
Wasserman, H. 26
Wa Thiong'o, N. 67, 68
Willems, W. 27
Wilson, Douglas 175
Wolff, H. E. 55
word formation, ways of 80–81
words derived from names 81
World Bank 65
World Food Programme (WFP) 171
World Health Organization (WHO) 3, 14,
    86, 106, 116, 153, 170, 174

Xiang, Y.-T. 8
Xinhua 72

Zamchiya, P. 171
Zhang, X. 109
Zigron, S. 103
Zimbabwean government 7, 25, 43
Zimbabwe Council of Higher Education
    (ZIMCHE) 30, 32
zvivharo zvepamuromo 87–88